s & Girls Clubs • Boys & Girls Clubs of Northeastern Pennsylvania • Brave Kids • Buckhorn Children's Home • California Museum of Science and In
ans • Central Florida Children's Home • Cerebral Palsy of Northeast Florida • Child Development Resources • Children's Aid and Family Services • Ch
rth Carolina • Children's Hospital of Southwest Florida • Cities in Schools, Inc. • Clarke School for Hearing and Speech • Classroom on Wheels • Colu
on of Indiana • Domestic Violence Project • Dreams Come True of Jacksonville • Duke Children's Hospital • Education for Tomorrow • Egleston Child
Wins! / Links to Literacy • Fairway House • Family First of Monterey County • Family Services of the Piedmont • Fatone Family Foundation • Fisher
ds of Retarded • George Mark Children's House • Georgia Council on Child Abuse • Girls Inc. of St. Louis • Girls Ranch of Arizona • Give to Colomb
fter League • Healing Hands • Hearts, Hands & Hooves of Northeast Florida • Heritage Classic Foundation • Hilton Head Heroes • Hole in the Wall G
ity Foundation, Delta Gamma Lectureship Fund • Kapalua Art School • Kenter Canyon Elementary Foundation • Kids Care • Leath Children's Center
ICI Ronald McDonald House, Milwaukee • Meeting Street • Meyer Center for Special Children • Minority Golf ssociation of America • Mom's Hous
r Foundation • Nationwide Children's Hospital • New Orleans Children's Hospital • Nicklaus Children's Hea ndation • North Carolina Hem
Arnold Palmer Children's Hospital • Our Military Kids • Pace Center for Girls • Palm Beach Habilitatio • Place of Hope • Porter Lea
Riley Children's Hospital • Ronald McDonald Children's Charities • Ronald McDonald House • Ro Charities of Memphis • R
eniors for Kids • Shell Junior Golf • Shriners Hospitals for Children • South Bay Children's Heal Special Olympics • St. Ber
es • Target House • The Achievement Academy • The First Tee of Monterey • The First Tee o oundation • The Lionheart Sch
unior Golf Program • United Way • University of Iowa Foundation, The Carver Family Cente eration • University of Wisconsin Ho
almer Hospital • Wolfson Children's Hospital • Women Playing for Time • Wood Trust Fund • helter • A Sporting Chance • A Stepping
• Angelwood • Arnold Palmer Hospital • Arrowhead Ranch • Assistance League of Las Vegas • A League of Phoenix • Assistance League of Ph
y Home • Betty Griffin House • Blessings in a Backpack, Hawaii • Blessings in a Backpack, New Jersey • Blessings in a Backpack, Phoenix • Blue Star F
Northeastern Pennsylvania • Brave Kids • Buckhorn Children's Home • California Museum of Science and Industry – Curator Kids Club • Camp Twin
rebral Palsy of Northeast Florida • Child Development Resources • Children's Aid and Family Services • Children's Bureau of Southern California • Chi
est Florida • Cities in Schools, Inc. • Clarke School for Hearing and Speech • Classroom on Wheels • Columbus College Foundation • Compassionate
Dreams Come True of Jacksonville • Duke Children's Hospital • Education for Tomorrow • Egleston Children's Hospital • Elizabeth Glaser Pediatric A
ily First of Monterey County • Family Services of the Piedmont • Fatone Family Foundation • Fisher House, Andrews Air Force Base • For Every Child
eorgia Council on Child Abuse • Girls Inc. of St. Louis • Girls Ranch of Arizona • Give to Colombia • Goodie Two Shoes Foundation • Great Lakes
of Northeast Florida • Heritage Classic Foundation • Hilton Head Heroes • Hole in the Wall Gang Camp • Hope Center • House of Hope • How 'Bout
rt School • Kenter Canyon Elementary Foundation • Kids Care • Leath Children's Center • Lena Pope Home • Leukemia Society of America • Love146
eyer Center for Special Children • Minority Golf Association of America • Mom's House of Endicott, New York • Morning Star Women's Auxiliary • M
hildren's Hospital • Nicklaus Children's Healthcare Foundation • North Carolina Hemophilia Foundation • Northeast DuPage Special Recreation Assoc
ter for Girls • Palm Beach Habilitation • Para Los Ninos • Place of Hope • Porter Leath Children's Center • Pro Kids Golf Academy • Quad Cities River
Ronald McDonald House • Ronald McDonald House Charities of Memphis • Ronald McDonald House of Fort Worth • SAFEchild • Salesmanship Clu
outh Bay Children's Health Center Association, Inc. • Special Olympics • St. Bernard Projects • St. Joseph's Villas • St. Jude Children's Research Hospita
erey • The First Tee of San Jose • The Kidsway Foundation • The Lionheart School • Thunderbird Junior Golf Foundation • Time for Teens • TPC Villa
he Carver Family Center for Macular Degeneration • University of Wisconsin Hospital and Clinics Authority • Venture Out • Violence Prevention Cen
ime • Wood Trust Fund • YMCA Youth Shelter • A Sporting Chance • A Stepping Stone Foundation • Adam's Camp • ALSAC / St. Jude Children's Ho
ance League of Las Vegas • Assistance League of Phoenix • Assistance League of Phoenix / Operation School Bell • Athletes and Entertainers for Kids •
Blessings in a Backpack, New Jersey • Blessings in a Backpack, Phoenix • Blue Star Families • Books-A-Go-Go • Boys & Girls Club of Denver • Boys &
ome • California Museum of Science and Industry – Curator Kids Club • Camp Twin Lakes • CARE USA • Carousel Ranch • Casa de Esperanza • Casti
s • Children's Aid and Family Services • Children's Bureau of Southern California • Children's Flight of Hope • Children's Healthcare Charity Inc. • Chi
and Speech • Classroom on Wheels • Columbus College Foundation • Compassionate Friends • Crescent Academy • Crisis Nursery • Crusade for Child
Education for Tomorrow • Egleston Children's Hospital • Elizabeth Glaser Pediatric AIDS Foundation • Emory University, Robert Trent Jones, Jr. Schola
atone Family Foundation • Fisher House, Andrews Air Force Base • For Every Child • Free Arts for Abused Children of Arizona • Friends of Oakland Pa
ch of Arizona • Give to Colombia • Goodie Two Shoes Foundation • Great Lakes Adaptive Sports Association • Greater Boston Food Bank • Greater Ha
l Heroes • Hole in the Wall Gang Camp • Hope Center • House of Hope • How 'Bout a Hug for Foster Kids Foundation • Hurley Medical Center • Inc
s Care • Leath Children's Center • Lena Pope Home • Leukemia Society of America • Love146 – End Child Sex, Slavery and Exploitation • Make-A-Wi
ociation of America • Mom's House of Endicott, New York • Morning Star Women's Auxiliary • Multiple Myeloma Research Foundation • Nancy Reaga
Foundation • North Carolina Hemophilia Foundation • Northeast DuPage Special Recreation Association (NEDSRA) • Operation Tom Sawyer • Orlan
os Ninos • Place of Hope • Porter Leath Children's Center • Pro Kids Golf Academy • Quad Cities River Bend Food Bank • Quad Cities United Way - F
House Charities of Memphis • Ronald McDonald House of Fort Worth • SAFEchild • Salesmanship Club of Dallas • Salvation Army • San Fernando V
Inc. • Special Olympics • St. Bernard Projects • St. Joseph's Villas • St. Jude Children's Research Hospital • St. Michael's Special School • Starlight Found
ndation • The Lionheart School • Thunderbird Junior Golf Foundation • Time for Teens • TPC Village • Unified Theater • United Friends of the Child
University of Wisconsin Hospital and Clinics Authority • Venture Out • Violence Prevention Center • Waccamaw Youth Center • Walter Reed Medical
orting Chance • A Stepping Stone Foundation • Adam's Camp • ALSAC / St. Jude Children's Hospital • American Cancer Society • American Cancer So
nix • Assistance League of Phoenix / Operation School Bell • Athletes and Entertainers for Kids • Atlanta Children's Shelter • AVON Walk the Course A
Backpack, Phoenix • Blue Star Families • Books-A-Go-Go • Boys & Girls Club of Denver • Boys & Girls Club of Las Vegas • Boys & Girls Club of Phoe
Curator Kids Club • Camp Twin Lakes • CARE USA • Carousel Ranch • Casa de Esperanza • Casting for Recovery • Catholic Charities Archdiocese o
Bureau of Southern California • Children's Flight of Hope • Children's Healthcare Charity Inc. • Children's Healthcare of Atlanta • Children's Home

Beyond the
FAIRWAYS
and GREENS

Beyond the
FAIRWAYS
and GREENS

A Look Inside the Lives of PGA TOUR Families

ISBN 978-1-935497-61-5
Library of Congress Control Number: 2012954689
Printed in Canada

Book design by Scott Stortz

Published by:

Butler Books
P.O. Box 7311
Louisville, KY 40257
(502) 897–9393
Fax (502) 897–9797

www.butlerbooks.com

Dedication

To the charities, the employees, and the volunteers we have partnered with over the past
25 years: your passion has been a source of inspiration.

Tribute

To our husbands: thank you for your support, patience, love, and encouragement.

Homage

To the PGA TOUR wives who are no longer with us: though gone,
you will forever live in our memories.

Gratitude

To our sponsors: without your belief in and contributions to our mission,
none of this would have been possible.

Sincere and Humblest Thanks and Gratitude

To our anniversary book co-chairs, Kelly Bettencourt and DeAnna Pettersson:
we are forever grateful. Your vision, leadership, passion, and dedication brought this project
from idea to reality. We could not have done this without you.

A Special Salute

As we celebrate 25 years of the PGA TOUR Wives Association, there is one key person who must be thanked, Sara Moores. Sara was there from the very start of the Association back in 1988. She is the executive director, but her role is much more than can ever be expressed on paper. She is employed by the PGA TOUR as Director of Special Programs and wears many hats. Sara is the glue that keeps us all together and we forever will be grateful for her dedication. It is with great honor that we take this opportunity and *"Salute Sara!"*

"I like to call Sara our rock and biggest champion. Although she is not a TOUR wife, she is the heart of the PGA TOUR Wives Association. She has been a source of strength and guidance for 25 years. One of Sara's greatest strengths is the fact that she always finds a way to make things happen. The Association comes up with grand ideas, and Sara has always worked with the members to make each idea a reality. As the names on the board of directors have changed over the years, Sara's has been the constant. Since our Association puts on an average of 20 functions a year, in a different city every week, with members from all over the world, we need someone who is 100 percent dedicated all the time. Sara is the thread that has been woven through all 25 years."

— Amy Wilson, PTWA President, 2008-Present

"Sara has supported us in our goals and made sure that we achieved what we set out to do. She always had a knack for convincing me to wake up at the crack of dawn to do television interviews; something I was not crazy about. It was hard to say no to her! She went above and beyond for us and always with a smile. She is an asset to the PGA TOUR, but more importantly, to the TOUR Wives and the Association that she has helped to mold. If it weren't for Sara, there would be no PTWA. We are grateful to her for her incredible hard work and dedication."

— Dory Faxon, PTWA President, 2004-2007

"I can never remember Sara ever thinking the PTWA could not succeed in an event or fundraiser. I feel that everyone that comes in contact with Sara sees her passion for the Association and its mission. Back in 1997-98 when a group of players and wives went to the TOUR about day-care concerns, Sara was put in charge of establishing what is now PGA TOUR Day-care; it went from volunteers in churches and hotel rooms to a staff, crates, guidelines, etc. — Thanks, Sara; every child on TOUR has benefited from you."

— Jennifer Day, PTWA President, 2001

From all of us Sara, thank you! We admire and respect you for all you are and all you have done!

Contents

PGA TOUR COMMISSIONER
TIMOTHY W. FINCHEM

For a quarter of a century, the members of the PGA TOUR Wives Association have been giving their time to help others in communities across the United States. We can all be inspired by their unselfish natures and their willingness to help those in need.

I commend the efforts of all the wives and significant others of PGA TOUR players over the past 25 years who have worked so diligently and selflessly to support and provide assistance to needy children and their families.

Born out of a charity golf outing during the 1987 PLAYERS Championship, which was hosted by First Lady Nancy Reagan and benefited THE PLAYERS Championship Village, the PGA TOUR Wives Association has grown into an organization whose events have raised more than $5 million for charity.

The impact of the PGA TOUR Wives Association is felt not only in terms of the monetary contributions made to charity, but in the many volunteer hours the members have given to community outreach projects across the country.

While their husbands and boyfriends are working in the spotlight inside the ropes in clear view of our fans and television audiences, these special women are working behind the scenes to give back.

This commemorative book highlights some of the reflections, stories, images, and memories of the past 25 years and I hope you will find it as inspirational as I have.

Again, I congratulate the PGA TOUR Wives Association on reaching this milestone anniversary, and wish them continued success as they begin their next 25 years of helping children and families across the country.

– Timothy W. Finchem
Commissioner, PGA TOUR

EMERIL LAGASSE

The PGA TOUR Wives Association has been a group near and dear to me for close to a decade. I've had the privilege of getting to know these women and the amazing work they do when they've been in New Orleans for the PGA TOUR event with their husbands.

What has really connected us is that we share a similar dedication and love for kids. I had introduced the ladies with the PTWA to a place that means a lot me, St. Michael Special School in New Orleans. I knew they would share my fondness for St. Michael because it helps students with major learning difficulties that hinder their ability to achieve success in a regular class setting. It has been an important cause to me for over 20 years and a place to which I've dedicated much of my foundation's time and resources. Over the years, when the PGA TOUR was in town, I conducted cooking demonstrations for the members of the PTWA and the students of St. Michael Special School after a morning of crafts and activities. The lunches were, of course, about learning new recipes, but what we all would take away each time was a fun, meaningful day spent together with great food and great people.

St. Michael is just one example of the kind of community effort this group of women gets involved with. I've always been impressed to see just how much they do. The PGA TOUR Wives Association makes it a priority to give back to the communities that host the PGA TOUR events. They mean business, too. They strive to empower members of so many communities with skills, education, and support. What's more is that they continue to grow to make an even more profound impact every year.

It's an honor for me to be involved with this very special book. This book illustrates the impact they have had on so many folks and communities through the years. But what's truly great about this book is that it brings folks right into the PGA TOUR families' homes and gives a unique look at personal stories and family recipes. Coming from someone who has shared thousands of recipes and personal stories, I can attest to just how much joy this book will bring you. It's an exceptional glimpse into the lives of an exceptional group of people.

– Emeril Lagasse

CLINT AND DINA EASTWOOD

My relationship with the PGA TOUR started in 1951 when I decided to conjure up a story and sneak into the Bing Crosby Clambake.

I was just a kid from Fort Ord, a corporal who wanted to watch a little golf and maybe catch a glimpse of Bing, Bob Hope, Phil Harris, or Rosemary Clooney. So I told the guy at the gate I was the assistant to Art Rosenbaum, former sports editor at the *San Francisco Examiner*. He bought it and I was in.

There are countless stories to tell, but a favorite is the day at Cypress Point when Jack Lemmon hit a shot left at the par 3 16th hole. It went off the cliff and landed in an ice plant, short of a 60-foot drop down to the Pacific Ocean. Greg Norman, Peter Jacobsen, and I started ribbing Jack to hit the shot. As he walked toward the ball, I grabbed Jack by the belt, Peter grabbed my arm, Greg grabbed Peter's arm and Greg's caddie grabbed his arm to make a human chain. We were laughing the whole time. It was a miracle, but Jack got the ball back into the fairway. Unfortunately, his next shot went into the ocean.

For over five decades, golf and the PGA TOUR have been a part of my life. Not only have I enjoyed playing with some of the best golfers in the world, I've also enjoyed being a part of a sport that gives back so much to charity.

The PGA TOUR Wives Association is an important part of the larger picture of philanthropy in the golf world. They are putting into action what each tournament does in its own community; raising money and awareness for those in need.

In my role as chairman of the board of the AT&T Pebble Beach National Pro-Am, I have gotten to know so many of the wives and watched their organization grow. Dina and I have gotten to know these women socially and work with them philanthropically.

Dina and I are honored to celebrate the PGA TOUR Wives Association's 25th anniversary with them. We hope you enjoy, as much as we have, getting to know this incredible group of women and the strides they have made to lift up children and their families around the country.

– Clint and Dina Eastwood

PAULA DEEN

There's so much joy involved in the act of feeding others, but for me, the greatest joy is feeding children. In my family, so much of our lives are centered around the dinner table, so it was heartbreaking to me when I found out just how many children in our country miss out on what most of us consider to be simple: a home-cooked meal.

Then I learned about the absolutely incredible things organizations like Blessings in a Backpack are doing. You see, while many kids get school lunches, they still go hungry at home. But just like the name says, Blessings in a Backpack fills backpacks with food to give to underprivileged children to ensure that they have something to eat at home, too. The magic doesn't stop there, though.

In working with Blessings in a Backpack, I met another group of generous women working just as hard to feed hungry mouths, the PGA TOUR Wives Association. For the last 25 years, these amazing women have been helping women and children while they travel the country. And y'all, I am just beside myself with excitement to be a part of PTWA's Anniversary Book. This book has got it all: food, family, and the best part is being able to help others, too. It's an honor to have one of my own recipes featured in these pages (*See* Lime Shrimp Lettuce Wraps, page 345). I hope y'all take a copy home to share with your own families.

And as always, I'm wishin' you love and best dishes from my kitchen to yours.

– Paula Deen

Introduction

When we started this project several years ago, we originally intended for this book to be a follow-up to our first book, *Taste of the TOUR*, a cookbook published in 2000. That publication contained recipes and short stories from our players' families. It sold over 20,000 copies and was a very successful fundraiser for our organization.

As this project developed, it morphed into something more; a celebration of our 25 years as a nonprofit organization. While we still pay homage to that first book with new recipes collected, this book focuses more on the story of the PGA TOUR Wives Association and life on the PGA TOUR, as told through the eyes of our player families. Through stories shared and photos taken from our family albums, you get an inside look at our lives *Beyond the Fairways and Greens*.

We hope you enjoy reading this book as much as we have enjoyed telling the stories. And know that through your purchase, you are helping us continue our mission of helping children and their families for years to come.

The PGA TOUR Wives Association

PGA TOUR WIVES ASSOCIATION OUR STORY. . .

The PGA TOUR Wives Association officially began at a charity golf tournament in 1987, a small event that intended to raise money for charity and be an enjoyable activity for everybody involved. Might as well have some fun, right?

At least that's what Patsy Graham, the wife of PGA TOUR veteran Lou, the 1975 U.S. Open champion, was hoping. Nancy Reagan apparently agreed. In 1987, Reagan was the First Lady of the United States, wife to US President Ronald Reagan. So committed was the First Lady that she left 1600 Pennsylvania Avenue and headed south to Florida.

To kick, or shall we say tee, off this inaugural event, Mrs. Reagan arrived at Sawgrass Country Club in Ponte Vedra Beach with the Secret Service in tow. She looked the part, in her navy skirt, red-and-white saddle shoes, and strictly for glamour purposes, a gold chain necklace. Reagan was in town for the TOUR Wives Golf Classic, a fundraising event featuring the wives of PGA TOUR players who traded roles for a day by becoming the players, with their husbands serving as their caddies, as they played an exhibition on the course that had hosted five previous PLAYERS Championships. Proceeds from the one-day event benefited the Nancy Reagan TPC Village, a Jacksonville, Florida, facility that was part of Reagan's "Just Say No" campaign against drug abuse.

Jack Nicklaus was toting Barbara's golf bag. Same for spouses Lee and Claudia Trevino; and there was Raymond Floyd hefting wife Maria's golf clubs, along with many other wives and their "caddies."

That first project was such a success that Graham and other wives had an idea. Their small get-together could evolve into something bigger, an actual not-for-profit association. It did, as the TOUR Wives Association formed a year later. After developing the plan, the mission statement and the appropriate filings took life.

"This group of women felt they could do more," said Sara Moores, the executive director of what is now called the PGA TOUR Wives Association, a position Moores has held essentially since the formation of the organization. "That first TOUR Wives Golf Classic was so successful that they thought if they could be successful here, in the shadow of PGA TOUR headquarters, why not in other places where we play, too."

Of course, they were right, and after one more year of the TOUR Wives Golf Classic in Florida, they took the show on the road, with the third annual event taking place at Oakbrook Golf Course in Chicago. The TOUR Wives Golf Classic is still very much a part of the Association's fundraising activities and has been played on many courses around the country.

Since that day in 1987, the PGA TOUR Wives Association has expanded its activities, traveling all over the country raising funds and in many cases, the spirits of those they touch along the way. It has also expanded its membership to include Web.com Tour wives, significant others of both PGA TOUR and Web.com Tour players, and individuals and companies who support the Association's charitable endeavors.

In those formative years as the organization matured, there was the tour of the Arnold Palmer Children's Hospital in Orlando, Florida, in 1991; a wine-tasting and silent auction in Las Vegas in 1993; a putt-putt golf tournament at Egleston Children's Hospital in Atlanta over multiple years; and a fashion show in conjunction with the 1995 PLAYERS Championship with proceeds going to the Children's Home Society Auxiliary. All the events had the same goal in mind: helping those in need.

"There really is so much to remember, so many things they've done over the years. It's difficult to narrow down all the good done into a sentence or two," Moores said. "I'm just so grateful to be affiliated with these women of immense talent and gifts who have big hearts and want to make a difference."

The women of the PTWA decided they wanted to leave some part of themselves in the communities they visited; it was the reason they created the organization in the first place. Today, as in the 1980s, they admit they're trying to leave a footprint and legacy beyond just what their husbands do on the golf course.

"I think we, as wives, get a stigma sometimes that we're always at the mall or we're ladies who lunch. I like seeing the surprised looks we sometimes see on people's faces when we come out to walk a few miles to raise money for a worthwhile charity, or when we're working with kids or we're volunteering at a food bank. It just makes me feel good, and I love being part of an organization that does so much to bring a focus on these important issues," said Kelly Warren, whose husband, Charles, has played on either the PGA TOUR or Web.com Tour since 1999.

About ten years ago, there was a seismic shift in the organization's thinking and purpose. The first years of the Association's existence consisted mostly of visits to hospitals and children's homes. In a purposeful way, the TOUR Wives started to get more and more involved with, as Moores said, "projects that gave them the chance to roll up their sleeves and get to work."

There are still hospital visits, but the scope has changed. Rather than simply visiting, there is now engagement with the patients that can take the form of arts and crafts activities, in-house festivals and just plain silliness. The repertoire of other activities has broadened to community outreach. Their activities range from packing non-perishable food items for underprivileged students in conjunction with Blessings in a Backpack, to helping build Habitat for Humanity houses, cooking and serving in soup kitchens, walking with the Avon Foundation to support efforts to stop domestic violence against women, picking vegetables from a garden that go to a local food bank, and handing out water for disaster relief.

"Members are always looking for new ways to serve. Yes, we have the tried and true, and we'll continue to do those things we've always done," Moores added. "But doing what was perhaps great 20 years ago is different today. While our mission hasn't changed, the way we are supporting that mission has."

"We take it seriously, and we have a powerful platform because of the publicity that accompanies professional golf and our husbands who play," said Amy Wilson, current PGA TOUR Wives Association president and wife of Mark. "I see it as a responsibility to use that platform to make a difference. The PGA TOUR Wives Association is an incredible opportunity for the women out on the PGA TOUR to make a difference as we travel the country to lift up children and their families."

CHARITABLE WORKS
1987-1993

1987
TOUR Wives Golf Classic at THE PLAYERS Championship

1988
TOUR Wives Golf Classic at THE PLAYERS Championship

1990
TOUR Wives Golf Classic at the Central Western Open

1991
St. Jude Children's Hospital at the Federal Express St. Jude Classic
Tour of Arnold Palmer's Children's Hospital at the Nestle Invitational
Riley Children's Hospital visit at the PGA Championship
Fashion show at the PGA Championship
Sale of gloves, hats and visors at multiple tournaments
Silent auction at the Southwestern Bell Colonial
Kapalua silent auction
Sale of Golf trading cards at multiple tournaments
Raffle to Hawaii
The Stress Seminar at the Hardee's Golf Classic

1992
TOUR Wives Golf Classic at the Anheuser-Busch Golf Classic
Implementation of Charity Visitation Program

1993
Silent auction at the Federal Express St. Jude Classic
Wine tasting and silent auction at the Las Vegas Invitational
The Boys and Girls Club of Metro Denver at The INTERNATIONAL
Arrowhead Ranch at the Hardee's Golf Classic
Bethany Home at the Hardee's Golf Classic
Mom's House at the B.C. Open

TOUR WIVES
GOLF CLASSIC

THE FIRST ONE

Patsy Graham was determined. Oh, she was told it would never happen and that was a mistake – telling her no. So she called the White House, over and over and over, and she finally got through. Patsy explained the concept and what she wanted. And Nancy Reagan, First Lady of the United States, agreed. She was coming to Ponte Vedra Beach.

Patsy and other wives of PGA TOUR players were putting on a golf tournament . . . with a twist. A nine-hole exhibition match . . . no rules except to have fun. And the professionals? Well, the tables were turned. This time, it was their turn to carry the bag and hand over the clubs. The signs posted around the fairway were self-explanatory: "PLEASE BEWARE – THESE PLAYERS ARE INEXPERIENCED – FOLLOW AT YOUR OWN RISK." They pretty much said it all.

The tournament raised money to help build a new facility in Jacksonville, Florida, that would help children and adolescents with substance abuse issues. The facility became known as the Nancy Reagan TPC Village and was part of Reagan's "Just Say No" campaign against drug abuse.

All of the big names were there, along with Mrs. Reagan and her band of Secret Service agents. PGA TOUR Commissioner Deane Beman and his wife, Judy, welcomed the First Lady, but it was Patsy and the other wives who captured her attention and maybe the attention of others, as well. The day was filled with missed shots, "whiffs," but most of all, a lot of good-natured ribbing and laughter. Everyone knew the real reason they were there, and why the TOUR Wives Golf Classic continues to be played even today. Most importantly, and unknowingly, the event laid the foundation for a group of women who, 25 years later, are still making a difference in the lives of so many children.

The Palmer family, taken during Thanksgiving, 2008, in Pennsylvania

The Arnold Palmer Family

Growing up in a family where your father is Arnold Palmer, nicknamed "The King," and a man who is generally regarded as one of the greatest golfers in the history of golf, should have been difficult. The constant media attention, traveling around the country following tournaments, just being in the spotlight of someone so famous. Not necessarily, according to his daughter, Amy Palmer-Saunders.

"During the earlier years on TOUR, there was less accommodation to families traveling with their children," says Amy. "Although we did accompany my parents some, they chose to keep our lives as normal as possible, which meant we were home more than not."

Amy and her sister, Peggy, were raised in Latrobe, Pennsylvania, where Arnold grew up. Latrobe is a small industrial town in western Pennsylvania, at the foothills of the Allegheny Mountains.

"We had a small-town upbringing, and that was by design. My mother, Winnie, tried to strike a balance between traveling and being at home. We were fortunate to have both sets of grandparents to help; we would stay with my father's parents in the winter and my mother's in the summer when my mom traveled with Dad. I was, as most kids are, not as aware of the pressures or rigors of my father's career and the celebrity surrounding him; we were protected from that."

Winnie made sure the children were able to participate in the hometown and school events that are so much a part of a child's life growing up.

Arnold and Kit Palmer

"We were fortunate that, in spite of the trips out of the country during our summer breaks, my parents would often compromise to allow us to be home for the end of the school year picnics and activities," Amy explains. "It was difficult for my mother to choose traveling with my father, or being home with us." They were a part of a community and they stayed where their roots were firmly planted. While Amy and her sister knew and were friendly with the other TOUR players' children, their friends were at home in Latrobe.

They were also lucky to have those opportunities to travel with their parents and see the world that few, at the time, were able to. But kids, being kids, they didn't comprehend a lot of that at the time.

"Looking back, I can appreciate the wonderful opportunities we had," Amy says. One that particularly stands out in Amy's memory was a trip to Paris. "My parents had taken me to an evening at a very famous restaurant in Paris as the guests of the tournament hosts. The restaurant was famous for its pressed duck. I was on the mend from

a flu bug I had caught while traveling. Upon serving of the famous duck, head and all, it was explained how the duck was pressed to draw the blood from the duck to make the *au jus* in which it was served. Needless to say, that was the tipping point for this 12-year old. My mother quickly rushed me out to a cab before I made a most embarrassing moment for us all. Such was life on the road with children."

That was but one trip they took together. Her parents would always look at what they could possibly do, and pick and choose what trips would be beneficial and educational to take the entire family on. More often than not, the children would remain at home.

Fast forward a few decades and things have changed. Amy now has four children and six grandchildren spread out over the southeastern United States. Sam, her son, is a professional golfer.

Winnie, Peggy, Amy, and Arnold Palmer

"Watching my father play was exciting. We, of course, always watched and rooted for him, but it was not filled with the pressures I now recognize as an adult. I did not realize the seriousness and magnitude of the game," said Amy. "Now, with Sam, I have such appreciation for what it takes to be successful in this sport. Definitely more nerves come with watching Sam now."

Does Arnold enjoy watching his grandson? "My father is very supportive of Sam, but he also wishes to teach him how to be tough and what is required to be successful."

Amy has become involved in her father's businesses. But the one venture that tugs at her heart and has become her passion is the one that started her interest in philanthropy and helping others when she was young . . . the hospital that Arnold and Winnie became involved with over two decades ago. The Palmers were solicited by community leaders in Orlando, Florida, as a way to bring exposure to the community of Orlando and to the hospital. Arnold had a "big picture" view of what that involvement could be and Winnie became involved in building the relationships within the hospital and the community; she quietly and effectively supported Arnold's vision. Amy saw how personally meaningful it was for Winnie to be involved and her mother taught her, through example, how to work with people in a collaborative partnership. Amy later learned, through her own experience, why the

22

Winnie and Arnold Palmer, with their daughter Amy, son-in-law Roy, and grandchildren, Emily, Katie, Annie, and Sam

to accommodate growing women's services and neonatal care. Upon completion of a connecting building and to honor both Arnold and Winnie's commitment, the new building was named the Winnie Palmer Hospital for Women and Babies. Winnie, too, had inspired many people who worked within the walls of this hospital.

The entire hospital has a culture of helping people and longevity in staffing, something that Arnold insisted be put in place if his name was to be included on the hospital. As a result, they honor employees and patients who are compelled to give a little more, who respect and celebrate what people do for one another. They created the "Spirit of Winnie Award" which they present to patients or staff who exhibit the spirit that Winnie did as she touched so many lives.

It all goes back to that small hometown upbringing; that willingness to help one another, to lend a hand, to make a difference. The Palmer family, through Arnold, his children, and his grandchildren, continue the legacy started those many years ago in a small western Pennsylvania town. Yes, he will always be "The King," but to so many, he and his family are much more.

community needed a multi-discipline hospital.

At 30, Amy was diagnosed with breast cancer that had spread. After researching the daunting treatment options, she had one criteria: she had to stay in Orlando. She had babies and a family at home and didn't want to leave them for treatment. The local hospital was partnering with MD Anderson and Amy began her treatment there. She saw the importance of having everything available for treatment in one place and how the community could benefit from that. That was an epiphany for her; she knew this needed to be a focus and her vision was to have one place that could take care of everything from babies to cancer treatment to heart issues; all specialties housed in one location. Her community needed a hospital that could provide those services.

The hospital now bears both her mother's and her father's names. With the hospital's exponential growth came the need for more space

Mulligan and Arnold

July 23, 1960: Jack and Barbara's wedding day

The Jack Nicklaus Family

It was an incident that happened a half century ago, but Barbara Nicklaus remembers the place and the message as if it happened yesterday.

It was during the Masters in 1962. Barbara was sitting on the veranda at Augusta National with several other PGA TOUR wives and she was bemoaning the fact she missed her baby — the first of five children, Jackie, was nine months old at the time. Barbara remembers how a lady who had been quietly knitting in a chair to the side looked up, pointed a finger at her, and said in a kind but stern voice, "Listen, little girl, you had Jack long before that baby was born and you hope to have Jack long after that baby's gone. Now you grow up and be a wife."

The lady was Aleta Mangrum, wife of Lloyd Mangrum, who had won 36 PGA TOUR titles, including the 1946 U.S. Open. Barbara said she was initially taken back by Aleta's comments, but soon realized she was absolutely correct and took her comments to heart.

"When Jack would call and say, 'Hey, I'm lonely, please come out for the weekend,' I would think, 'Gee, I have two babies in diapers — it's easier here at home.'" Barbara said. "Then I would see Aleta's finger, and my answer would be, 'I'll be there as soon as I can!'"

"I did not see Aleta for about ten years, but when I did, I told her, 'You have no idea what you did for my marriage. You made me a better wife.'"

Just like her husband, Barbara soon became the gold standard by which TOUR Wives were measured. Somehow, she seamlessly handled the responsibilities of raising five children — Jack II, Steve, Nan, Gary, and Michael were all born between 1961 and 1973 — while nurturing the career of the greatest golfer of his time, if not all time.

1973 PGA Championship at Canterbury – Jack carrying Gary (age 4) off the 18th green after the second round

1973 Champion of PGA Championship at Canterbury

Jack once said Barbara's support and stability "have meant at least 15 major championships to me." A strong statement for a player who won a record 18 professional major championships. But their 52-year marriage has been stronger than titanium. Barbara might not have been directly behind her man in the literal sense, but she was always nearby, among his large gallery.

"He never made me feel like a golf widow," Barbara said. "He made me a part of his life — his partner."

For proof, Barbara told a story that disputes the common belief that Jack was so focused on his golf that he was unaware of the surroundings. At the 1989 U.S. Open at Oak Hill, Jack questioned Barbara after a round about where she had gone on the eighth hole.

"You've got to realize, there are 40,000 people on that golf course, so I couldn't believe he would notice," Barbara said. "I had stopped to talk to Laura Norman. I said to Jack, 'You've got to be kidding? How did you know?' His response was: 'I know how you walk and I always know where you are.'"

"It made me feel good. I didn't think he had a clue where I was on the golf course."

Barbara's efforts were certainly made easier by Jack's vow, when he turned professional in 1961, that he would never be away from the family for more than two weeks at a time. They broke that rule only once, when Barbara and Jack took both sets of their parents to South Africa for 17 days.

Jack was also known to go the extra mile, literally, to support his kids. It was not uncommon for him to fly all night so he could catch one of his son's football games. "The kids kind of got used to it," Barbara says, "But now that they're grown and have families of their own, they say, 'Wow, Dad really made an effort to support us and be with us when we were growing up.'"

Barbara said she also was fortunate to learn from two seasoned TOUR Wives in Winnie (Arnold) Palmer and Vivienne (Gary) Player. This wasn't surprising, considering their husbands comprised golf's Big Three, meaning the three families often traveled together for outings.

"Winnie was just the absolute best," Barbara said. "I've never seen anyone who handled her life, Arnold's life and their lives together better than Winnie. She would tell me that if she got mad at Arnold on a Tuesday, she wouldn't say anything to him out of fear it might hurt his play in the tournament. And by Sunday, she would forget why she was mad at him."

Barbara came a long way from the mom whose first plane trip with little Jackie from Columbus to Miami for the PGA TOUR's stop at the Doral Resort started with an $80 luggage overcharge when she thought it was best to bring her own portable crib, sheets, and diapers with her on the plane, because "my son wasn't sleeping in a hotel bed or on hotel sheets."

"Jack was like, 'You don't think they sell portable cribs and sheets in Miami?'" Barbara says, smiling. "I think he wanted to put me back on the plane." She quickly learned that hotel beds and sheets were just fine.

From Miami, the PGA TOUR would wind its way through Florida during March, with the Nicklaus car full of golf clubs, a portable crib, and a not-so-fresh diaper pail. Not exactly like today's world of private jets and courtesy luxury cars for the modern stars.

"I guess it was tougher traveling then, but we didn't know it was tough at the time. That's just what we did," Barbara said. "We looked out for each other. If there were ten players and their families staying at

Jack and son Jack II walk off the 18th green at the 1986 Masters.

Courtesy of the Jack Nicklaus Museum

the same hotel, and one of the husbands was playing really well, one of us would help watch their children so that his wife could go to the golf course and support her husband."

Despite never playing golf — except for a few fun rounds — Barbara was honored as the PGA of America's First Lady of Golf for her many contributions to the game and numerous charitable causes. First and foremost is the Nicklaus Children's Health Care Foundation, which Barbara and Jack founded in 2005 to help provide support for activities that advance and enhance the diagnosis, treatment, and prevention of childhood diseases and disorders. The Foundation, which has raised more than $22 million in its relatively brief existence, originally was created to support programs in south Florida, but since has grown nationally without losing focus on the helping hand given to the children and families in the community where the Nicklauses live. The NCHCF

Nicklaus family photo (Not pictured: Finley Catherine Nicklaus, daughter of Mike and Traci Nicklaus)

serves as the primary charity of The Honda Classic, a PGA TOUR event played at the Jack Nicklaus-redesigned Champion Course at PGA National, just minutes from the Nicklauses' North Palm Beach home.

The Foundation also has partnered with the Memorial Tournament, Jack's PGA TOUR event outside his hometown of Columbus, to support Nationwide Children's Hospital — the Memorial's primary beneficiary since the tournament began in 1976. Closer to their Florida home, Jack and Barbara's foundation has partnered with Miami Children's Hospital and has opened two facilities in Palm Beach County — a Miami Children's Hospital Nicklaus Care Center and a newly opened Miami Children's Hospital Nicklaus Outpatient Center. The latter is a 23,000-square-foot facility with a state-of-the-art rehabilitation center, after-hours pediatric urgent care, along with a myriad of pediatric sub-specialists.

While some TOUR Wives relish the spotlight, Barbara has never sought it. She has always been content to remain in the background.

"I know this is going to sound corny," she says, "but when the song 'Wind Beneath My Wings' came out, I thought, 'That's all I've ever wanted to be for Jack. I always wanted him to be proud of me.'"

Even though Jack quit playing competitively in 2005, Barbara still takes calls from younger TOUR Wives seeking advice. When asked if she had one favorite piece of advice, it was obvious she still remembered that long-ago talk from Aleta.

"Just be 100 percent supportive, through thick and thin," Barbara said. "Don't stop being a wife just because you become a mother."

Gary and Vivienne Player celebrate their 50th wedding anniversary during the first round of the 2007 MasterCard Championship at Hualalai, held at Hualalai Golf Club in Ka'upulehu-Kona, Hawaii, on January 19, 2007.

The Gary Player Family

Gary Player was only 14 years old when he first saw his future bride, Vivienne Verwey. She was working part-time behind the counter in the pro shop at Virginia Park Golf Club in Johannesburg, South Africa, where her father, Jock Verwey, was the pro. "From the beginning, I was attracted to Vivienne like a nail to a magnet," said Gary. "With her set of legs and golf skills, how could I not? I believe she used that to her advantage when we would bet a bit on the course . . . a great distraction."

Gary and Vivienne, along with her brother Bobby, who is also a pro golfer, essentially grew up on the golf course together. Vivienne's father came to be Gary's mentor during his teenage years, and as the daughter of the talented golf professional, Vivienne herself was an accomplished and promising young player, winning a number of national championships in South Africa. Vivienne's golf career boasts something even Gary never achieved: two holes in one in the same round.

Gary and Vivienne dated for five years before Gary headed to Melbourne, Australia, to compete in the 1957 Ampol Golf Tournament. Upon leaving, he declared he would marry Vivienne if he won. When the 19-year-old Vivienne received the news of his victory, via telegram, a photographer captured her jumping for joy. That photo was later voted "picture of the year" in South Africa, and they married in January of 1957. "Frankly, I simply could not have achieved what I have, both on and off the course, if it were not for her tireless love, support, and companionship," says Gary.

With Vivienne at his side, Gary's golf career has been nothing less than stellar. In 1965, at the age of 29, Gary became the third man in history to win golf's career Grand Slam: winning the Masters, the U.S. Open, The Open Championship (a/k/a British Open) and the PGA Championship. With an impressive 165 tournament wins, including nine major championships on the PGA TOUR, and nine Senior Tour major victories, Gary's record has made him the most successful

Gary and Vivienne Player's wedding day, January 19, 1957

international golfer of all time.

"Golf has been a great bond between us," says Vivienne. "I love golf, and I cannot imagine life without it as it has been extremely important over Gary's career and even before. I grew up on the golf course and our shared love of the game was always important."

The game of golf evolved into the business of golf for both Gary and Vivienne. Gary is a well-known golf course architect with over 325 design projects completed around the world. In addition, their businesses include real estate development, golf events, apparel, magazine publications, wines, and even horse breeding. Their philanthropic efforts are even more important to them. Vivienne sits on the advisory board of Black Knight International and on the board of directors of The Player Foundation. The Player Foundation, which was established to aid education for underprivileged children around the world has, under Vivienne's efforts, raised over $50 million dollars since 1983 and celebrates its 30th anniversary in 2013.

Married now for over 55 years, the Players continue to travel the globe together. "Gary and I have had a very eventful and wonderful life through golf," says Vivienne. "I have met many wonderful people through the PGA TOUR and share many memories with fellow PGA TOUR wives."

With six children and 21 grandchildren, Vivienne spends less time walking the golf courses and more time with her family. However, she still remains as dedicated as the day Player turned pro in 1953.

First baby Jennifer Player, 1959

"Behind every successful man is a woman," says Gary. "But, behind every successful professional golfer is an exceptional woman. She has been an exceptional mother to our children, a wonderful grandmother, and I salute her."

Gary Player and his family at Gleneagles, Scotland, in the late 1960s

The Raymond Floyd Family

Raymond Floyd sized up the situation like any good caddie would. He calculated the distance, the trajectory, and fiddled in the conditions. Then he paused and added one more variable — the experience level of his player. He pulled the club and said, "Hit this one." His player — wife Maria — shook her head. "I can't hit that club," she said. Raymond didn't miss a beat. "You can't hit any club," he grinned. The group, Jack and Barbara Nicklaus, Greg and Laura Norman, Lee and Claudia Trevino, cracked up. "It was a hoot," Maria said.

The event was the first PGA TOUR Wives Golf Classic. It was 25 years ago and it didn't take much to get them to agree to be part of the three-hole exhibition. Maria, Barbara, Laura, and Claudia were close friends, and "their guys," as Maria called them, were four of the most respected players in the game.

"Everyone just wanted to have a little fun and raise money for a good cause. The guys were interfacing and having a good time," Maria said. "It was a fun event, and we're all friends. At the time, the whole TOUR Wives Association was just coming together."

Barbara's children were in their 20s, Maria's were a few years younger, and Laura was juggling teenagers. They had raised their children together at tournaments and motels and on long-distance car trips. They had been through everything together — teething infants, rambunctious kids, the ups and downs of their husbands' games, major championships, and everything in between. Now this, another girlfriend moment.

Raymond and Maria, with their children: Raymond, Jr., Robert, and Christina

"Being a professional golfer's wife is amazing," Maria said. "I wouldn't trade it for anything. There are so many ups and downs, but the friends you make are for life."

Maria and Raymond had been giving back on their own for decades, but when Patsy Graham came up with the idea of the TOUR Wives Association, Maria and her girlfriends were in. They teed it up in that first event to raise money for First Lady Nancy Reagan's TPC Village for children and adolescents with drug problems. "It was a very passionate thing for those of us early on," Maria said. "Everyone who was a member participated in one way or another. We all believed in it."

They sold charity tickets at tournaments. They toured hospitals and got involved. Then, as they moved from the PGA TOUR to the

Raymond and his kids, playing golf

Champions Tour, they took that same mind-set and platform with them and created the Champions Tour Wives. Their first project was a needlepoint blanket to auction off.

"We were all going to needlepoint a square for the blanket," Maria said. "We all had our little square — it was like 15 by 15. I got tendonitis in my elbow from that and it took three years to go away. I don't know who gets tendonitis from needlepointing, but Maria Floyd does. Everyone made fun of me."

That's what friends do, right? Get you through whatever obstacle is in front of you. Maria remembers the day she, Barbara, and the late Winnie Palmer were trying to find something — anything — to do during the practice round days at one British Open.

"Our entertainment was going from bakery to bakery to find out who made the best scones," she chuckled.

Twenty-five years later, the TOUR wives still have the same dynamic. They're friends who join friends to reach out and make a difference. "It's bigger and better than ever," Maria said. "It's a powerful organization with a lot of powerful ladies, who come together for the same cause. We were kind of like a momma and poppa association and now it's big time."

Maria chuckles as she remembers the days before day care when she would watch, say, Jill McGee's son if Jerry was playing early and Raymond was playing late. She remembers the birthday parties they threw in motel rooms. "We all pitched in and did," she said.

There's a picture at the Floyd house labeled "Watson, Norman and Floyd." It's not what you'd expect. It's three five-year-olds — Meg Watson, Morgan-Leigh Norman and Christina Floyd — having fun. It's a reminder of the old days and the friends that still remain close.

"We all had the same thing in common," Maria said. "We were traveling with our families and it was hard to be close with our friends at home. We all understood each other and that was an integral part of our tight-knit friendships."

The TOUR wives took off because of that.

"We had the best time," she said. "It wasn't just about golf. It was about life and life experiences. Golf was the mitigating factor."

Which brings us full circle to another day — this one in 1992 — when Maria shared yet another moment with her girlfriends.

Two days earlier, Maria and Raymond had lost their Miami Beach area house in a fire. Maria was asleep with the children at home, and Raymond was in San Diego playing at the Buick Championship of California when the fire broke out. Firemen had been able to salvage a few things that night, but the house was a total loss.

They were picking through things when Barbara Nicklaus and Laura Norman drove up and handed Maria a Chanel handbag. "They said Chanel cures everything," Maria said, chuckling. "It was so perfect, so girlfriend. So very much needed."

Chanel didn't cure everything that day, but that moment and those friends started the healing. The next week, Maria told Raymond to go play the then Doral-Ryder Open and she would take care of the house. He did and won.

"He won at almost 50," she said. "It was very profound. Professional athletes have to dream and believe. And he did. It took the pressure off losing the house."

Maria and Raymond rebuilt; trophies were replaced; and friends sent them so many pictures to make up for the ones they lost that they now have more than they started with.

And the girls? They're still only a phone call away. "You really do need your girlfriends," Maria said. "They're still two wonderful friends."

Maria Floyd passed away on September 7, 2012, shortly after this story was written. Maria was one of the founding members of the Association and her belief in its objectives and drive to succeed helped mold the organization into what it is today. She was an incredible advocate for helping those in need and will be greatly missed by her entire TOUR family.

The Floyd family

Julie and Bill Haas and Jay and Jan Haas at the 2011 Presidents Cup in Melbourne, Australia

The Bill and Jay Haas Families

Jan Pruitt made a one-dollar bet on Jay Haas at the 1977 Heritage Classic, and it turned into a marriage now in its fourth decade.

"It makes me sound like I picked him, but I didn't," she said.

The truth is she didn't know much about Jay, who was early in his PGA TOUR career after a brilliant college career at Wake Forest. Her family annually made an early-spring trip to The Heritage at Harbour Town Golf Links on Hilton Head Island, South Carolina, where they had a house near the seventh green. It was an easy spot from which to watch the par-3 seventh. In a family pool, someone suggested to Jan that she put a dollar on Jay, so she did.

When Jay came to the seventh hole, he was leading the tournament, so Jan and her father walked the next five holes to watch Jay play. She didn't get close enough to him to get a good look at him, but she enjoyed watching him play.

The next day, Jan pulled her mother out to walk a few holes watching Jay, who was no longer leading the tournament. When Saturday rolled around, Jan and a friend went out to watch her future husband. By that time, he had noticed the blonde who kept showing up in his gallery.

"He asked someone to find out who I was," Jan said. "A guy introduced himself and asked if I wanted to meet Jay. I said not really. I just had a bet on him and he was fun to watch."

As fate — or perhaps Cupid — would have it, the guy who offered to introduce Jan to Jay was staying in a house two doors down from where she and her family were. He gave Jay the phone number, he called Jan, and the two went to dinner in Hilton Head.

Later that year, Jan was in school at Florida State and Jay came through town to play in the Tallahassee Open. They had dinner again. Now they are parents of five children and have three grandchildren.

For 30 years, Jay played The Heritage at Harbour Town. He contended, but never won. Now his son, Bill, regularly plays the Harbour Town event, keeping a family tradition alive.

"Being from South Carolina, the tournament was always important to us," Jan said. "A lot of times it was on Easter, so we'd spend the holiday there. We would always go. When Jay Jr. was just ten days old, I drove him to Hilton Head."

Perhaps Jan Pruitt was destined to marry a golfer. The game was a central part of the family fabric in Greenville, South Carolina. Her grandfather owned a golf course. Her brother, Dillard, played the PGA TOUR and is now a TOUR official. She has been around the game — and the people who play it — her entire life.

Early in their marriage, Jay and Jan decided she would not try to follow her husband's nomadic schedule week-to-week. She preferred to stay home in, first, Charlotte, North Carolina, and later Greenville, where they settled 30 years ago. "Everybody's approach is different," Jan said.

As they had more children, more responsibilities came. Jay had his schedule. The children had their own. "We always talked about wanting the children to have a sense of community. We both grew up with that," Jan said.

2011 Presidents Cup - Captain's Assistant Jay Haas with his wife, Jan

"You can have a close family even with your dad traveling a great deal and we wanted them to have the sense of school and church and what we had. The TOUR is so much more family-friendly today than when our kids were younger, and traveling with two is different than traveling with five. We didn't have a nanny. We wanted our family to be as normal as possible. It's a little easier to travel with kids today. The way we did it worked for us."

Though Jay won nine times on the PGA TOUR, he and Jan didn't push their children to golf. While son Bill ultimately won the FedEx Cup title in 2011 and Jay Jr. has had success in mini-tour golf, it was just another sport played in an athletic family. "The boys didn't seem interested until they were older. They liked faster sports like basketball and soccer. We were of the mindset that we wanted the kids to play all sports, not just specialize," Jan said.

Bill and Julie Haas, with their dog, Dock

They played a lot of basketball. "We averaged nine to 11 basketball games a week during the season," Jan said. And daughter Fran was a ballerina, who had practice six days a week. "When we decided to have children, I had a commitment to whatever the kids were involved in," Jan said.

While Jan was busy getting the kids to practices, games and recitals, she had no idea that Julie, Bill's future wife, was living just a few miles away.

Bill and Julie grew up in the same city of Greenville, South Carolina, but attended different schools and went off to different colleges. Despite having many mutual friends and only living a few miles apart, their paths never crossed until they had both moved back to Greenville after finishing school. A chance meeting at a restaurant downtown turned into three years of dating. Bill and Julie were married in June 2011 in Highlands, North Carolina.

Three months after they were married, Bill and Julie found themselves with Jan and Jay in Atlanta for the TOUR Championship. "We were so excited just to make it to Atlanta, knowing anyone could win the TOUR Championship, but thinking the title of FedExCup Champion was probably out of reach, with Bill starting the week pretty far down the points list," shares Julie. "The week went by so fast, and in what feels like the blink of an eye, Bill was in a playoff with Hunter Mahan, with both the TOUR Championship victory and FedExCup at hand. I was standing outside the ropes with Bill's parents when Bill hit his second shot on number 17, the second playoff hole. We saw the ball roll off the green, into the water, and heard the loud moans and sighs of the crowds. Much to everyone's surprise, the ball

2011 FedExCup Champion Bill Haas, with his wife, Julie, his parents, Jay and Jan Haas, and his brother Jay Haas, Jr.

had stopped just off the bank and was only halfway submerged in the lake. The ball was playable, and Bill hit an incredible shot that landed just a few feet from the hole. Bill made par and the playoff continued.

"I was standing next to Jay and Jan again when Bill had his final putt to secure the victory and the FedExCup. It was the most surreal, amazing moment, made so much better surrounded by family sharing in our joy. We all caravanned home to Greenville that night to find our house covered in toilet paper and balloons, and all of our friends were waiting to celebrate."

Months later, Jan said she still gets chill bumps when she thinks about seeing her son win the biggest prize of his golf career. "It's

so different watching your child have success," she said. "You want everything in the world to go right for them.

"With your husband, you feel like he can manage whatever and will be okay. But to watch your child and see him succeed, it's hard to explain. You want life to go well for your children. To see things fall their way and to see them happy, it's a blessing."

Julie and Bill's wedding, the FedExCup, and a trip to Australia for the Presidents Cup made 2011 a year the Haas family will never forget. Bill and Julie love living in Greenville, just miles from both sets of parents and all of their siblings. The sense of family and community that Jan speaks of is still growing strong for them all.

The Curtis Strange Family

Curtis and Sarah Strange, celebrating his win at the 1988 U.S. Open Championship

It was an amazing 48 hours.

One minute Sarah Strange was getting married, the next she and Curtis were dancing with their wedding guests at the tiny airport in New Bern, North Carolina. Car doors open, music blaring. Police politely shut it down and told them to get on the plane.

Two days later, she was standing in Winnie Palmer's kitchen in Latrobe helping fix dinner. Her job was to shake a little cinnamon into the applesauce. Sarah was so nervous she dumped in the entire box. "We had brown applesauce," Sarah said. "Winnie never said a word."

That night in Latrobe was the beginning of what would be a long, close friendship between the two women. It was also a whirlwind start to marriage and life on the PGA TOUR.

Make that life on the TOUR back in the day.

Sarah chuckles as she tells the stories. Today, Curtis splits time between the Champions Tour and an ESPN broadcast booth. He was inducted into the World Golf Hall of Fame in 2007, and they've retired to the Crystal Coast in North Carolina where Sarah is tirelessly working to fund the new Crystal Coast Hospice House.

But there is always time to reminisce about those first few years on TOUR — years when Curtis's back-to-back U.S. Open titles, those Ryder Cups teams he played on, and his Ryder Cup captaincy were

The Curtis Strange family

still a dream. One that felt a million miles away standing in Winnie's kitchen.

Arnold had played in an outing with Curtis — they had that Wake Forest connection — and afterward flew them to Pennsylvania in his private plane — a luxury for two North Carolina kids who had sold Sarah's car just to bankroll their start in life. And, did we mention, they had moved their wedding to Friday so Curtis could play in the event and make a check?

Two months later, they had been around the world: Belgium, Indonesia, Japan, and Australia. And one hotel in Asia was about to change a policy, thanks to Sarah and Curtis.

"We didn't have any money, so we were eating at Kentucky Fried Chicken and McDonald's and I was washing clothes in the sink and hanging them all over the room to dry," she said. "I didn't go back the next year, but the girls told me there were signs all over the hotel — 'Don't do laundry in the room.'"

Back then — in 1977 — gas hovered around 60 cents a gallon, Apple wasn't even a year old, and VHS recorders had just gone on the market. It was before there was exempt status, a top 125, a Web.com Tour, day care, courtesy cars, player dining, and most young players were just making it. Eating out meant cooking with an electric skillet or a hibachi outside the motel room.

The good news? There were two qualifying schools each year, which turned out to be a blessing for a lot of folks, including Sarah and Curtis.

At the end of the around-the-world trip, Curtis finished second to Jack Nicklaus at the Australian Open, but he came up one shot short at the fall Q-school. "We truly didn't think the sun would rise the next day," Sarah said. "We were so young. I was 20, he was 21. We both hadn't finished college. Now what?"

Spring Q-school, of course. And it was at Pinehurst where Curtis had won the North & South Amateur twice. All Sarah could think was, "Hallelujah!" He got his card and they hit the road.

The stories followed. Sarah was sitting out in the sun at an affordable motel one day in a city which shall remain nameless, when she looked up.

"The maid was shaking her finger at me and asking, 'Does your mother know where you are?'" Sarah said. "I told her yes, I had just talked to my mother. I realized later what she meant when I saw cars coming for an hour or so and leaving."

And there was the car they rented with Phil and Kitty Hancock in Carmel. "To get the car to start, we had to open the door and put wires together," she said. "Curtis had one, Phil had one. I was in the driver's seat pushing the gas. When it started, Curtis slid in and pushed me out the other side of the car so Phil could get in."

She chuckled. You did everything to make the cut each week so

Curtis and Sarah Strange

Paul Lester

you didn't have to Monday qualify. If you struck out on both, you didn't make a cent that week. Everyone was frugal and everyone stuck together. "You've known each other's children and now their grandchildren," she said. "We even got to know each other's parents. It was a little smaller world back then."

Everything was scaled back. Even the motel — not hotel — rooms.

Thomas came along first in 1982 and when David arrived three years later, two adults and two cribs were more than some rooms could handle. "I pulled a bottom drawer out of the dresser, lined it and that's what David slept in when he was three weeks old," Sarah said. "And when he was a little older and would be taking a nap, I'd have a shoe holding the door cracked so it wouldn't lock, and Thomas and I would be sitting on the floor in the hallway reading or playing so David could sleep."

With no day care, the wives knew where every park and zoo was on TOUR. They knew which weeks weren't family-friendly, too. And, when they could, they'd pile in a station wagon or Suburban, and head out on the road.

his first U.S. Open in a playoff over Nick Faldo and backed it up a year later with a second win at Oak Hill. He came close to winning three in a row at Medinah Country Club, but finished third.

In between those two Open Championships, Sarah battled breast cancer. Fifteen years later, she had a recurrence and underwent a double mastectomy, but today she's cancer-free and helping others cope. "To know that you can help someone, give them a little peace, answer a question," she said, "that's important."

So, too, is the area's need for hospice, and Sarah, who is president of Hospice House, has helped raise $4.5 million in 18 months — including funds from Curtis's annual fishing tournament — to fund it.

"It's been the most rewarding thing I've ever done in my life," she said. "The need is so great. I never thought I could do anything like this, but God has put the right people in the right places at the right time."

Some are just stopping by. "One man saw the sign at church, and stopped and wrote a check for $5,000," she said. "He said, 'I just lost my wife; I'm going to need this one day.' It's just incredible how kind and wonderful people are and the depth of their hearts."

Curtis and Tom at Father/Son Challenge

One of the toughest times for Sarah was the week after David was born. Curtis had opened with an 80 at the Masters, but came back and was leading going into the back nine Sunday. He lost the tournament with bogeys on the 13th and 15th that day, and tied for second behind Bernhard Langer. She had to watch it on television.

"To have to sit there and watch it . . . I remember him coming home, driving in," she said. "We met each other in the garage and sank to the floor and we sobbed. I couldn't tell you how long. That was one of the hardest things. He won without me, but it was the worst when he didn't win and I wasn't there."

Three years later, Curtis was the best player in the world. He won

Curtis and Sarah moved to their tiny fishing village seven years ago, and built their little piece of heaven on the coast. They're grandparents now and when they're not playing with Thomas, Jr. they're paddle boarding or boating or just chilling out.

This, too, was a dream back in the day when Curtis was grinding on the course, and Sarah was reading to Thomas in a hallway. Yes, some things have changed. But some haven't.

Curtis still mows the grass and wields his weed eater. Sarah is still burping babies and telling stories of that road. "It's been a lot of fun times and great memories before children, during children, now with grandchildren." It all started that night in Winnie's kitchen.

The Scott Hoch Family

With age, of course, comes context.

Not long ago, Sally Hoch overheard the details of a young player's dazzling honeymoon trip. It was filled with several exotic ports of call, five-star accommodations, and lots of bells and whistles.

She sighed. When Scott and Sally got married in the summer of 1981, they spent two days in Myrtle Beach, South Carolina, before heading off so Scott could defend his title at what is now the John Deere Classic. Mind you, that was two days in the middle of July, when the humidity along the Atlantic Coast is as high as the temperature.

Today, Sally and Scott are set financially. But back then? It was much more of a grind. Very different; and Sally, for one, absolutely

The Hoch Family

Scott and Sally Hoch

appreciates the stepping stones of their journey — the travels, the travails, and everything in between.

Like many TOUR families of that era, the Hochs often took the road less traveled — in a minivan, with two kids, two dogs, and roughly nine suitcases. At first, there was a lot more grits than glitz, though they are undoubtedly the richer for it.

When Scott started his first full season on the PGA TOUR in 1980 as an All-American out of Wake Forest, it was three years before the all-exempt program began, and the majority of the fields played in Monday qualifiers. They lined up by the dozens trying to get a foot in the door.

"Rabbits, they called them," Sally said. "If you didn't make it, it was off to the next tournament site for the next week, and you practiced until the next one. You might not have eaten so fancy that week if you didn't have a paycheck."

Although Scott won as a rookie and became one of the steadiest players in TOUR history, the glamour came years later. It was preceded by musty hotels with paper-thin walls, nights often spent with host families, and plenty of airports.

Scott was one of those road warriors who loved to play. In 21 seasons, he played 25 or more weeks; in three of those seasons, he played 30 weeks. It's no wonder that Sally sought out the Yoda-type advice of Barbara Nicklaus, who had juggled her husband's Hall of Fame career and raised five children along the way.

"She said to travel with Scott on the road as much as possible," Sally laughed, "and don't let them know you can iron, and don't let them know you can sew."

They didn't have a choice when it came to child care. It was all but non-existent, except for the Western Open and then-Colonial National Invitational, which had day care options.

The Western Open's children's program was a favorite because it included field trips to water parks, miniature golf, and other outings. Once, as the pros were playing over at Cog Hill, a tornado blew through the Chicago area while the kids were on a field trip, and a park ranger had to shepherd the kids into a secluded area. As winds kicked up, the ranger grabbed hold of the children to keep them from being carried away.

Scott won 11 times on TOUR and is now on the Champions Tour, although he missed much of 2012 following his third wrist surgery. Sally can't believe this is their 32nd year on the circuit. "Time flies," she said. And she has loved every minute of the ride.

"For a little North Carolina girl, the TOUR allowed me to see the world, and meet and dine with presidents," she said. "I am just so appreciative of that, and the people we've met and the life we have been able to lead, because of the opportunities the TOUR has given us."

The Steve Pate Family

Sometimes, the best memories are made away from the golf course, when silliness prevails and professional golfers become big kids.

For the Pate family, Kapalua, Hawaii, has many special memories. Sheri reminisces about those special years on TOUR.

"All the golf families stayed at the Kapalua Bay Hotel and Resort," she says. "We attended dinners together, hung out at the beach and pool, played games, and just got to know each other outside the game of golf. Our daughters formed lasting friendships with other TOUR kids as they roamed the Kapalua grounds and were spoiled by their 'aunt' Debi Rolfing and the lovely Kapalua staff. These people become not only good friends, but our family on the road.

"One of the more memorable afternoons at the pool featured several players, including my husband, Steve Pate, along with Fred Funk, Duffy Waldorf, and Billy Andrade entertaining everyone by performing a water ballet for all to watch.

"Swimming caps donned, routine choreographed, the show was on! Maybe it was too much time in the sun, or maybe it was just them letting their hair down, but the guys had a blast and the spectators enjoyed it even more. Laughter joined the enthusiastic encouragement of the crowd for the ragtag group of ballet swimmers. It was hilarious! A memory we will never forget . . . and one we'll never let them forget, either!"

Synchronized swimming at Kapalua Bay Hotel and Resort - Steve Pate, Fred Funk, Duffy Waldorf, and Billy Andrade

Steve and Sheri Pate, with their daughters, Nicole and Sarah

Doug and Pam Tewell

The Doug Tewell Family

They met in church when they were in the sixth grade in Stillwater, Oklahoma. Who knew that 50 years later, they would still be together on a journey neither ever could have dreamed.

Doug started playing golf at the age of 12, after caddying for his father on Saturday afternoons. He graduated from Oklahoma State University and spent two years as a club pro before he and Pam started their nomadic life in the world of golf.

Doug and Pam began their great adventure on the PGA TOUR in

1975. Pam says, "We had experiences I would never even have imagined. We traveled the USA in our Buick station wagon with a three-week-old (son, Jay) and a six-year-old (daughter, Kristi), a Crock-Pot® and a Double Mac. We stayed in Days Inn and Howard Johnson hotels. We thought that was pretty cool. Life moved very fast for us. Doug's career grew as the TOUR grew. Our parents were awed and proud. We met new people from everywhere and made many new friendships that continue today, some 37 years later.

"TOUR life also exposed us to many interesting people and places. One particular and perhaps embarrassing memory was at the first players' dinner at TPC Sawgrass. We were waiting on the arrival of the two "surprise" guests, Bob Hope and Gerald Ford. As we sat there, our daughter, Kristi, blurted out, 'What's so big about Bob Hope and Gerald Ford?' She just wanted out of there and, of course, after that, so did we!"

Along with these memorable experiences came opportunities that would change this Oklahoma family in the most fundamental of ways. Both Doug and Pam realized that their life on TOUR was giving them a platform that they, too, could use to help change other people's lives in dramatic and needed ways. Other women traveling with their spouses felt the same way and decided to collaborate to raise money to give back to the communities who supported the tournaments where their husbands were playing.

Immediately, Pam became involved with and helped organize what is now the PGA TOUR Wives Association. She played in the very first TOUR Wives Golf Classic in 1987 and would continue her involvement throughout the many years Doug was on TOUR. When he qualified for the Champions Tour, she eventually became president of the Champions Tour Wives organization.

"We raised money, lots of money, and gave it away all across the country. What a rewarding experience it was," Pam said.

Doug retired from competitive play in 2007. He and Pam now live in Edmond, Oklahoma, along with their children and five grandchildren who all live nearby. They have taken their desire to help others to the inner city, working primarily on projects that help inner-city children and families by providing them with opportunities for a better life through education and development of life skills.

"Whoever would have thought this quiet, young couple from Stillwater, Oklahoma, would have all of these wonderful opportunities. We've been able to follow a dream, grow personally, and raise a family who also embraced these opportunities. We've been able to help others and make a difference not only in our home communities, but around the country," she says. "We are truly blessed."

Hale And Sally Irwin

The Hale Irwin Family

It had been one long emotional Monday at Medinah Country Club: a 19-hole playoff; a birdie on the final hole, and a third U.S. Open trophy.

Hale and Sally Irwin were still pinching themselves as they packed up the car for the five-hour drive from Chicago to St. Louis. This wasn't supposed to happen. Hale had gotten in on an exemption. Then he sank that 45-foot birdie on the final hole Sunday afternoon to get into the playoff with Mike Donald, and took a lap around the green, slapping hands with the gallery. And Monday? He had trailed until that sudden death putt found the bottom of the cup.

Now, the oldest U.S. Open champ in history at 45 — and one of now just six players to win three or more Opens — was starving. He'd been through the ceremonies, the interviews, the back slapping. What he hadn't found was dinner. The concessions were shut down and the club's food service was over.

Then, the volunteer committee chairman, Don Larson (who went on to serve as tournament chairman for two PGA Championships and the 2012 Ryder Cup), scrounged up some cold pizza from the volunteer tent and shared it with Hale and Sally.

"We were standing there drooling," Sally said. "Don brought us the pizza and I don't remember what kind it was. I just remember it was delicious."

Yes, major championship wins were different back then. Instead of today's week-long roller coaster of appearances and events, they packed the car and headed out or called home.

Sally has the three magazine covers from Hale's three Opens up on the wall at home and each one has a story. The '90 Open was the most emotional, while the 1974 win at Winged Foot Golf Club was a solo event for Hale. They had just moved into a new house and Sally was pregnant with their son Steven.

"My daughter Becky and I were sitting on unpacked boxes watching the tournament on TV," Sally said. It was also the year of Hale's white belt. "The kids gave us grief until a few years ago when white belts came back again," Sally said.

The 1979 win at Inverness County Club was a family affair, but there was one amusing moment. Hale had braces at the time and when friends invited them over for corn on the cob, French bread, ribs, and salad, he couldn't even eat dinner.

Five years after that third Open, Hale turned 50 and proceeded to turn the Champions Tour upside down. In the next 12 years, he won 45 Champions TOUR events to go with his 20 TOUR wins. "Funny," Sally said, "when he graduated from Colorado, he didn't even know what it

Becky Irwin family

was like to play golf year-round."

Hale was an academic All-American defensive back for Colorado and, in 1967, he was an All-Big Eight selection in football, as well as the NCAA individual golf champion. "When he started out in May 1968, he was learning as he went," Sally said. "I graduated two weeks before we got married and our honeymoon was in Oklahoma City at a partnership tournament."

She loaded down an old Pontiac Bonneville with clothes, clubs, practice balls (tournaments didn't always provide them), an electric skillet, spices, an ironing board — you name it — and they drove. When they had a break, they stayed with Sally's parents in St. Louis, and all their wedding presents were stored in the basement for their first four years of marriage.

Steven Irwin family

"Looking back now," she said, "to the days when Becky would ride her toy motorcycle through the airports and Steven followed behind in an umbrella stroller, we wondered what the future held."

Which brings us to one more loving reminder of great times in Hale and Sally's five-decade journey in the game that is framed and up on the wall along with those Open covers.

Not long before Hale jumped to the Champions Tour, he was playing at the AT&T Pebble Beach National Pro-Am when the Irwins and President George H. W. Bush and Barbara were invited to what they thought was a small party. It wasn't, so they opted for a casual dinner in Carmel.

"They gave us butcher paper and crayons to draw with at the table and we were all hiding our drawings," Sally said. "Barbara drew a very good Millie (their dog), Hale drew the 18th green looking out toward the ocean, 41 (Bush) drew the 18th from the ocean looking in. They were all pretty good except mine. I drew rabbits, which is all I can draw."

Hale Irwin, at the 1990 U.S. Open

Frank and Selena on their wedding day, with Frank's daughter, Bianca

The Frank Nobilo Family

It was a simple ceremony in a stunning setting in the Bahamas.

Just Selena and Frank Nobilo, his eight-year-old daughter Bianca, Ernie Els and his then-fiancée, Liezl, on a beautiful day in a marvelous garden. Nothing fancy mind you, just a lot of love and five pairs of bare feet. Perfect.

Well, the perfect solution. When Selena and Frank started talking marriage, they quickly realized that planning the wedding would be

quite a kerfuffle.

They lived in Orlando. Selena's parents lived in Malaysia. Frank's family was in New Zealand. And most of their close friends were in England. Trying to pull that one off was daunting, even for Selena, who ran an event management company in London.

So, they turned Liezl and Ernie's scheduled holiday into a two-family affair and decided to "elope." It was so easy, so sweet. The girls wore summer dresses, Frank's linen shirt was untucked, and Ernie came in shorts. The bare feet? A must for a post-ceremony stroll along the beach.

"It was so difficult to find a date and place of common ground with everyone all over," Selena said. "We decided to bite the bullet and run away. We had every intention of having a big party when we got back, but of course that never happened."

When Selena moved to Orlando, it was a leap of faith. She and Frank met in Spain when he was playing on the European Tour and her company was managing events for both golf tournaments and Formula One races — another of Frank's passions. For several years, she would work all week, fly out to watch him play, then fly back to work a Formula One event.

They moved to Florida when he got his PGA TOUR card, and she knew she would eventually have to sell her business, but she also knew it would all work out. It took her five years to get her work visa and, even though she was traveling full-time with Frank, something was missing.

"I'm a bit of a doer, so I got involved in the TOUR Wives Association," she said. She spent five years as a member of the board of directors of the organization and served as vice president of community outreach. She also worked on charitable efforts in their hometown community.

They've been married 14 years now, and Selena has transitioned from TOUR wife to wife of a Golf Channel analyst, and a freelance event coordinator. Bianca graduated with highest honors from Warwick University and is attending the London School of Economics to pursue a master's degree.

Five months after Selena and Frank's wedding, they took a whirlwind three-day trip to South Africa where Selena was in Leizl's bridal party. The wedding was stunning and just as much fun because all of Ernie and Leizl's families and friends were there.

This brings us to one final detail about that marvelous tiny wedding in the Bahamas.

Frank, Bianca, and Selena Nobilo

Because the school system in Malaysia wasn't very good, Selena and her brother went to boarding school in England, starting when she was seven. Since they spent so little time with their parents, Selena had always promised herself one thing — her dad would walk her down the aisle.

"It was the one thing I could do for him, so going away and getting married wasn't an easy decision at all," she said. Not, at least, until her father wrote Frank a letter five months before they were married:

"It would be my dream to give Selena away, but I'm old enough to know dreams don't always work out the way you want them to," he said.

He gave them his blessing, then ended the letter with this:

"As the cherry blossom protects the mountain, so we ask you to protect Selena."

"Every time I read that letter," she said, "I cry."

She also laughs.

In the midst of blessings and requests, her father also found the lighter side. They were doing him a favor actually, he said, because the father of the bride didn't have to pay for anything.

Kirk and Cathi, with their children, Conor, Sam, Alexis, and Kobe, at the Wall-E premiere

The Kirk Triplett Family

One day Johnny Depp walked into the Disney offices and asked Dick Cook if he had a family-type project on his desk. A movie his kids could see. Cook said he had a pirate script in development. Depp said he was in. His agent just shook his head, shot him the "what-*are*-you-thinking look" and put his hand over his face.

True story. One that made Cathi and Kirk Triplett shake their heads and chuckle when the former head of Disney Studios recounted that moment. A few years later, the Tripletts and two of their four kids

were on hand for the premiere of the third film in the trilogy, *Pirates of the Caribbean: At World's End*.

It's funny, they thought, how much of a role Disney has played in their PGA TOUR life. Cook and Kirk met a little over a decade ago at the Bob Hope Classic, and struck up a friendship that had nothing to do with movies until Cook invited them to premiers like Pirates 3, *Wall-E, The Proposal*, and the re-release of *Mary Poppins*, complete with real penguins. But that's jumping way ahead.

The Tripletts have been a Disney family from the start. Kirk always made room on his schedule to play the Children's Miracle Network Hospitals Classic at Disney World. In fact, he used to call it a major because, for him, it was major family time. In fact, the gang would hit the Disney Park twice a year. They'd go in the summer and again after Thanksgiving for what Cathi called a "pre-Christmas kickoff."

"We'd take the kids out of school for three days, stay at the Grand Californian, and have a really fun few days that didn't have any golf involved," Cathi said. "It was so special for everyone."

It was even more special as their family grew in very unique ways. It took Cathi and Kirk three *in vitro* treatments before she got pregnant with twins Conor and Sam, now 17. Six days after they were born, the boys made their PGA TOUR debut at the 1996 Phoenix Open, then hit Pebble Beach the following week.

They always wanted a big family, so they tried several more times, but it just didn't work out. Enter Debi and Mark Rolfing. Together, they facilitate foster families and adoptions from their home in Hawaii. In March 2000, Debi called about a baby that was going to be born and put up for adoption in Sacramento; Cathi and Kirk didn't hesitate. "In the space of a week, we went through home study, evaluation, and certification. Just over a week later, I watched Alexis be born!" Cathi said.

Two years later, Debi called again. This time, she was fostering a

Triplett children and Eeyore

The Triplett family, with a Disney Adventure guide (on right)

newborn and looking for a family. It just so happened that Kirk had said to Cathi that very morning, "Aren't we about due to get another baby?" So when Cathi got the call from Debi, it was fate. Because they were current on their certification, Kirk and Cathi were able to meet up with Debi six days later and bring home 11-day-old Kobe. "We have it all going on," Cathi said. "We have two big Irish twins, Lexi is full Hispanic, and Kobe is half Japanese, half African-American. We are a blended family."

The Tripletts have become a resource for others looking at adoption and *in vitro* on TOUR. They have also started their own charity — FORE Adoption, to help children get placed with families and to heighten awareness of how many children are in foster care that need to find their forever families.

Cathi has always been an advocate for helping others. She'd been part of the PGA TOUR Wives Association before the children arrived. She helped organize their first fundraising publication, *A Taste of the TOUR,* in 2000 and, for 14 years, was tournament director for the

TOUR Wives Golf Classic. The golf tournament, where the wives play golf while their professional golfer husbands caddie, has provided many laughs over the years. One of the funniest moments, she said, was when Rose Lietzke stepped to the tee and set up sideways. "Bruce didn't come out that year," Cathi said. "I'd never seen anyone turn sideways, but she said that's the way Bruce told her to do it. She was right. It was pretty scary, but she hits a massive hook, so that was what she had to do."

Since they lived in Scottsdale, Cathi took the idea of the tournament to the Thunderbirds, who put on the Waste Management Phoenix Open. "Like many other tournament sponsors, they are always looking for ways to draw the best possible field to their tournament," Cathi said. "So when I presented the idea of hosting the TOUR Wives Golf Classic, they were more than happy to oblige." She ran six events there and one in Callaway Gardens, Georgia, when she was six months pregnant with the twins. "It wasn't too pretty," she said, "but it sure was a lot of fun."

Which brings us back to the family Disney vacations, son Conor,

The Triplett family at Walt Disney World

and another Disney moment. Cook knew that Conor had an interest in becoming a Disney Imagineer, and invited Cathi and Conor on the "grand tour" of the Burbank studios. They met Dwayne "the Rock" Johnson and saw a preview of *College Road Trip*, but the highlight of the tour at the Imagineer Studios was going on a prototype for the park's *Toy Story* ride.

"I can't even begin to tell you how special that was," Cathi said. "We were sitting on a basic wood platform on some school chairs. We had these mock up 'guns' that were in front of a makeshift screen. You could see all the nuts and bolts of what had gone into creating the ride, and it was awesome."

They are a Disney family. Always have been. They have been on five Disney cruises, including one to the Mediterranean, and a Disney Adventure in Yellowstone. Kirk's friendship with Cook? Like the call from Debi Rolfing or the meeting Depp had at Disney, it simply opened the door to a Triplett adventure.

The Mark Calcavecchia Family

The builder was due to break ground on Brenda and Mark Calcavecchia's house — Villa Nahar — on the banks of the Loxahatchee River when he got a call from Maui. It was the Calcavecchias asking him to hang on; there was a little change. They were going to tweak the plans to add a two-lane bowling alley.

Some 18 months later, Brenda and Mark moved into Villa Nahar. The lanes were sanded, finished and oiled, the disco ball was spinning overhead, and they were ready to bowl.

This is the way the Calcs roll. Literally. They both grew up bowling, so why head down to someone else's lanes when you could have your own? And this is no bare bones two-lane alley. It's 2,000 square feet of up-to-date Brunswick technology on the screens and maintenance for the lanes. There is an arcade game area, seating areas, a sound system cranked with an eight-CD best of the '70s set, and an area stocked with a full selection of bowling balls and shoes in every size. The only requirement — which is on every party invitation Brenda sends out — bring your own socks.

"It's been the coolest thing we've ever done because every party we have, everyone wants to bowl," Brenda said. "Even those who don't bowl have fun, too. You don't think of going to a bowling alley in a home."

"When we were building it, the people who had to approve the plans kept asking, 'What's this giant long space?' They thought it was some golf training facility for Mark. They thought it was for swinging and video taping and putting greens. And we said, 'Nope, it's a bowling alley!'"

The alley is soundproofed, decorated with an Art Deco flair and a zebra rug, six arcade games and bar areas. And a few bowling Barbies, and maybe a seasonal one, too, from Brenda's stunning Barbie collection (500-600 dolls). Brenda's obsession — her word — even led to Brunswick making her a custom 12-pound pink Barbie bowling ball. "They only made them in eight-pound balls for children," she said.

The best part of the story? The idea to build the alley came from an interview Mark did at the 2008 Mercedes Championships. When asked who was a better bowler — him or Jeff Sluman — he answered, "Jeff," because Jeff had a bowling alley. Brenda said they should get one and … they did.

Mark and Brenda threw a party each year during The Honda Classic, but that has fallen by the wayside since Mark moved on to the Champions Tour. They do have other parties, some impromptu. One night they were in their PJs around 9:00 o'clock when someone rang the gate bell. Neighbors Russ and Jackie Cochran dropped by to roll a game or two.

"We try to shut the lanes down at 1:00 a.m., but sometimes the party has lasted until 3:00 a.m.," Brenda said. "I've seen people bowl barefoot and we've hosted formal parties where girls are in their beautiful gowns bowling."

She's seen a few wipeouts, too. Right after it was installed, there was extra oil on the lane and Mark took a face plant.

Who's a better bowler? It depends.

Brenda and Mark Calcavecchia on their wedding day

Mark and Brenda's bowling alley, in Villa Nahar

Straight-up, Mark is the winner. But Brenda can take him down when they bowl left-handed. It was a coincidence, but she realized this while nursing a sore right wrist from caddying for Mark. Since she's ambidextrous, she tried bowling left-handed and rolled a 120. As good as he is right-handed, Mark struggles to bowl well as a lefty.

Brenda caddies for Mark about 90 percent of the time on the Champions Tour. She started on the PGA TOUR, but she was on the bag less than half the time back then. "Why not?" she said. "You're out there walking anyway, so why not caddie? It's great exercise." And she's been on the bag for two individual wins as well as two team event wins.

The two met at the Memorial Tournament when she was working as a CPA and squiring clients around the event. Her last name was Nardecchia, and she just happened to be standing near Mark and teased that they must be related. A few months later, she took clients to Akron for what is now the World Golf Championships-Bridgestone Invitational. Mark saw her and asked where they'd met. They had dinner that night. "We've talked every day since then," she said.

He's the one who knew they'd be together first. "We were talking about music and I told him I'd seen Rush, his favorite band, about 10 times — every concert since 1982," she said. "He said he knew right away we were in love."

They married on May 5, 2005, (05-05-05), during the Italian Open. Mark played in the first round, they showered, drove two-and-a-half hours to Lake Como by themselves for the ceremony, took a boat trip, had a nice dinner, and drove back so Mark could play in the second round. They plan to go back for their tenth anniversary. In the meantime, Brenda's disco ball — which reminds her of growing up roller skating and bowling in the '70s — will be spinning on the Florida coast.

When they were building the house, they discovered it was tradition to name houses in the neighborhood, so the Calcavecchias rolled with a combination of Mark's Italian roots (villa means home) and Brenda's Jewish ancestry (Nahar is Hebrew for river). As for those two lanes that held everything up? They're always open. Just remember to bring your own socks.

Mark, with wife and caddie, Brenda

The Brad Faxon Family

In May 1999, Dory Ricci was about to send out her wedding invitations. It was seven weeks until she was going to marry her long-time boyfriend and he called off the wedding — that day. Envelopes were ready to go.

Three days later, her cousin Ted Fisher told her he had a great guy for her. It was one of his squash buddies — Brad Faxon. She said, "Tall, red hair? Golfer? Divorced with three kids? That Brad Faxon? No, thank you," she said. "He is so not my type."

A month later, she gave in to her cousin's cajoling and went out with Brad. One date was all it took and they were both, as she put it, smitten.

Brad jokes that he ruined Dory's law career. She was in her final year at Rhode Island's only law school — Roger Williams Law School — when she met Brad. She never intended to practice, but instead wanted to use the critical thinking to work in human resources for her family's textile business. That plan, however, got tossed out the door, too.

Dory still shakes her head. Life really is what happens when you're busy planning it. From a whirlwind courtship to a wedding to mom of three children to a daughter of their own, Charlotte, in less than two years . . . and then there was the TOUR. "I never thought about what was ahead and this blessed life we have," she said.

The TOUR Wives Association was equally blessed. When Dory started traveling with Brad, she got involved with the Association's events.

"I loved the women out there," she said. "They were warm, wonderful people. When they gave Charlotte a little shower, I was amazed. I think Char got 50 dresses." A few years later, Dory became the Association's president and channeled all that critical law school thinking into taking the Association to the next level.

"We had this tremendous amount of talent at our fingertips and we needed to utilize it," she said. "So we started the ball rolling and got more people involved. It was important that we showed people who we were involved with and the places we wanted to be involved in. We wanted to be hands-on help." Dory nurtured the Association for four years before handing the presidency off to Amy Wilson in 2008.

Giving back is a family affair. Brad and Billy Andrade founded the Billy Andrade/Brad Faxon Charities for Children, Inc., which has raised more than $15 million for Rhode Island children in need. For that and more, Brad has been honored with the 2005 Payne Stewart Award and two awards from the Golf Writers Association of America — the 1999 Charlie Bartlett Award for unselfish contributions to society and the 2012 Jim Murray/ASAP Sports Award for his relationship with the media.

"The thing I love most is that Brad has been recognized through not just wins, but through other awards, for who he is and how he treats people," Dory said. "He's such a caring person. A lot of people can say they've won, but not many can say they've won these awards; awards that are testament to what kind of people they are."

Brad and Dory Faxon

Charlotte, Sophie, Melanie, Emily, Dory, and Brad

All of which brings us back to fate, the whirlwind courtship, and a laundry bag on the floor of a San Diego hotel room.

She is blessed that her cousin was persistent and that life throws as many great curves as bad ones. It turned out a good portion of the family already knew Brad from the golf world. Dory's parents and grandparents were members at Newport Country Club; her dad and his dad were golf buddies; and Brad even knew her dad. So when she told her dad she was going out on a date with Brad, he was thrilled. Brad, he said, is a great guy.

They dated for seven months and she studied for the bar exam in places like Hawaii and Pebble Beach. She was frustrated. She was tired. During the AT&T, Brad called her dad and asked permission to marry her. The answer was absolutely.

Brad planned to propose Sunday afternoon on Ocean Drive. He had the ring shipped in and they were pulling out of the parking lot when his then-caddie, Bruce Clendenen, knocked on the window.

"He said, can you give me a ride to the caddie parking lot?" Dory said. "Brad was quiet, so I said, 'Sure. Of course. Get in.' That completely derailed his proposal that afternoon. He was ready for it to be nice and romantic. It was an amazing setting, his favorite place in the world and favorite golf course."

They flew to San Diego that night and Dory was so frustrated

68

Brad and Dory

studying for the exam, that she was in tears on the hotel floor. "Brad's fumbling around in his laundry bag while I was crying," she said. "Then he pulls out the ring and asked, 'Would it make it better if I asked you to marry me?' I was shocked."

She said, "Yes," and Brad told her the whole story of what he had planned. "That romantic proposal turned into an unromantic one from a laundry bag," she said laughing. "I just remember saying, 'What? I don't care.'"

They got married seven months later; Char was born 15 months after that. They've been married a dozen years now and today, life is still throwing them a few curves, but they just laugh through them. "Looking back to where I was that day in 1999, to end up in this life . . .," she said, pausing. "It's pretty amazing."

The Faxon girls - Emily, Melanie, Sophie, and Charlotte

The Peter Jacobsen Family

Jan Jacobsen had one unbreakable rule when it came to her three kids and traveling — if they flew out to watch their dad play, they had to be in school Monday morning. No argument. No exceptions.

The Jacobsens, you see, lived in Portland, Oregon, and back in the day, non-stop flights were seldom an option. Two, maybe three planes to get to where you were going, and the same number to get back. Missed your flight? Too bad. Flight delayed? Sorry, you're going to school.

So when air traffic was slow out of Rochester after the 1995 Ryder Cup, oldest child Amy — then 15 — missed her connection in Chicago and the airline didn't want to book her on another flight. "My kids were so well traveled that she told the lady, 'I'm 15, so if you don't put me on a flight, you're responsible for me. I'm alone. I can't go to a hotel. Where am I going to go? I'd suggest you put me on a flight tonight.'" They did; she got in at 3:00 a.m. and Jan wasn't budging. "To this day, she's still mad at me about that," Jan said. "But she had missed the whole week, so she was going."

It may seem harsh, but it worked. It had to. No tournament was just a short flight away. It was 2,700 miles to Miami, more than 1,700 to Chicago, about 1,800 to Texas, and 2,400 to New York. Whew!

"The flying and the amount of travel over those years were kind of daunting," Jan said. "You couldn't just come home for the night." In fact, there were times during the season when logistics meant the Jacobsens would be gone two months. Any time they traveled, there were a lot of red-eye flights and 4:00 a.m. wake-up calls just to get where they were going.

"We tended to have long flights and, of course, no electronics back then, so I would get the kids bags full of brand new crayons, markers, puzzle books, and even paints one time," Jan said. "That turned out to be a one-time-only activity, though, as Mickey decided to paint the windows, tray table, and his sisters!"

If that wasn't enough, the kids all had bright red hair, so they stood out in any crowd. "As I told them one time, whatever you do you will always be noticed," Jan said. "Someone will always say, 'One kid had red hair.'"

Usually that was Mickey, whose motto was 'I-was-gone-why-do-homework.' When he was 10, he and his remote-controlled car had the entire waiting area on its toes during a long flight delay. "He drove it in and around passengers who couldn't figure out who was controlling it," Jan said. "It was quite entertaining for everyone."

The time changes from the Northwest were just as tough as the flights. Amy was one month old when Jan took her to the Buick Open in Grand Blanc, Michigan, and mom figured she would sleep through the night. She would have — on Pacific Time. Instead, Jan and Peter were driving around at midnight trying to get her to sleep. She finally nodded off about 2:00 a.m.

Jan and Peter Jacobsen

Amy, Kristen, Jan, Mick, and Peter Jacobsen, flying to a tournament

The night before the final round, Phil and Kitty Hancock knew it was tough and offered Peter a bed in an adjoining room. "He jumped at the chance of a good night's sleep and I was happy not to be worrying about him," Jan said. "The end of this story is pretty fantastic. He came from 7 shots back to win his first TOUR event. Then he finished second the next week — all with a baby keeping him up most nights."

In case you're wondering, Peter and Jan did try driving across country the first two years they were on TOUR. They didn't consider a third, in part, because of trips like the one in 1977 when the car broke down just outside of Lyman, Wyoming.

"Peter gets the car off the highway and there are no cell phones,

obviously, and no phones anywhere," Jan said. "A big truck came by and gave Peter a lift into town. He said, 'I'm not leaving my golf clubs out here alone. You've got to stay here in the car.' So he leaves me, the dog, and the clubs alone in the car in the middle of nowhere."

They got the car fixed, but they didn't have any cash or credit cards, so they called Peter's father. "He called a bank," Jan said, "and had the bank call the shop to say it was okay to take a personal check."

Much later, the Jacobsens found themselves creating Thanksgiving Day memories at the La Quinta in Palm Springs. Peter was a commentator on the Skins Game, which was played that weekend. "We all had a wonderful time, but one thing missing was turkey," Jan

Amy, Kristen, and Mick Jacobsen

said. "We ate at a few restaurants that offered turkey dinners like Tony Roma's and Marie Callender's, but our kids just wanted grilled cheese. I think it was 2002 when we finally had Thanksgiving in the house and I had no idea how to cook a turkey. I soon found out that is the easiest part of the meal."

Today, the Jacobsens are still flying long distances. Jan and Peter and Mickey, an attorney, are all in Florida. Amy, who works for her dad's production company, her husband and two young sons are in Portland, and Kristen is a neurologist in New York.

The funny thing is, when the family all gets together, Peter, who is known for his uncanny ability to entertain people with imitations of players and celebrities, is the quiet one. "Maybe because he finally has a chance to sit back, relax and not be the one expected to entertain," Jan said. "But I think it's mostly because we don't give him a chance."

As for all those miles they've flown over the past 37 years? They're still stockpiling them, although they did splurge in 2004 when the whole clan went on the road again — on free tickets — to the British Senior Open.

"Between Peter's tournament play and commentating for NBC, we don't spend much time in one place," Jan said. "But then that's the life we've always known and loved . . . most of the time!"

The Kenny Perry Family

Lesslye Perry was about six when she and four-year-old Justin and two-year-old Lindsey walked down the runway at THE PLAYERS in a children's fashion show. Cute kids. Cuter clothes. Precious moments. An inside look at the kids behind the players.

A week later, there was a chicken pox outbreak in the TOUR family. "They were all exposed there and broke out when they got home," Sandy Perry said. "It was before the vaccine, so it affected everyone. Very few kids didn't get sick."

Ironically, that happened to be one of the few times the Perry kids were at a tournament during a school year. Back then, it wasn't as easy to pack the kids in the car and head out. Schools were less likely to budge on time missed, private school wasn't always an option, and homeschooling was just starting. So when the kids hit school age, every family had to make a decision.

With the kids starting to get involved in sports and spending more time with their friends, Sandy and Kenny put it to a family vote of sorts. The decision? Kenny would travel, and Sandy and the kids would stay home.

"We just tried to make a total family decision," she said. "It was a tough one and one you have to make for your family. There's no right or wrong."

So, until Lindsey graduated from high school in 2006, Sandy stayed home and shuttled them to dance and golf and gymnastics and baseball and swimming and . . . you name it, the Perry kids did it all. Lindsey focused on dance, and Lesslye dedicated her time to cheerleading, and was a Tennessee Titans cheerleader for two years. Justin played baseball and basketball, but wound up playing golf at Western Kentucky, Kenny's alma mater.

The years put a lot of miles on Sandy's car, but she wouldn't trade the time with her kids for the world. "They all tried many sports," Sandy said, "and we let them weed it out on their own."

And, unlike today when you can text, Skype, or FaceTime with dad when he's on the road, the Perrys made do with phone calls from Kenny. Back then, most players phoned home from the free long-distance landline phones in every tournament locker room. It took coordination with all the kids' activities and Kenny's tee times.

"We needed to figure out when Kenny was going to call so we would be home," she said. "There were no cell phones. It wasn't like you could text your husband all the time. And in the locker room, people were always there listening to what you were saying."

When Kenny did come home after a few weeks away, he didn't come bearing gifts for everyone. He just walked in the door and turned his focus to family. "The present was he was at home," Sandy said.

Today, the Perrys have come full circle. Justin now caddies for Kenny

Sandy and Kenny, celebrating on the green after his win at the 2009 FBR Open

Sandy and Kenny, on their wedding day

on the board of directors and as vice president of membership for two years. During that time, she resurrected the Big Sister, Little Sister program, patterned after the sorority model. She didn't want anyone to feel alone like she did that day in family dining.

"I thought it was important to develop friendships," she said. "There were girls coming out here from what was then the Nationwide Tour or from the mini-tours. It's good to have someone to help you — someone to call and ask.

"It really, really helped me get to know the younger wives. I was away from my daughters, so I could relate because they were about the same age. It was fulfilling getting to know a whole other group of wives."

"It's an odd life," she said, "filled with travel, sacrifices, and lots of moments when dad is playing a tournament and mom winds up being both mom and dad." As it was, their plan worked perfectly and even when Kenny was on the road, his heart and passion for giving back was at home.

In 1992, Kenny and Sandy bought 142 acres of land, then borrowed money to build an affordable public course — Country Creek. The course opened in 1995 and it may be the only place where 18 holes and a cart on a weekday is only $30. Kenny still pops behind the counter at times to ring up a green's fee or two.

Now, there are grandbabies to bounce and elderly parents to care for. Kenny still plays a few TOUR events, and he and Sandy travel together as much as they can on the Champions Tour. "It's awesome," she said. "We love doing it because we spent so many years apart; we're thankful for being together."

when he plays PGA TOUR events and Sandy started traveling again after Lindsey graduated in 2006. She was able to catch the last few years of Kenny playing full-time on the TOUR, as well as recent years when he transitioned to the Champions Tour. But when she first came back out on the TOUR, she felt a bit out of place. "I walked into family dining and knew no one," she said. "So I decided to get involved."

Sandy embraced the PGA TOUR Wives Association events, serving

The Perry Family – Kenny and Sandy, daughter Lindsey, son Justin and daughter-in-law Brittany, grandson Rowdy, daughter Lesslye Perry Harris, and son-in-law Justin Harris

Kenny and Sandy

Target House/
St. Jude Children's
Research Hospital

Comedian and entertainer Danny Thomas is best known for his starring role in *Make Room for Daddy*, but his legacy lives on through the St. Jude Children's Research Hospital in Memphis, Tennessee. As the founder, he has had a profound influence on the public, as well as on PGA TOUR and PGA TOUR players and wives.

The FedEx St. Jude Classic is a summer TOUR stop and most commonly know as "St. Jude's" by those out on TOUR. The shortened name is in no way intended to offend the sponsor or throw off the spectators, but everyone seems to know what tournament the players are talking about. "It's really ingrained with the players and the TOUR," says J. D. Peeples, a marketing executive with St. Jude. "We understand we're not the biggest or most important event on the PGA TOUR schedule, but it's amazing how many top players come to play in the tournament each year because they know of the great work the hospital does and they want to support that."

In 1970, the Memphis Classic's name changed to the Danny Thomas-Memphis Classic at Thomas's behest so that all the charitable proceeds could be directed back to the hospital. Since the first St. Jude-associated event, the FedEx St. Jude Classic has raised more than $21 million for the hospital. The PGA TOUR Wives Association early on recognized the importance of St. Jude and the relationship it has with the tournament and the competing players. This explains the Association's acknowledgement and support of St. Jude and Target House.

Target House is a facility where children who are undergoing long-term treatment for cancer or other life-threatening diseases can stay with their family for no charge. When a new family arrives in Memphis, ready to move into Target House, Karri Morgan, the facility's manager, likes to hold an orientation to help the new residents understand what amenities Target House offers. She talks about the 800-square-foot; fully furnished apartments that include a kitchen, bathroom, and living room, and can

Sarah McGirt and Erin Gainey, with an honorary caddie, during the FedEx St. Jude Classic

PGA TOUR Players – Billy Horschel, Bobby Gates, William McGirt, and Will Claxton show off their faces, painted by children from St. Jude Children's Research Hospital

accommodate the patient and three other family members. Morgan covers everything from laundry facilities to the gym and even how residents can go about getting things like a haircut.

Lauren Gates and Arjun Atwal interact with kids from St. Jude Children's Research Hospital during the Honorary Caddie for a Day event, at the FedEx St. Jude Classic

More times than she can remember, though, Morgan has done the orientation outside, often in the blazing Memphis heat. Sure, her office might be more comfortable, but when the patients who will be receiving care at the St. Jude Children's Research Hospital gets to Target House, their new temporary home away from home, they often see the playground — nicknamed The Park — and once they see The Park, they're hooked.

Goodbye, air-conditioning. Hello, bright sunshine.

"These kids have been through heck and back, so the chance for them to just be kids and play on the playground, doing what kids are supposed to do, it is a thrill to see them get excited," Morgan says. "We hold orientation on the playground since the kids see The Park as the coolest place on earth."

Target House opened its doors in 1999, providing a place for families to live in Memphis while a child receives long-term care at St. Jude's. Morgan has been with Target House from the beginning, and as she talks about the colorful playground, complete with all the slides, climbers, and swings, the passion with which she speaks seems to increase.

"The PGA TOUR Wives Association donated the original playground that came with Target House when we opened," Morgan says. "It has since been renovated to become Americans with Disabilities Act-compliant, but it has and will always be know as 'The Park.' When I think of a park, I think of my parents driving me to a place away from my house," Morgan continues. "But here, we have a park right in our backyard, and it's a great place for kids to come and be kids. They quickly make friends on the playground, but it has also been a place where parents in similar situations can watch their kids have fun, and talk and bond with other families who are going through the same gamut of emotions."

Back when Target House was still a dream, Ann Herron, wife of PGA TOUR veteran Tim Herron, brought the idea to the TOUR Wives Association Board of Directors. She felt the playground donation was a worthwhile project, and the board agreed. Through the years, Target House has been one of the major beneficiaries of TOUR Wives initiatives.

Jonathan Byrd and friend

In recent years, the wives have added an art aspect to the FedEx St. Jude Classic's tournament week. In one of the hospitality tents, patients from the hospital and Target House have an opportunity to make arts and crafts, and even do a little face painting — on PGA TOUR players.

The Park – Playground built by the PGA TOUR Wives Association

"While you would think the players who had their faces painted would immediately go and wash the paint off, some of them, like William McGirt, went right out to the tournament practice green and started putting with their faces still painted," Peeples says.

"The PGA TOUR Wives Association has always been very supportive of our mission. I think most of these women look at the sick kids and think, 'That could be us,'" Morgan adds. "The kids don't get to leave Target House very much, and it's hard when you are bald because of chemotherapy or you have muscle atrophy. But when the kids visit Target House or are able to go to the golf course during the FedEx St. Jude Classic, the TOUR Wives and their husbands treat the kids like the kings and queens that they are."

Thank you for your support on behalf of the kids of St. Jude Children's Research Hospital.

CHARITABLE WORKS
1994-1999

1994

TOUR Wives Golf Classic at the Phoenix Open
Silent auction at the Phoenix Open
Children's Hospital at the Freeport-McMoRan Classic
Fairway House at Shell Houston Open
Chickasaw School of the Woodlands at the Shell Houston Open
St. Jude Children's Hospital at the Federal Express St. Jude Classic
Mom's House at the B.C. Open
Children's Hospital of Wisconsin at the Greater Milwaukee Open
Fashion show at the Greater Milwaukee Open
Golf in the Garden at Egleston Children's Hospital at the BellSouth Classic
Silent auction at the BellSouth Classic
International Boy's Club at The International
Arrowhead Ranch at the Quad Cities Classic
Quilt raffle at multiple tournaments

1995

Fashion show, the Children's Home Society Auxiliary and TOUR Wives Association
at THE PLAYERS Championship
Auction and raffle at the Freeport-McMoRan Classic
Gourmet Golf Gala at the PGA Championship
TOUR Wives Golf Classic at the Buick Southern Open
Los Amigos School at the Northern Telecom Open
Winn-Dixie Hope Lodge at the Doral-Ryder Open
Golf in the Garden at Egleston Children's Hospital at the BellSouth Classic
Acadiana Boys & Girls Club at the NIKE Louisiana Open
Boys & Girls Club of Raleigh-Durham at the NIKE Carolina Classic
Ronald McDonald House at the NIKE Ozarks Open
McLeods Children's Hospital in Florence at the NIKE South Carolina Classic
Hospital visits at the NIKE Cleveland Open
Silent auction at the NIKE TOUR Championship

1996

Tin Cup movie premiere and auction at the PGA Championship
Friends of Retarded at the Shell Houston Open
United Hospital Medical Center at the Buick Classic
St. Jude Children's Hospital at the Federal Express St. Jude Classic
Canuck Place Children's Hospital at the Greater Vancouver Open
Children's Hospital Medical Center of Akron at the NEC World Series of Golf
Mom's House at the B.C. Open
Arrowhead Ranch at the Quad Cities Classic
Loma Linda Hospital at the NIKE Inland Empire Open

Boys & Girls Club of Raleigh-Durham at the NIKE Carolina Classic
Lake County Hospital at the NIKE Cleveland Open
University Orthopedic Institute Hahnemann University at the NIKE Philadelphia Classic
Fashion show at NIKE Wichita Open
Silent auction at the NIKE Ozarks Open
Silent auction at the NIKE TOUR Championship

1997

Gourmet Golf Gala II at the Nissan Open
Everybody Wins! Links to Literacy program in Washington, DC
TOUR Wives Golf Classic at the Michelob Championship at Kingsmill
Fashion show and luncheon sponsored by Southern Bell at the La Cantera Texas Open
"Taste of the TOUR" at THE TOUR Championship
Martha's Kitchen at the Bob Hope Chrysler Classic
Boys & Girls Club in Phoenix at the Phoenix Open
Children's Home Society at the Buick Invitational
Boys & Girls Club of Raleigh-Durham at the NIKE Carolina Classic
Boys & Girls Club of Richmond at the NIKE Dominion Open
Boys & Girls Club of Knoxville at the NIKE Knoxville Open
Silent auction at the NIKE Ozarks Open
Silent auction at the NIKE TOUR Championship

1998

St. Jude Children's Hospital 10-year Anniversary Celebration at the FedEx St. Jude Classic
Golf Jam at the Hard Rock Café at THE TOUR Championship
Everybody Wins! Links to Literacy program in Washington, DC
Everybody Wins! Links to Literacy program in Atlanta, GA
Golf in the Garden at Egleston Children's Hospital at the BellSouth Classic
Boys & Girls Club of Hartford at the Canon Greater Hartford Open
Early Works Children's Museum at the NIKE Huntsville Open
McLeod Children's Hospital at the NIKE South Carolina Classic
Boys & Girls Clubs of Knoxville at the NIKE Knoxville Open
Boys & Girls Clubs of St Louis at the NIKE St. Louis Golf Classic
Youth Emergency Services (YES) at the NIKE Omaha Classic
Silent auction at the NIKE Ozarks Open

1999

Disco Mania Fundraiser at the Phoenix Open
Rock the Greens, a TOUR Wives Association benefit concert presented by
Lucent Technologies at the Sprint International
First Tee / Everybody Wins! Links to Literacy program in Washington, DC
Everybody Wins Gala at the Kemper Open
Target House fundraiser for a new playground at the FedEx St. Jude Classic
Target House Family BBQ, St. Jude Children's Hospital at the FedEx St. Jude Classic
Golf in the Garden at Egleston Children's Hospital at the BellSouth Classic
Camp Arrowhead at the John Deere Classic
Fashion show at the NIKE Wichita Open
Boys & Girls Club of Gulfport at the NIKE Mississippi Gulf Coast Open
McLeod Children's Hospital at the NIKE South Carolina Classic
Silent auction at the NIKE Ozarks Open

The Tom Lehman Family

Tom Lehman was on a mission. He had finished up a tournament in Amarillo and was driving straight through to California to meet his wife, Melissa, and go to a wedding. He needed a shower badly, but there was no time to stop for the night. No money to waste on a room, either. So Tom turned to nature. "It was pouring rain," he said. "I was stinking so bad that I just got out of the car and took a shower."

Welcome to the mini-tours and trail of state opens. The stepping stones to the Web.com Tour and PGA TOUR. No one ever got rich playing the litany of options out there, but they did learn a whole lot about life. Sometimes that tournament check you just earned would bounce. Other times, your car was your room. And sometimes, the rain was your shower.

"We would have weeks on the mini-tours when, if it was a good week, I'd get a bag of Oreos because we could afford them," Melissa said. "Or on a lean week, we would go to the movies, but no popcorn, no drinks. We were so young and we had no money, but we pieced it together."

Almost three decades after that shower in the rain, Tom has a major on his résumé and he has gone where no player has gone before or likely ever will go. He's the only player to earn Player of the Year honors on every tour — the then-Ben Hogan Tour in 1991, the PGA TOUR in 1996, and the Champions Tour in 2011.

But when they got married in 1987, money was tight. Tom had

Melissa and Tom

bounced around the PGA TOUR for a few years in the early 1980s, but had settled into a life that was a jumble of events from South Africa and Southeast Asia to the Dakotas Tour, Golden State Tour, T. C. Jordan Tour, and every state open in the vicinity. Melissa even doubled as a caddie at times to save money, and they shared meals. One night in Japan, where everything was expensive, she spent eight dollars on a pint of Häagen-Dazs® — which they split.

"It was all about how to work it out and finding your way in the world," she said. "He missed the cut in Taiwan and Korea, and he was going to have to qualify for the tournament in Japan, so we had the conversation about do we want to pursue this?

"I did have to caddie for him because we couldn't afford the

Melissa and Tom Lehman

Tom, with Thomas and Sean

The Lehman family – Melissa, Tom, Rachael, Holly, Thomas, and Sean

caddies. They were tiny ladies who caddied with carts and they were fast. Luckily, Tom outdrove everyone, so I had a chance to catch up."

Melissa felt a little better when they cleared their first hurdle. "When he was fully-exempt on the Hogan Tour, that just seemed like a better way for him to get his PGA TOUR card," she said. "It was by playing well all year, not just one week at Qualifying School."

She was right. After two wins on the Ben Hogan Tour, he earned his PGA TOUR card. At that point, Melissa was no longer worried about every penny flying out the door. But it really wasn't until he reached 125 cuts made — not long before Thomas, their third child, was born in 1995 — and they were vested with lifetime membership and insurance that she took a "big, deep breath."

"Every time we would get to a level, I would think, 'Oh, my gosh, can it get any better than this?'" Melissa said. "Yes, it did. And it did again."

Tom just missed making the Ryder Cup team in 1993, but Melissa, who didn't think it was that big of a deal at the time, just said, "You're tired; let's go home." It didn't take long for her to figure out it was a big deal. Tom made the next three Ryder Cup teams, captained the 2006 team, and played on three Presidents Cup teams.

Melissa and Tom have four children now: Rachael, 23; Holly, 21; Thomas, 18; and Sean, 10. They look back on the days when they'd travel with a deck of cards and battle each other or whoever was around in Gin Rummy or Spite and Malice or Hearts, and smile. Those penny-pinching, sketchy motel days, those long trips with the kids, turned into those three Player of the Year awards.

"It's a blessed life and golf is a fabulous game," Melissa said. "I had no aspirations. I didn't know what golf would provide. It's a special sport. Who can play football when they're 53? When you look out there and see people you've known for 25 years, you know you're blessed."

The Lehman children – Thomas, Holly, Rachael and Sean

Tom and Melissa, during Halloween with Holly and Rachael

Sonya and David Toms, at the Gala Celebration for the 2011 Presidents Cup in Melbourne, Australia.

The David Toms Family

Four hours before kickoff, David Toms is in the car heading to Tiger Stadium. He's a little fidgety and seriously tense. Wound tighter than a drum, actually. He wants to get to the locker room to say hello and then to the field to watch warm-ups.

This isn't just another game. It's LSU football.

Without traffic, it's about five minutes from the Baton Rouge home he bought just for games at the stadium. But on a game day? He has to deal with everyone headed to the game and all the tailgaters along the

way. Trust his wife. It's not a pretty picture.

Sonya Toms shakes her head. "I can't ride with him. If you get in traffic with him, he's like a crazy man. He gets so fired up about football." The whole family does, actually. They're just not all as tightly wound as David, who was a three-time All-American at LSU.

Sonya and David, who both bleed purple and gold, have 20 season tickets to dole out each weekend and the requisite subtle purple wardrobe items in their closets.

"Sometimes," Sonya said, "we're like Ticketmaster trying to figure out who's sitting where. And every once in a while, if we're short a ticket, we just tell David to stay on the sidelines."

During football season, Carter, 16, heads to the sidelines and locker room with his dad and sometimes even dares ride with him to the stadium. Anna, 8, goes to the field too, often in her cheerleader uniform, to see the mascot, Mike the Tiger, and the cheerleaders.

Home games mean an all-day tailgate party at their house. It starts Saturday mornings — sometimes Friday night — when they all watch ESPN's Game Day and maybe an early game or two if the Tigers are playing late. After the game? It's back to the house for more food, fun, SportsCenter, and maybe another game.

Tiger football is their passion.

Life moves fast in the Toms' house and not just for football. Their downtime, which always revolves around another sport, moves even faster. Every sport has become a family affair.

Everyone but Anna hunts, but it won't be long until she joins in. Sonya picked it up a few years ago, and loves not just the sport, but the incredible beauty of the quiet, dark mornings when everyone is sitting in the blinds waiting for the sun to come up.

Skiing means everyone on the slopes. And the lake? That's where they hang out. "We're not home a lot in Shreveport when David's off," Sonya said. "We are always doing something and it's some other sport or activity.

"About eight years ago, a good friend of mine said, 'The Toms, you like to recreate.' I said I guess you're right. We are always going from one thing to the next, but life's short and we like to have fun."

David is at the point in his career where he can take six weeks off in the summer and hang out with the family at the lake. He can make his fall golf schedule around Tigers games. They've watched LSU win a split national title in 2003 and an uncontested one in 2007, but missed their loss to Alabama in 2011. In case you're wondering, they have Tigers season baseball tickets, too.

By November, the family is heading to Arkansas to hunt — mostly

David and Sonya enjoy an LSU football game with their kids, Carter and Anna.

on non-Tigers game weekends — and by January, they're ready for a week or two in Colorado. Then it's the lake and . . . they're back to football. Whew.

That doesn't even take into account the kids' sports. Anna plays the piano and loves tennis almost as much as Sonya. Carter played baseball when he was younger, but is now on his high school golf team. And David has been known to get that same fidgety game-day-like focus before one of Carter's matches.

"When David's at a tournament, and say he has the lead, he's not the same kind of nervous," Sonya said. "When it's golf, he's very quiet, very focused. He's already zoned in. He can control that."

The rest? Not so much. Even that game-day drive, which gets frenzied because he doesn't like to be late. "He's like Mr. Punctuality," Sonya said. "Three o'clock to him means 2:30 and to us, it's 3:10."

Which brings us to Thanksgiving week 2011. LSU was hosting Arkansas, and the Toms and some more family were hunting. David knew it should be a quick plane ride to Baton Rouge, but it wasn't. Air traffic had everything backed up and they wound up flying into an airport 45 minutes from the stadium.

"We weren't cutting it completely close," Sonya said, "just a lot closer than he likes to cut it, and he was trying to contain himself. We made kickoff, but he was a nervous wreck."

The Jeff Maggert Family

Jeff and Michelle take advantage of having the whole family together at Thanksgiving. Captured in this photo are their five children: Matt, Macy, Jake, Madeline, and Phillip.

Years before Jeff and Michelle Maggert met, President George Bush, Sr. called Jeff to play golf in Houston a few times. Michelle says they formed a friendship through golf. When she and Jeff started dating, President Bush sent her a note wishing the couple well and signed a golf ball decorated with the presidential seal that she still has in her office.

Jeff and Michelle have twins, Jake and Madeline. "From a young age, they preferred to play with cell phones over their toys," says Michelle. "They would pretend to talk to one another from different places in the hotel room, talk to their grandma and grandpa, their brothers and sister, and their imaginary friends. It was quite fascinating to watch them carry on these conversations with people as if they were actually on the phone with them."

One time though, they managed to make a call. Unfortunately, it was to the office of President George Bush, Sr. "They were connected to a wonderful lady on the other end and she quite enjoyed receiving a call from a two-year-old," laughs Michelle. His office called Michelle back just to make sure everything was okay.

"To say I was a bit embarrassed was an understatement," Michelle said, "but looking back, it is something we will always remember and laugh about. Most importantly, we appreciate the fact that even a president can have a sense of humor when it comes to two-year-olds and their imaginations."

The Skip Kendall Family

Skip and Traci Kendall

The Waste Management Phoenix Open is well known amongst players and fans for its famous 16th hole. Fans come prepared for the day with a taunt for every player as they grace the tee on the par-3 hole. Traci Kendall shares a story about their experiences surrounding the event.

"In 2010, Skip finished tied for fourth place at the Mayakoba Golf Classic, which earned him a last-minute entry into the Waste Management Phoenix Open. It was great news, but it meant we had to scramble to get flights from Cancun to Phoenix. We needed five seats, but there were only four seats available; one in first class and the others in the last row of coach. I insisted Skip take the seat in first class because he had just finished playing and my sister, my kids, and I would wedge into the seats that were left. Several PGA TOUR players were also on the plane and saw as I took the children to the back and Skip took the seat in first class. They now kid him that the "king" sits in first class while the family moves to the back.

"As it turns out, my sister, whom I had asked to join us, ended up meeting her future husband, Steve Flesch, that week. Now we all enjoy this tournament. I particularly love watching Skip play the 16th hole. As soon as he walks on the tee box, the crowd serenades him with 'Skippity do da, skippity day. My, oh my, what a wonderful day. Plenty of sunshine, heading my way. Skippity do da, skippity day' . . . and the crowd goes wild!"

"Getting to the tournament is such a minor inconvenience when you have the fans who greet and support you as they do at this tournament. There's nothing like the fans of the Waste Management Phoenix Open!"

Skip, Traci, Remi and Brady prepare for trick or treating with their "dressed up" golf cart as transportation.

Chris and Amy DiMarco

The Chris DiMarco Family

Growing up together, Chris and Amy DiMarco went to the same middle school and their parents were really good friends who hung out at their local country club together. Their families would go to University of Florida Gator football games together and Amy cheered for Chris's football team. Chris and Amy did not start dating until their senior year of high school, but that's when they fell in love.

They dated all four years of college and married a year after they graduated. "Once we were married, I started traveling with Chris full-time and became his caddie," explains Amy. "I caddied for him during the Canadian Tour in 1992, where he won the Order of Merit, and I caddied for him during the Nike Tour in 1993. He finished ninth on the money list and earned his PGA TOUR card for the following year. I started out caddying for him on the PGA TOUR in 1994, but that lasted about six months. We decided it was time to start a family so my caddying days were over." It was almost a decade later before Amy put the caddie bib back on.

"Chris got invited to play in the Abu Dhabi Golf Championship in 2006. He thought it would be great for us both to go, sort of like a mini vacation. I could relive my caddie days, although I hadn't caddied in nine years and didn't really have an interest in caddying. I was leaving three busy kids at home and was looking forward to spending time together. I said, 'Okay let's do it!' Abu Dhabi is beautiful and they put us up in the palace, which was the most spectacular place we had ever stayed in. I can remember thinking, "Wow, this is vacation!" But, who was I kidding? I was going to be caddying!

"Chris played okay the first day and shot a 71, 1-under par. There were a lot of caddies who did not have a bag and they kept asking me if I wanted them to take my place and caddie for Chris. I thought really hard about it and was thinking it would probably be a good idea, since Chris was playing so-so and I wanted a little vacation time. The second day, Chris shot a 67, 5-under par, and made the cut. Chris was several back off the lead and I remember saying to Chris, 'Why don't you get a 'real' caddie and I will enjoy the weekend?' He said, 'Amy, you got me through the cut. Let's just finish this out and see what happens.' Not exactly what I wanted to hear.

"We went shopping that night at the local mall and stopped by a watch shop. I noticed a green Daytona Rolex watch that I fell in love with. Chris said to me that if we won the tournament, he would buy me the watch. I told him, 'You're on!'

"On Saturday, Chris started out with a double bogey; I almost

Cristian, Amanda and Abigale DiMarco

dropped the bag right there. I told him to get it together. 'We are going to win this tournament and I am going to get that watch!' Chris then shot 11-under par on the next 17 holes, and ended up shooting a 63, 9-under for the day and was leading the tournament. I was so excited and so glad I hadn't given up his bag.

"On Sunday, Chris played great, too, and shot a 67, 5-under par, enough to win the tournament by one shot, at 20-under par. It was one of the best moments in our lives together! I gave him a kiss on the 18th green wearing the caddie bib. And, as he had promised, I got the watch!"

The Michael Allen Family

Michael and Cynthia Allen with their daughters, Christy and Michelle

Traveling when you have some idea of where you are going can be challenging, but traveling outside the country before cell phones and GPS was particularly difficult at times. Cynthia Allen shares her story.

"When Michael and I were first married (more than 20 years ago), we drove everywhere. We were heading to a tournament in Toronto, and had to be there by noon the next day to make Michael's pro-am tee time. It was past midnight when we crossed the Canadian border and checked into a hotel to get a few hours of sleep before continuing our drive to the tournament.

"We didn't realize it until the next morning, but we should have left much earlier to get Michael to the course. After much anxiety, we made it with just enough time for him to run to the tee. As he ran off, he told me to go check into the Holiday Inn, Mississauga. To my delight, I was able to find the hotel and get us checked in.

"Later that evening, I waited for Michael to arrive . . . six o'clock, seven, eight, and then 9:00 p.m. rolled past. First I was mad, but then became frightened that something had happened. I went to the front desk and this is when I learned there was another Holiday Inn in Mississauga. What a relief! I called the other hotel and . . . no Michael registered. With no other recourse available, I went to the course early the next morning to see if he was there.

"By eight o'clock in the morning, I was at the course sitting in the car watching as player after player arrived. Finally, there he was . . . in the exact same clothes as the day before. I ran over, thinking he would be as anxious as I was to see him, but he said sternly, 'Where have you been?' 'At the Holiday Inn Mississauga!' I told him. 'No, you weren't,' he replied. 'I called and they said you weren't there!'

"Turns out we were both given faulty information. He was at one, and I was at the other; with both of us panicking because we couldn't locate each other. Cell phones have taken this particular worry away, and I am grateful every time for that particular convenience!"

The Michael Bradley Family

Michael and Jennifer Bradley

Brooke, James, Michael, and Jennifer, enjoying a family vacation

Like many player spouses, Jennifer Bradley left a career to become part of her husband's traveling support team, but quickly learned she needed something to keep her busy. She found her challenge at the course. Here's her story.

"In 1994, I started doing the Darrell Survey, which is an equipment survey that takes place every Thursday on all tours in the United States. A Darrell Survey employee records what each player has in his bag — the number and brand of clubs, and anything else in or around the player's bag. This helps to verify that both the players and manufacturers are in compliance with their contracts.

"Patti Inman, wife of player John Inman, also did the survey and took me under her wing. Soon I was a staple on the first or 10th tee on Thursdays. I got to know a lot of the players as well as a lot of the caddies, many of whom I remain friends with today. I loved digging into the players' bags, listening to the banter between the guys, and being included in on inside jokes.

"In 1996, at the Doral-Ryder Open, I was very pregnant and still working the survey. My husband was playing in the Open and shot an opening round 64. Player Jay Don Blake came to the tee I was working and asked if he could rub my very pregnant belly for good luck, as it appeared it had clearly worked for my husband. I laughed and, since I was good friends with Jay Don and his wife Marci, said, "Of course, please rub the Magic Buddha." Jay Don proceeded to snap hook it right into the water off of the tee. I laughed and reminded him that perhaps the good mojo worked only for my husband. It was priceless!"

The Greg Norman Family

Gregory and Morgan-Leigh Norman used to eye the crowd in front of them at a green and look for an opening. Sometimes it meant hitting the ground and crawling between spectators' legs; other times, it was sliding through a kid-sized crack. A wiggle here, a quick dart there. Gregory was a master at it by age four.

The whole idea was to get to the rope line. Say "excuse me" along the way, and pull the but-that's-my-dad card if needed.

The end game? Getting a glimpse of your dad at work.

"It's not just another golfer; it's your dad," Morgan-Leigh said. "You want to see him play. We kind of dreaded when he was playing well on Sunday because you knew how many people would be out there, so you had to get creative and find your way to the front."

It wasn't easy, considering their dad was Greg Norman, the dashing Australian with white-blond hair who was the number one player in the world for 331 weeks, and is still one of the most popular players period. "I think I always understood it or appreciated it," she said. "When you're out there walking around with thousands of people just watching your father, you grasp that."

Gregory even made a game out of it when he got a little older. Instead of crawling through the crowd, he would sprint ahead of it and scramble up a tree to find a good spot. "I was so short and it was always so packed," he said. "I had fun doing it. And I'd do the same thing 18 times in a row."

It was driven home, too, when the family would go out to what was supposed to be a quiet dinner. They couldn't go 10 or 15 minutes without someone coming up to ask for an autograph or a picture. "We'd go out with friends' families and no one interrupted you for photographs or autographs," she said.

But there was also a normalcy to growing up Norman. They had a strong family dynamic and two of the most important nights of the week were Sunday and Monday. On weeks when they didn't travel, Greg would fly home as soon as he could and they had dinner together.

"We were away from the chaos and drama," she said. "Those are the moments you appreciate the most. You work so hard traveling around, watching, that you appreciate just being there having dinner and hanging out together. We felt really normal, despite dad being the number one golfer."

Morgan-Leigh went on the road at two weeks old. Gregory came along three years later. They grew up with other famous players' children such as Michael Watson, Christina Floyd, and Amy, Kristen, and Mickey Jacobsen — all in the days before child care was available. So, when they were on the course, they had not one, but several moms watching them.

"The moms would group up and be there for support and they all always looked after us," she said. "We weren't going too far."

One exception was an afternoon in Chicago during the Western Open. The Western was one of the few tournaments with child care and on this day — Gregory was six or seven — some of the kids had gone swimming at a county pool. A sudden storm came up and a tornado touched down.

Gregory and Morgan-Leigh, with their father, Greg Norman

A ranger grabbed Gregory and some other kids and got them to safety. "I remember getting locked up in a stone room," he said. "They had us all in there. I didn't really know what was going on, but you could hear it outside. It sounded like a jet engine." His parents found out after the fact and they were just happy that everyone was safe. Gregory's take at that age — it was pretty awesome.

When they got older, the kids wouldn't necessarily go to the course, but they would hang out. At one British Open, Gregory taught Mickey Jacobsen to play snooker and they spent most of the week with cue sticks in their hands.

Sometimes the Normans would fly to an event on a Friday when Greg was in contention; other times they would head home Friday night if he missed the cut. A win would mean a family celebration on the flight home; a tough loss meant a quiet night. "I remember being somber (after losses)," she said. "A lot of times we'd just adjust — Dad's close to a win, let's fly out or change of plans, we're going home."

Then there was the 1993 British Open. Greg closed with a 64 at Royal St. George's to win his second Claret Jug and Morgan-Leigh couldn't watch it or talk to her dad. She was at Camp Waldemar in Texas and they had a rule that campers couldn't just call their parents because they missed them. "I remember how disappointed I was," she said. "I'd been there for so many close calls and I wasn't there for the win. We worked it out and I got to talk to him the next day."

Greg and Morgan-Leigh

Greg didn't push his children toward golf. Morgan-Leigh played soccer and swam. Gregory played golf for a bit, but turned his attention to kite boarding and became one of the top boarders in the United States.

Today, both have a hand in the family business. Morgan-Leigh is entering her seventh year with the business and is the global director for Greg Norman Estates. Gregory is building cable parks — practice facilities for surfers, kite boarders and wake boarders — and working for Great White Shark Enterprises. "It's a family business and we want to keep it that way," Gregory said.

Morgan-Leigh went to culinary school after college and studied wine. She never thought she'd work for her dad. Then, she was working

as a chef in the wine industry seven years ago when her dad made her an offer she couldn't refuse.

"He said, "Okay, you've earned your stripes. I'd love to have you become involved,"' she said. "Wine and food are my passion. It's a great opportunity to work with my dad. Fun to have not just a father-daughter relationship, but a working one, too."

But some things never change — especially when she goes to a tournament with packed galleries and thinks about the old days when she was still a kid. "I go out on the golf course now," she said, chuckling, "and I'm thinking I wish I could still crawl between people's legs to get up front."

Greg and daughter, Morgan-Leigh, at one of the Greg Norman Estates Vineyards.

Lisa and Stewart, with their sons, Connor and Reagan, holding the Claret Jug following Stewart's win at the 2009 British Open.

The Stewart Cink Family

Stewart Cink knew he was losing the battle, but couldn't bring himself to let go. That receding hairline from his late 20s had been reduced to what wife, Lisa, referred to as a "monk band." It wasn't pretty.

So when she saw Stewart taking off his cap at the end of the 2008 Wells Fargo Championship, she kept the DVR recording for him to see. "He was balding pretty bad," she said. "When he watched it and he could see himself from the back and how ridiculous it looked . . . he went into the bathroom and shaved it off."

"He loves it. Other than the fact that when you first shave a head it looks purple . . . he's got a good bald head. It was a real improvement. It almost looked more natural to have that."

Five years and a British Open Championship later, Stewart's dome is as much part of his off-course signature as Twitter and his Big Green Egg. He makes sure to take his cap off between shots during practice rounds so he can lose the white lines from the seams of his cap. "Tan maintenance," he calls it.

Lisa and Stewart Cink

Photographer Chris Condon/PGA TOUR

And the other two hobbies? He's one of the TOUR's top tweeters — only his Nike teammate Tiger Woods has more followers — and Lisa tweets, too. "It's just a nice banter, especially for him," Lisa said. "He says it's a way to connect with golf fans. He responds to all the messages he gets."

His passion for smoking meats in the Big Green Egg led to a second grill from a competing company — Primo — and has gone from a backyard barbecue for family and friends, to hosting a barbecue contest, entering a few barbecue contests, and a couple of semi-catering gigs.

It's a bit ironic, though, that Lisa stopped eating red meat and pork just as Stewart was morphing from good, to super good, and from grill master to master smoker — and please don't confuse the two. Grilling is direct heat; smoking involves wood chips and is a lot more complex.

The Cinks' first barbeque contest was for their community, benefiting a newborn intensive care unit and a crisis pregnancy center where Lisa volunteers. The crisis center is, in fact, one of the Cinks' most important charities, because when Lisa got pregnant at 19, she turned to a center in Atlanta for help. Connor was born when they were 20 and sophomores at Georgia Tech. Reagan came along three-and-a-half years later.

The Cinks enjoy hiking together as a family.

"When I went to the crisis center, the lady told me she had gotten pregnant at the same age and she had gone through exactly what I was going through," Lisa said. "Just hearing her say that was an epiphany. It was like, 'Oh wow, people get through this? This can actually turn out good and we can be normal people?' It was a huge help, so if I could be that person for somebody else, yeah, I want to do that."

During that time, Stewart was on full scholarship at Georgia Tech, so he couldn't work. Lisa didn't get in-state tuition — despite being married and having a baby in Georgia — until their last quarter. "I borrowed every dime I could," she said. "We were on Medicaid,

food stamps, and had help from WIC (Georgia's assistance program for women and infants). It was a humbling position to be in. We got denied for welfare, then lost food stamps with one quarter left."

Lisa worked as a waitress and a telemarketer, and Stewart, a three-time All-American and top player in the country in 1995, planned to play in the U.S. Amateur, but instead turned pro.

As the agents were pitching their services and potential contracts, there was only one thing on Stewart's and Lisa's minds. "All we cared about was we had a $400 Visa bill we had to pay off," she said. "We were so stressed. They said, 'Really? That's what you're worried about?'"

Stewart finished tied for 18th in his first event as a pro at the Canon Greater Hartford Open, but he didn't know what he earned. "We went to Waffle House the next day, and grabbed a newspaper to look up how much he had won. It was a little over $15,000. That was when we exhaled and said, 'Okay, this is going to be okay.'"

A few months later, he tied for fifth at the BC Open and put another $38,000 in the bank and, while it wasn't ever about the money for them, it did ease the strain. He wound up playing the Nike Tour in 1996, won three times, and led the money list, playing well enough at the U.S. Open (T-16) to make it into the 1997 Masters field.

"It was a great place for Stewart to play [the Nike Tour]," Lisa said. "It gave him the stepping stones for his career; it gave him confidence."

Back then, they weren't old enough to rent a car — you had to be 25 — so life was as challenging as it was when they were in college. When they went to buy their first house, they got asked for two years of tax returns. "We had to say, we don't have them," Lisa said.

It wasn't long until Lisa was staying home with the boys, who were busy with school and starting hockey. Her friends at home knew little, if anything, about golf or Lisa's life on the road. "Having one foot at home and one on the road, you live that dual life," Lisa said. "It's interesting how [the difference] comes out in friendships. One friend, who didn't know anything about professional golf, thought we didn't make any money unless Stewart won."

And the kids had a little trouble at first figuring everything out. Dad played golf for a living, so since Mom played tennis, that must be her job and she must get paid, too. Over the years, Stewart and Lisa explained the difference and much more.

"One day we got home from a tournament and they came piling on the bed and asked, 'Mom, Dad, can we order room service?' I told them no, we're home. They asked again. They really didn't know what

normal was."

They soon learned. Connor is now at Clemson, and Lisa is, happy to say, concentrating on academics, while Reagan is a defenseman for the Atlanta Fire, a junior hockey team that competes locally and nationally. "His team went to nationals a few years ago, and one of his tournaments coincided with the Deutsche Bank Championship so we got to see both the same week," Lisa said.

One of the best trips ever started with one heck of a kerfuffle at the Atlanta airport in July 2009. Stewart wanted to take the boys to play a few courses in Ireland on their way to the British Open at Turnberry, so they planned to fly over four or five days early. When they were checking in for their flight, they found out the boys' passports had expired — minors' passports were only good for five years and not ten.

Luckily, they knew someone in Washington, DC who could help them straighten it out, so they flew up there that day, then flew back to Atlanta and were on their way to Ireland the next day. "Stewart wanted the boys to play the courses and we didn't get to Turnberry until Tuesday. Getting to a major on a Tuesday is crazy," Lisa said.

Although Stewart got sick and spent half his time early in the week at the medical trailer, he beat Tom Watson in a playoff to win the 2009 Open Championship. A magical week for the family that ended with all four of them dangling their feet over the edge of a bunker for a photo op with the Claret Jug.

"He wasn't playing well coming into the week," Lisa said. "There was no indication. I think [it happened] because all the pressure was off . . . That was so special."

Life moves fast around the Cink house. Even when they think they know what's around the corner, they don't. Stewart has catered a couple of barbecue events, and when Georgia State coach Joe Inman called, Stewart figured he was calling him to do a clinic at a college tournament. Wrong. Inman called to ask him to fire up the Big Green Egg and serve barbecue to the teams.

The Joe Ogilvie Family

Colleen, P.J., Kaitlin, Lauren, and Joe Ogilvie

Photo by Jennifer Eisnaugle Conklin

Colleen and Joe Ogilvie were more than thrilled as their family grew. But traveling with a crew of five can be pretty hectic. Colleen shares how they made sure to keep family their focus and give each child their own special time on the road.

"Our family grew from three in 2003, to four in 2005, and to five in 2006. We were happy, perhaps a tad exhausted, and also a little overwhelmed with all our little [wonderful] people. We realized that we needed to make a few adjustments with our travel schedule.

"One evening, Joe and I went on a date and came up with the perfect plan; each child would get their very own trip with Mom and Dad to one of Daddy's golf tournaments. It evolved in such a beautiful way to make each child feel special.

"By default, the trips enable Joe and I to acknowledge the child's value and special attributes [when siblings were not around to chime in]! Kaitlin consistently attends the AT&T Pebble Beach National Pro-Am; Lauren likes the warm weather events like the Mayakoba Golf Classic, the Shell Houston Open, and the Justin Timberlake Shriners Hospital for Children Open; while P. J. has traveled to the John Deere Classic and the Shell Houston Open. We all love to watch Joe play and cheer him on.

"Our motto is 'family first.' It's our goal as parents to encourage the kids to be the best they can be. Joe is a great role model. He makes a living doing what he loves and it's encouraging for our children to see his dream be a reality."

The Bob Heintz Family

You never know who you're going to run into when you travel on TOUR. Here's a story Nancy Heintz shared.

"Bob's rookie year on the PGA TOUR was in 2000. We arrived at the Bob Hope Chrysler Classic and Bob, his caddie, our two children, and I were trying to get all of us, our luggage, and Bob's golf clubs into the courtesy car. It wasn't looking good as we struggled to fit everything into the car. At that moment, Davis Love III walked up to us and said, "Never gonna' happen, Bob!"

"We all laughed and with a little muscle and fortitude, managed to somehow fit all of our travel items, and ourselves, into the car. As we drove away from the airport, fully loaded and crammed into the car, Bob started to jump around like a little boy. He excitedly exclaimed, "Do you believe it?" "No," I replied. "I didn't think we were going to make it all fit." "No, not that," Bob said. "Do you believe Davis Love knew my name!"

Nancy and Bob, with their children, Eryn, P.J., Daniel, and Brody

The Justin Leonard Family

"How do you do it? And can you teach me your secret?"

Amanda Leonard laughs. Funny that people would think of her as the go-to source for anything and everything children. Best crayons? Best double stroller? Formula? Potty training?

Somehow she's become that woman, that mom. You know the one. Calm in the face of a half-day delay in the airport. Laid back when everything goes wrong. Always smiling. Her kids are, too. And, by the way, everyone has to ask — how do you juggle four children?

Funny, but she wondered the same thing when she met Jan Haas at the 2000 PGA Championship. Only Jan had five children in tow. "Jan was literally the first person I met in player dining," Amanda said. "What a great woman — so filled with grace. I immediately looked up to her."

Another inspiration was Mia Parnevik, who has four children. "She is so laid back," Amanda said. "She told me it's so much fun. You'll love it."

She was right. After they had their first child — daughter Reese in 2003 — Amanda and Justin couldn't wait to have another. Avery came along 18 months later; Luke was born the following year; and Skylar came four years later.

Amanda will tell you there is really no magic or secret answer to raising four children under the age of ten. Just priorities. "Justin and I are very intentional about how we prioritize things," she said. "For us, it's God first, our marriage second, and our children third. Everything follows behind that. They see this neat marriage and our love, and they benefit from it. They see it, they feel it, and they're secure with themselves."

They're equally committed to traditions, too. Take Friday nights. It's family movie night, no matter what. The kids pick the movie and Justin whips up gluten-free chocolate chip cookies.

"We turn down plans because of it," Amanda said. "Very seldom do we skip it. And when we moved into the house, one requirement was a big

Amanda and Justin

basement with a big couch for movie night."

Saturday nights belong to Amanda and Justin. It's their date night. "The only reason we don't go is if we're on the road and there's no one to watch the kids," Amanda said. Those days are about as infrequent as bad days around the Leonard house. Instead of fretting over what's around the corner, Amanda and Justin make the most of each day.

"I think every day is what you decide it will be," Amanda said. "It's how you embrace it. You can wake up in a hotel room and say, 'Oh this is so boring. I'm missing my yoga class back home and the kids are missing gym.' Or you can wake up and realize what a special thing this is — what an opportunity to travel and be together as a family."

The Leonards explore every city. The Golden Gate Bridge. Trolley cars. Times Square. The San Diego Zoo. Broadway. "My kids have seen so many Broadway plays because when a tournament gives you tickets, we all go," Amanda said. "Most nine-year-olds haven't seen one Broadway play. And Luke loves it. At three, he would sit through a whole play."

Another must in the Leonard house? Laughing. And lots of it.

Take the 2005 Bob Hope Chrysler Classic. Amanda was pregnant with Avery and they were driving from San Diego to Palm Springs when Reese threw up all over the back seat of the car. Once they found a place to stop, they cleaned it up, laughed and kept going.

Monday night, Amanda got sick and Tuesday night, Justin woke up with it. The next morning, he could hardly bend over to tie his shoes, but he played. They laughed and, well, he got the last laugh. "Somehow he goes out there and wins the tournament," Amanda said. "Sometimes what seems like the worst week ever turns into a blessing in disguise. You laugh your way through it and life turns around."

"Or you party in the car. When a great song comes on while Justin is driving, it's dance party time. Everyone sings and dances in their seats."

At the same time, they also make giving back a part of their lives. The three older children get a five-dollar allowance each week; one dollar goes to savings, one dollar goes to church or a charity, and the other three dollars they can spend however they would like. If they do not complete their chores, one dollar is taken back per chore forgotten. They've also helped Amanda stuff backpacks for a Blessings in a Backpack event, baked and sold cookies for victims of the Haiti earthquake, and Avery raised $750 on her own for a woman's shelter.

One of the most gratifying times came last summer when Amanda, Reese, Avery, and Luke worked at Camp Mak-A-Dream, a camp for children with cancer, hosted by Young Life. "They were being exposed to the different needs that are out there," she said. "These kids shared their stories and we'd have dinner with a different family each night. It was eye opening and amazing to see. You see so much joy in their hearts just to be alive."

It's no wonder everyone marvels at her parenting skills. Last summer, Amanda and the kids were stuck in the Philadelphia airport for ten hours, and didn't arrive in Hartford until 2:00 a.m. Some parents would have gone a little crazy. For Amanda, it was a breeze — and another chance to celebrate the day. "It wasn't a hassle, it was one more day you're alive and we've got this great family," Amanda said. "That's what's made a difference; what has made the whole ride so enjoyable."

That and those priorities. Last year, Luke's sixth birthday fell during the 2012 British Open, so the kids stayed home. Amanda went to the Open, but came home early, in time for Luke's party. "Some people think it was crazy," Amanda said. "It didn't faze me. It was 19 hours over, 19 hours back. When you're balancing six people's lives, that's kinda what you have to do."

"Along the way you create memories. If you don't, life can pass you by. Sometimes you have to look for them and we do it with joy. That's what makes the whole journey fun."

The Leonard Family – Justin, Amanda, Avery, Skylar, Luke, and Reece

The Nick O'Hern Family

Photo by Craig Johnston

Nick and Alana, with their girls, Riley and Halle

Nick and Alana O'Hern were married in 1994 and started traveling together in 1995 on the "Troppo Tour" in Australia.

"This tour took us along the east coast of Australia to some pretty remote locations and all the traveling was done in a camper van we nicknamed J. C. (just cruising). Our first experience traveling had us leaving one tournament very early in the morning and driving 13 hours to the next.

"We were out in the middle of nowhere when a rock flung from a passing road train and smashed right through our windshield. We knew we could not drive like this and needed to get to the closest town for repairs. We got about 15 minutes down the road, when another truck came zooming by, and with all the pressure built up through not having a windshield, it blew the top half off of our camper van.

"We crawled to the next tiny little town with Nick driving and me hanging from the roof, trying to keep the lid on. Nick found a saddlery shop and managed to pop rivet the pop-up roof back on. This town did not have much going for it, let alone a windshield, so with a schedule to keep, we rummaged some plastic from a nearby store and spread it across the front. We drove 12 hours looking through plastic and stopping every couple of hours to cut out windows because the plastic became too cloudy to see through.

"We were fried by the time we made it to the next tournament and were not surprised when Nick did not make the cut or any money at the next event. To this day, we are still unsure if this tour is called the Troppo Tour for the tropical climate or for the way it made you troppo (crazy) being on it!"

The Chris Riley Family

Chris and Michelle, with their daughters, Rose and Taylor

For two college golfers from Louisiana and Las Vegas, the last place you'd expect to find romance is in Japan. Yet, that's exactly what happened for Chris and Michelle Riley.

Michelle played golf for Louisiana State University and Chris had just graduated and finished his collegiate career at University of Nevada — Las Vegas. Michelle recalls, "The tournament in Japan is called the Goodwill Games and they take about 25 collegiate golfers from the United States to play the Japanese golfers. We stayed in private housing in Japan, which was quite the experience for someone like me who had never been out of the United States.

"Chris was staying with a host family and he would come over with his host. We would all sit on the floor drinking tea, but were unable to communicate! Chris had me laughing the entire trip and we were great friends by the time we left Tsu City eight days later. After that, I caddied for him a few times, and when I turned professional, he returned the favor and caddied for me."

Clearly the Rileys' lives have been centered around golf since that fateful trip to Japan. Michelle explains how, for the Riley family, special events coincide with their golf schedules.

"I remember a lot of important things based on what tournament we were playing during the time they occurred. For example, Chris and I got engaged during Doral in 2002; we found out I was pregnant at the Bob Hope Classic in 2004; and our first daughter was born the weekend before the Ryder Cup in September of 2004. Our second daughter was born during the St. Jude Classic in 2007, and her first airplane trip was at seven weeks old to the US Bank in Milwaukee . . . You get the picture! It always comes back to golf."

Halloween at the Rileys

The Tim Petrovic Family

The bell. It's tucked right there in the third stanza of "Bohemian Rhapsody" — just after a couple of long *Mamaaas* and well before you get those iconic sing-a-long lines involving *Galileo* and *silhouetto* and *mama mia*! It's just a little tinkle following the line, *Sends shivers down my spine.*

Classic Queen. Classic Petrovic.

That bell tells you volumes about Tim and Julie Petrovic. Even after 21 years together, when the song starts playing, he sings along, then looks over at her just in time so she can pretend to ring the bell.

It's one of their things. They started it when they were dating and now it's part of a journey that's been filled with highs and lows, near evictions, newspaper routes, scrubbing floors at pizza parlors, watching latchkey kids after school at the YMCA, traveling the country in an RV,

singing, chasing the dream, then winning on the PGA TOUR.

"It's been a roller coaster ride," Julie said. "We've hit the bottom and we've hit the top."

Today, life is good. Julie home schools their two daughters and when Tim isn't playing, he's relaxing with his guitar, playing everything from The Doors to Nirvana to the Eagles and Clay Walker or helping their oldest — Bayleigh — pick out a current hit on the piano or computer by ear. Tim taught himself how to play both the guitar and piano, and Bayleigh is following her dad's lead.

The guitar is a Robby Krieger signature Gibson, a present from his one-time idol and now friend Robby Krieger of The Doors. Tim has been on stage with him as well as Clay Walker and Tommy Thayer of Kiss. "He doesn't play with the guys," Julie said, "because that trio is way too good, so Tim just sings."

Julie will tell you it's a blessed life, but it almost wasn't a life at all. In fact, their first two dates were pretty much disasters in her mind. Tim? He wasn't taking no for an answer.

They met at a health fair when he was helping a friend sell mobile phones, and she was a last-minute stand-in at her company's booth. She missed breakfast and thought she was being sneaky, taking pieces of a bagel from his booth. He noticed and eventually asked her out. On that date, he ordered her a salad that she didn't like. She told him as much, but he wouldn't change the order and he wouldn't let her leave until she agreed to a second date. He leaned against her car door until she finally obliged.

The second date was worse. Both thought the other stood them up. "There were two entrances to the restaurant," Julie said. "I was at one, he was at the other, and we never saw each other."

And the third? It only happened when Julie called him to ask why he blew her off. They agreed to meet again to go dancing. "I walked across the room to meet him, he met me halfway on the dance floor, dipped me back, kissed me and that was it," she said, chuckling. "I was so flustered; I couldn't talk for ten minutes. That's hard for me. I talk a lot."

The bumpy start turned into a road filled with more lows than highs. Tim was struggling to find his game and relied on throwing newspapers and selling mobile phones to make ends meet. When they moved to Florida to play in what was formerly called the Nike Tour in 1993, his sponsor pulled out.

"I caddied for him to save money; we went three-quarters of a season before the money ran out," Julie said. "We recognized he had a talent, but couldn't get it to click. We maxed out my credit cards and we had an eviction notice."

Her parents paid their back rent and she found a job waitressing. That led Tim to a spot on the closing crew at the restaurant, which meant he scrubbed floors. He moved up to pizza delivery, worked at a YMCA, and even delivered orders for Julie when she worked for Avon. She called the time "character building," but it was also downright scary.

But five years later, it all changed. They worked their way out of debt and bought their first house. In 2001, Tim earned his PGA TOUR card at the Buy.com Tour Championship.

"We're at the ceremony and I was sobbing my eyes out," she said. "I had a two-and-a-half-month-old on my chest and a two-and-a-half-year-old next to me. I was trying to take a picture and couldn't because I was crying so hard. It was a whole new era for us." The era has included a win at the 2005 Zurich Classic of New Orleans, invitations to majors, and the FedExCup Playoffs.

"Funny," she said, "looking back, you see a journey that has been filled with incredible experiences." They can now smile at the lows as well as the highs and the magic moments that started as something silly. However, 21 years later, they are still like that bell — he always looks for it in the song and she never forgets to ring.

Tim and Julie, with their girls, Bayleigh and MacKenzie, and dog, Toby

The Glen Day Family

Their story begins when a professional golfer who didn't have two nickels to rub together started flirting with the girl behind the counter at the 1988 Arkansas Open in Little Rock. She gave him a golf cart for free for all four tournament days, but he didn't even ask her to dinner.

Turns out, he had a girlfriend. The counter girl, who was working to earn money for college that week, was heartbroken, but she still cut a little story from a magazine later that year when he won the Malaysian Open.

More than two decades later, the clipping is still in the original 50-cent frame from Walmart and Jennifer Day won't let any decorator tell her to put it away. And Glen Day? He chuckles that those four free carts cost him plenty over the years.

Those carts and that Arkansas Open also started what would be a litany of major milestones for the Days — all associated with tournaments. "We don't remember dates," Jennifer chuckled. "We remember tournaments or hotels. Everywhere we go, we have a story."

They felt Whitney, their oldest daughter, kick for the first time at Bay Hill in 1994. To be specific, it was at the Marriott on International Drive in Orlando. "She's now 18 and, every time we go by there, we still think of that," Jennifer said.

Later that same year, Jennifer was having contractions during the first round of the Deposit Guaranty Classic. Glen shot 74, but was disqualified for not signing his scorecard. "All he could think about was getting to the clubhouse to call and see how I was," Jennifer said. "There were no cell phones then, so he had to get to the locker room to call me."

Jennifer and Glen, with their daughters, Whitney and Christina, on the Swilcan Bridge on The Old Course at St. Andrews

A year later, at the Memorial Tournament, the PGA TOUR was filming them for "one of those days-in-the-life-of-a-player shows," Jennifer said. "The crew got to the hotel early and just as Glen and Jennifer were about to walk out the door, Whitney started walking."

Christina was born two years later, the week of the Phoenix Open. It just happened to be one of the same years the Super Bowl was in Phoenix and Jennifer was due the Monday after the tournament, but she wouldn't wait. In fact, four TOUR babies came that week.

"I called Glen and told him I was having the baby and if he wanted to be a part of it, he better get home," Jennifer said. "He came home from Phoenix and when I went in, the doctor told me I was in labor."

Two years later, Christina walked her first 18 holes at the Phoenix Open. "I think I spent $48 keeping her happy and quiet that day," Jennifer said.

There's a story about Glen's lone TOUR win, too — the 1999 MCI Classic. They had just moved into a new house, and Jennifer and the girls weren't at the tournament. The painters had pushed all the furniture into the middle of the room, and Jennifer and friends were sitting on boxes covered with plastic watching the tournament.

The kids were in the pool. "Not how you imagine your husband's first win," she said. Over the years, Jennifer and Glen had a little joke. She'd ask him to tug on his ear when he got on TV. During the final round that week, he bent over to do something and . . . he pulled his ear.

"I thought I was going to fall out of my chair," she said. "When he called me, he asked if I'd seen him pull his ear. I told him I did and couldn't believe he remembered. He was still at the course waiting to see where he placed; he thought he was going to be one shot short. He was wrong. He won."

Now, after a long wait, Glen is on the comeback after undergoing foot surgery in 2011. What was originally diagnosed as gout was re-diagnosed two years later as damage to both a ligament and tendon in his foot. He's bouncing back and they're just waiting for that next moment.

Until then, there's always more to tell about that meeting in Little Rock. Jennifer came from a golf family that included her father, Bob Ralston, who was a teaching pro and knew Glen from tournament golf. A year after breaking Jennifer's heart, Glen asked her out. Her mom wasn't happy that he was five years older, while her dad liked the idea of having a pro-pro partner.

Two years later, they were married and Glen was standing on the first tee at LaQuinta during the final day of Q-school when Jennifer broke the news. "I told him, you need to play good because we're fixing to have a baby," she chuckled. "He needed incentive."

He qualified and, though they didn't realize it at the time, it would be one more major tournament moment to add to the list.

The Day family celebrates Glen's 1999 MCI Classic win.

The Rich Beem Family

Michael, Rich, Sara, and Bailee Beem

For Sara Beem, life on TOUR has been a time of bonding with the women who all share the same challenges and triumphs. It's a part of what makes the PGA TOUR Wives Association such a tight-knit group of women. They often refer to each other as friends, but make no mistake, they consider each other family. Sara shares these sentiments in her story.

"It's amazing to go back 13 years and see what we've been up to. Our lives really revolve around family and golf, and we wouldn't have it any other way! Golf has taken us all over the world, and we have met some amazing people along the way. Some of my closest girlfriends are PGA TOUR wives. I've raised my kids with those women! From pregnancy highs and lows to the first day of kindergarten, they are the ones that have been there every step of the way. We entertained our kids at every park, museum, aquarium, and zoo in the country. We also were there for each other to congratulate and celebrate the victories, and to have a sympathetic ear when things weren't going so well on the course. As much as our lives revolve around the game of golf and our husbands' careers, it's nice to have some "girl time" with your best friends. I'm so thankful for the friendships and lifelong relationships that have been formed through our time on TOUR."

Michael and Rich, at the Par 3 tournament at the Masters

The Omar Uresti Family

Anita and Omar Uresti, with their children, Isabella and Omar

Lisa Tullet, Memory Market Photography

In many tournament cities, local families sign up to "host" visiting players by allowing them to stay in their homes during tournament week. The host family typically provides lodging, food, and sometimes even transportation. This is especially beneficial to rookie players who haven't yet established substantial career earnings. Many players and families have made lifelong friends with their host families and return to see them every year. However, not all are so lucky. Omar's wife, Anita, provided this story.

One week, Omar and his brother, Rusty, who was caddying for Omar that week, were set up with an older couple as their host family. The first morning, they were presented with a list of chores they needed to complete for the host couple that day. It started with mowing the lawn and vacuuming the living room.

Omar proudly sports the burnt orange of the Texas Longhorns, where he was a former All-American.

After returning from the golf course at the end of the first day, they were given a bill that read "milk, 50 cents; cereal, $1.50." It became clear that this couple was not aware of what the expectations were as a host family. Needless to say, Omar's focus needed to be on the golf tournament, not chores. So he made a polite excuse, thanked them for their hospitality and moved to a hotel for the rest of the week.

Sometimes the best home away from home actually *is* a hotel.

Crew, Bo, Trace, Olivia, and Carrie, outside the Augusta National Clubhouse

The Bo Van Pelt Family

It was pouring down rain during the final round of the 2000 Buy.com Upstate Classic and nothing was going right, except some of Bo Van Pelt's shots.

His wife Carrie was on the bag — not caddying in the true sense — rather just toting the clubs to save money. Caddies were required even when there wasn't any money to pay them. Carrie stepped in for the summer — well, part of the summer.

Bo had started the day with a chance to win, but that wasn't going to happen. "He was hitting it everywhere — in the trees, in the rough," Carrie said. "I didn't appreciate a caddie's job until that day. It's way easier walking in the fairway. I was like, why did you hit it there? And he's getting mad."

Then, he comes up way short on a par-3, but he doesn't know it. "He walked up like it was over the green and I asked where he was going," Carrie said. "He said he was looking for his ball and I said, well, your ball is way back here."

That did it. They'd been walking apart most of the day; they were barely talking and he was about to shoot a closing 78. Her future as a

Olivia, Carrie, Trace, Bo, and Crew enjoy game day at Oklahoma State University.

snacks and Bo's favorite — a McFlurry.

Bo made it through qualifying school in 1998, and they were off and driving. "That was a crazy year for us," Carrie said. "We were newlyweds, and Bo's golf game definitely had more downs than ups. We were completely overwhelmed."

Carrie would drop Bo off at the golf course, then sit in her car and read until he teed off. Bo was intimidated finding a spot on the range while standing there with players who were his heroes and he rarely went into the clubhouse. He ate at the caddie trailer and sometimes Carrie did, too.

He lost his card and played on what was then the Buy.com Tour the next few years and learned what he needed to do to turn everything around in 2004 with a big year on the TOUR. It's gotten better every year. "It's been a long process to get where he is now," Carrie said.

Carrie admits she is "super high-strung." Bo's as laid back as they come. His easygoing attitude helped when their first two children were born 18 months apart, to the day. They're now 12 (Olivia), 10 (Trace), and 7 (Crew).

"I'm surprised he doesn't just fall asleep on the golf course," Carrie said. "We definitely balance each other out. I take care of the agenda. He thrives with chaos . . . He doesn't need a strict routine and that's what made traveling with him so much fun."

They do indeed balance each other out — always have and forever will. Bo was mad at himself going into the fifth round at the 1998 qualifying school. He shot a fourth-round 70 and wasn't happy.

"I didn't know much about it all, but I said, 'I don't understand. I don't see why are you so upset,'" Carrie said. "Isn't that just golf? I don't understand how you know who is good. One day someone plays bad and the next day they play well. So how do you know?"

Bo paused for a minute and said he didn't know. Two days later, after rounds of 65 and 72, he earned his card and called Carrie. "What you said got me my card," he said. "It made me laugh. You were right. Everyone does have a bad round. I just needed to have a better one."

caddie was not looking bright.

"About 30 minutes into the drive to the next event, he finally said, 'You know I didn't marry you because I needed a caddie. I just need to play better,'" Carrie said. "Now we're laughing about it."

They laughed a little later that night, too, when they checked into a dingy motel, and Carrie laid down on top of Bo because she didn't want to touch anything. Then their dog jumped on top of Carrie. "That was probably the longest day ever," she said, laughing. "Bad day, a bad hotel, and I got fired. It was like, 'What are we doing?'"

It was also one of maybe three grumpy moments ever between Bo and Carrie. When they left Oklahoma State, they were two kids rumbling down the road in Bo's old black Toyota 4Runner. They loaded it down with clubs and clothes and the dog, and entertained themselves by challenging each other to sing along with the radio.

"Neither of us can sing to save our lives," she said. "It wasn't much of a contest."

Carrie and Bo didn't meet until their senior year at Oklahoma State and their first date was a Big Head Todd concert followed by a stop at a 24-hour Waffle House. A year later, they were on the road where she swears they each gained 20 pounds with vending machine

The Jim Furyk Family

As the 2011-2012 school year came to an end, Tabitha and Jim Furyk headed to John Love Elementary to deliver summer reading books and journals to their favorite students and Blessings in a Backpack recipients. They thought they were doing something special for the kids that day, but when they got to the school in Jacksonville, Florida, the students had another idea. They wanted to thank Tabitha and Jim for making a difference in their lives through Blessings in a Backpack. One class made posters, another sang songs, and another recited a poem they wrote for them. It was a celebration, complete with hugs to go all around — from 200 children.

This was Jim's first opportunity to be one-on-one with the children who benefited from the Blessings in a Backpack program — one of the selected organizations that their foundation supports. After such a heartwarming reception, Jim declared to Tabitha, "That's it. That's what I want to do." Tabitha said, "He realized at that moment, being able to feed hungry children was going to be a priority."

"There are people who are reaching out to feed children around the world and we have children in our own community and country who need our help," remarked Jim. Tabitha said "Blessings in a Backpack is addressing that need and we are proud to be supporting their programs."

That one school and 200 students have blossomed into four schools and 800 students, but that's just one piece of their foundation puzzle. Two other powerful area charities they support through the foundation are Wolfson Children's Hospital and Community PedsCare, a palliative care program for pediatric patients. All too often, the patients overlap.

They met Olivia in 2010. She was having brain surgery on a cancerous tumor and they were helping raise awareness and money for a children's oncology tower at Wolfson. She was eight, the same age as their daughter, Caleigh, and they were amazed at how poised and mature Olivia was. They kept in touch for a long time, but then came an untimely silence in their communication.

Tabitha said, "She was an amazing little person who doesn't get to see tomorrow. We want to do all that we can to ensure that the best care is available for these young patients so that they can live a full happy life." Wolfson is doing some amazing things in oncology and hematology. Due to their advances in transplantation programs, children with life-threatening cancers and blood disorders are being cured at a higher rate than ever before. Supporting an organization that can help so many is exactly what the foundation is about.

Reaching out and caring is what drew Tabitha (who got her degree in education) to Jim in the first place. She had no idea who he was when she saw him at the 1994 Memorial Tournament. "He was having fun with the kids in the autograph line," she said. "Other guys walked past and didn't give the kids the time of day, but Jim took the time to make it a special moment for these kids. He traded hats with kids, and was teasing them about why they weren't in school. It was different with Jim." And that extra bit of care impressed her.

Later that day, she was standing by the 18th green, waiting for her clients — she was working for Muirfield Village Realty at the time — and Jim walked past and said hello. "I apparently tried to say hello," she said, "but nothing came out."

Jim stood behind her trying to figure out his next move. Her boss

Jim, Tabitha and their children, Caleigh Lynn and Tanner, cheer on the Ohio State Buckeyes, Tabitha's alma mater.

saw what was happening, walked up and introduced himself and invited him to dinner with his fiancée and his associate, Tabitha. Later Jim asked her to go over to Ohio State's Scarlet Course with him to see his former Arizona coach and the team play in a tournament. "We ended up spending the rest of the week together," she said. "At the end of the week, he handed me a plane ticket to DC; I left after work Thursday and flew in to meet his parents."

Jim missed the cut, so they put on their tennis shoes and went sightseeing for the weekend. By then, they had already discussed marriage, but neither was in a rush. They dated for the next five-and-a-half years and married in 2000. "Strong family values are what brought us together," she said.

It's also the basis for their foundation, which they started in December 2010, just after Jim won the FedExCup. "After such an amazing win, we felt like the timing couldn't be better," she said. "We always wanted to do it. We had supported charities in Jacksonville, Florida, in my hometown of Columbus, Ohio, and in Pennsylvania where Jim is from. With the FedExCup prize, it just made sense. We're trying to make a difference in the lives of those children and families who need our help. We decided that by creating a foundation and holding annual events, we could raise awareness, as well as much-needed donations, to these wonderful charities."

Jim and Tabitha hold an annual fundraiser called "Furyk & Friends," which includes a celebrity golf classic held in March in Ponte Vedra Beach, Florida, and a party the evening before, complete with top chefs from their favorite restaurants and a concert for all who are participating. They have had a tremendous outpouring of support from celebrity friends from the NFL, NBA, and PGA TOUR, as well as musicians and actors.

Tabitha and Jim hold the FedExCup trophy, after winning the 2010 FedExCup Playoffs.

holding a three-year-old during the first year of the event.

"The boy had no muscular use of his arms and legs, and he was curled up in Ben's arms," Tabitha said. "Ben left in tears and wrote us a check for $5,000. Today, the boy has braces on his legs and the little guy is walking around all on his own."

"Our kids volunteer at this event and it is great to see the kids interact together and help one another." Tabitha said. "Showing our kids how important it is to help others is so important, participating in these events helps shape their personalities. Lots of players like the Leonards [Amanda and Justin], the Mickelsons, the Duvals, and the Petrovics [Tim and Julie] bring their children to the event to be a part of something that is so special. These kids face so much, but they're so full of life. They're living every moment to the fullest extent," said Tabitha. "There's simply nothing more inspiring than to see that sparkle in a child's eyes."

And Tabitha and Jim? They just feel blessed to be able to help and make a difference.

"It has become a fun event that does so much for the children in our community," said Tabitha. Over the past two years, they have raised half a million dollars and continue to grow the event.

The one charity that pushed them over the edge philanthropically was Community PedsCare, which helps kids with life-threatening or life-limiting diseases, as well as their families. This unique organization helps provide comfort, support, and care when families are in need. Each year, they host "Halloween Doors and More," where an area of the building is transformed into a fantasy world with costumed characters such as Darth Vader, Sponge Bob, Cinderella, and Jack Sparrow walking around greeting the children. Doors are decorated to provide an enchanted experience for the children to do their trick-or-treating. Patients come in costumes, in wheelchairs or in their hospital beds with breathing tubes and IVs to have fun and enjoy just being a kid.

That event inspired Tabitha to start the annual These Kids Can Play event at THE PLAYERS Championship in 2007 for groups of children from PedsCare and Wolfson. Since the start of these events, Tabitha and Jim have become close to the families that come to enjoy these events and understand how important it is for them to be there. Their passion for these children has become contagious. She remembers Ben Crane

The Furyk family, on the sidelines at a Pittsburgh Steelers game

The Steve Flesch Family

Dina, Steve, Griffin, and Lily, in Carmel, California

When Traci Kendall, wife of TOUR player Skip Kendall, asked her sister to join them at the Waste Management Phoenix Open to help with their children, the last thing Traci thought might happen was she would be introducing her sister to her future brother-in-law. However, that's exactly how Dina met her husband, Steve Flesch. Dina remembers the week well.

"I really needed to get back to my job as a flight attendant, but I wanted to help my sister and Skip out and see my niece and nephew. I agreed to come to the tournament that week and found myself in family dining with them on Friday night. Steve was sitting a couple of tables from us and I could tell he was looking at me. The next day, Skip told me that Steve had asked about me and would it be all right if he contacted me. We talked on the phone a few times and met a couple of weeks later at the Puerto Rico Open. Since then, we've never looked back.

Dina and Steve on their wedding day,
September 10, 2011 (9/10/11)

"Steve proposed during the 2011 AT&T Pebble Beach National Pro-Am on the beach in Carmel in front of both of our families. We married in September of the same year. I'm so blessed to have someone who makes me laugh every day. "

The Larry Moody Family

Ruth and Larry Moody

Traveling on the PGA TOUR means that we are often away from our homes, our families, and our places of worship. Larry Moody has served as chaplain to the PGA TOUR players for many years. His wife, Ruth (aka "Ruthie"), shares her memory of their time with TOUR families.

"My involvement with women on the PGA TOUR began in 1981 when my husband, Larry, began teaching the TOUR Fellowship. When our youngest left for college in 2000, Larry asked if I would travel full-time with him. I agreed and have never regretted that decision. I have loved spending individual and group time with the wives and girlfriends of the players. These wonderful women are an extremely capable, intelligent, funny, and caring group of gals. I love them all. What I enjoy most is being a listening ear and sharing encouraging words with these amazing women who daily juggle an unusual and demanding life with grace and style."

Ashley and Stuart Appleby celebrate after Stuart shot 59 in the final round to win the 2010 Greenbrier Classic.

The Stuart Appleby Family

Ashley didn't travel much when she was younger. Her family would take the occasional road trips to the East Coast or travel west to Chicago, but that is the farthest her travel extended. On the other hand, Stuart Appleby, a native Australian, was traveling the globe pursuing his golfing career.

A mutual friend set them up on a blind date the Sunday after a tournament in Ohio. They both felt something special, but Stuart wasn't sure about jumping into a relationship. He had lost his first wife in a tragic accident, and the wounds were still tender. Ashley understood the emotions Stuart was going through. Her grandparents owned a funeral parlor in Canton, Ohio, and she was comfortable talking about loss and the feelings that go along with losing a loved one.

After their first meeting, Stuart traveled back to Sydney, Australia, to see family and go to the Olympics, while Ashley finished her degree at Mount Union University. The two kept in touch and saw each other a few times before she graduated. After graduation, Ashley traveled as far west as she could possibly go, and met Stuart at a tournament in Hawaii. They began dating steadily. He adored her kind and generous heart, while she believed she had found her soul mate.

The Appleby children, Max, Rex, Mia, and Ella

juggling life on the road, exploring different cultures and eating out nearly 300 nights a year! Stuart and Ashley married in December of 2001 and continued their nomadic lifestyle for five years before starting a family. They now have four children — three of whom were born in Melbourne, Australia, and one that was born in Orlando, Florida.

The Appleby family travels together, and both Stuart and Ashley make it a point to learn about each city they visit. They want their children to learn about and appreciate the different cities and the history, people, and culture each one has to offer. With a new and different location also comes new food to try.

"We consider ourselves 'foodies' and ask locals and tournament volunteers for restaurant recommendations for the week," says Ashley. "We want to try new places and taste the local flavor. The kids have pretty sophisticated palates for children their ages."

Ashley learned quickly that life on the PGA TOUR meant traveling, not just around the United States, but around the world. The gypsy lifestyle can take some getting used to and she found herself

Nowadays, Ashley is no stranger to travel. The Applebys embrace the new location, culture, and, of course, the food they learn about and experience at every tournament stop.

Stuart and his caddies at the Par 3 tournament, during the Masters

The Bob Estes Family

Bob and Liz Estes

Sometimes real life can imitate art. Liz Estes shares an experience she and Bob had during tournament week.

"During one tournament, we were staying at a hotel-casino, which we both really enjoyed. Unfortunately, Bob missed the cut, and we decided to pack up and leave as soon as possible the next morning to get home. We got up at 4:00 a.m. to catch an early flight, and called down to the valet to retrieve our car. As we walked up to the elevator, out the window we could see our car waiting at the curb, but by the time we got down to the valet, the car was gone!

"The valet had inadvertently left the keys in the car after he'd parked it and, during the short elevator ride, someone had walked up and stolen our car — a car covered in tournament stickers. Needless to say, without a car, and now the necessity of meeting with police, we missed our flight. The police arrived, took a report, and we eventually made our way to the airport and finally home.

Lo and behold, the police did find the car. A group of kids had seen the movie *The Hangover* and decided it would be fun to live out the movie. In this particular case, life imitating art won't be as funny for these kids as the movie was.

The Frank Lickliter Family

Diane and Frank Lickliter celebrate their nuptials with their twins, Steele and Storm.

Ask Frank and Diane Lickliter what drives them to keep giving back and somewhere in their response you're sure to find the answer is the United States Armed Forces. Frank, who has been a spokesperson for the Wounded Warrior Project since 2005, knows firsthand the sacrifices that are being made by the military.

Frank's dad, Frank R. Lickliter, Sr., served proudly in the US Navy for many years, mostly aboard aircraft carriers. Frank now serves as a representative of the Navy Seal Foundation. Diane describes Frank as "a great patriot who has always embodied a deep and passionate love for his country." When asked about his efforts to give back, Frank said, "I have been blessed with family, friends, health, and prosperity. Through golf, I've met amazing people who have made incredible sacrifices; sacrifices not for themselves, but for the well-being of the whole country. These men and women and their families are very special to me."

Diane says that Frank is one of very few civilians who have had the honor to fly with both the Blue Angels and the Thunderbirds. She laughs and says that, possibly just as amazing, he managed to keep down lunch both times.

The lifelong friendships that have been formed between Diane, Frank, and the men and women they've touched through their charitable outreach are just one benefit of giving back.

Frank, with a U.S. military veteran, warming up on the range

The Brian Gay Family

Never say never.

That's pretty much what Kimberly Gay told her husband, Brian, in 2005 when he swore he was done with Harbour Town Golf Links — not coming back.

Why? The problem — years of self-imposed high expectations topped off with a missing parking pass. He didn't have his one day and he couldn't get into the players lot. He said, "I am never going there again," and Kimberly said, "Oh, yes you are — you're going to win this one day."

She was right. Oh, it took a while — four years to be exact.

This is the guy who struggled and hung in there through three trips to Q-school, with several close calls, swing changes, as well as confidence highs and lows. The birth of daughters, Makinley and Brantley in 1999 and 2004, introduced new challenges and a new phase to Brian and Kimberly's lives.

They are a couple who, like so many, are as much defined by their perseverance as they are by their success. "As a family we're completely committed to this life," Kimberly said. "Even though the girls have full

128

schedules at home, his dream became our dream."

It's only fitting since they started the journey on the eve of the 1996 U.S. Open – Brian's first PGA TOUR event – when he asked her to marry him. The irony? She knew nothing about golf when they started dating.

Kimberly was working for a pharmaceutical company when she met Brian at the Gainesville Airport. Two weeks later, they saw each other at a Florida football game. They started hanging out and she eventually asked Brian for a date. It was then that she threw herself into learning the game. He headed to the Walker Cup, and she studied the game and even took lessons.

Golf and supporting Brian's career quickly became her passion. Her organizational skills were perfect for dealing with travel logistics on TOUR, and planning their wedding.

"We got married before wedding planners," she said. "I did transportation packets for family and guests. I sent them out and gave them all the details. I do that for everything. It's the way we stay organized. I always say I'm more of an organized mess."

Their next decade was defined by that perseverance. Brian got his TOUR card their first year of marriage, but was forced to go back to Q-school twice. Even when his game matured, he kept coming up short of a win. Finally, things came together at the 2008 Mayakoba Classic in Mexico, where there was a little premonition attached.

After the second round, Brian was in contention. Makinley and Brantley were visiting defending champion Fred and Sharon Funk's daughter and son. Taylor Funk, who caddies for his dad, told them simply, "Your dad is going to win — I know it." He did.

Kimberly and Brian celebrated with a private flight home after Mayakoba — and were surprised by friends at their Orlando home — waiting to celebrate. Celebrate they did — until the wee hours of the morning.

A year later, Brian was closing in on his second PGA TOUR win — yes, Harbour Town at the Verizon Heritage. Kimberly had the celebration — and a big surprise — covered.

"We had rented this small condo — a third-floor walkup — and I didn't let him sit around," Kimberly said. On the eve of his 10-shot victory and after an intense workout, the girls met him at the door and

Kimberly and Brian, with their daughters, Makinley and Brantley, celebrate Brian's 2009 win at the Verizon Heritage Tournament.

insisted on riding bikes around the island. "We didn't want him thinking about golf," Kimberly said.

She coordinated with three dozen family members, including her 80-year-old grandparents. On that Sunday morning, she met everyone and asked that they stay out of sight. They could go to the golf course, but they had to fade into the gallery. She handed out passes, making sure everyone knew what to do.

By the time she headed to the course, Brian was 3-under for the day. He opened birdie-eagle after two holes. Kimberly walked the course as usual, while keeping in touch with the family. Brian was unaware of anyone's presence until the 18th hole when he spotted an uncle, and then Kimberly's parents. "He then saw his mom and almost lost it," she said.

At that moment they all appeared. The celebration lasted long into the night.

A few weeks later, Brian won the St. Jude Classic in Memphis, Tennessee and they had another celebration — their third in 14 months, which they joyfully shared with Brian's caddie, Kip Henley and his family, who are from Tennessee. There was even more reason to celebrate, as this win made Brian eligible to play in the U.S. Open at Bethpage Black.

"We feel there are things so much bigger than us that have been involved in these victories," Kimberly said. "That's what has made it so much fun — to be able to share them."

Amy Sabbatini, with her children, Harley, Tylie, and Bodhi

The Rory Sabbatini Family

There's always a little drama when you're RV-ing.

You cut a corner too close and scratch up the side just as you're driving the new purchase out of the dealership. You go airborne in an intersection. You take out the exhaust pipe in a drive-through. There are no hook-ups at the RV lot and tanks are full, which means bathroom facilities are up the road. Then there are those pesky curbs.

Amy and Rory Sabbatini were towing their Jeep to Colorado when they stopped in a small Texas town to get gas and headed out of town. Amy's dad was driving that shift.

Suddenly, a woman in the next lane kept pulling up and waving. After a few times, Rory asked his father-in-law if the Jeep was still behind them. It wasn't.

"So we turn the 45-foot RV around," Amy said, "and the Jeep is on the side of the road. The sheriff was there and people were taking pictures of it on the curb."

As Amy will tell you, RVs are a lot of metal rolling down a road. They're also a home — not just a hotel room — on the road.

"I think it's fabulous," Amy said. "We're constantly trying to convince people. Some people prefer room service and beds made, but I love that I can manage my 500 square feet all by myself. The children have a constant environment and their toys. They may be in a different city, but they're in the same bed. It gives a little bit of consistency in an inconsistent world."

It also gives them their own pillows, sheets and towels, a dishwasher, washer/dryer, a collection of TVs, an Xbox, and room for the family pets. No need to re-pack every week. No schlepping a young family with luggage through the airport. No waiting on room service.

"It's a suitcase rolling down the road," she said. Put your clothes on the shelves and go. Rory was a little skeptical at first, but a decade later, he wouldn't have it any other way.

"He's an engineer type, very mathematically inclined," Amy said. "If something goes wrong, he can fix it. And, inevitably, there is always something breaking. It gives him something to do. He goes mad in a hotel room."

Rory and Amy were on the cutting edge of RV life on TOUR. Today, it's commonplace, with tournaments providing parking spaces for the week. The area turns into a little neighborhood with plants on picnic tables and the players standing over their grills.

"What's unique is it allows you to foster relationships with other families that normally you wouldn't get to know," Amy said. "We're in a little circle, we're all out there grilling and you bring your chairs and drinks."

There are hidden complications, though. One year Amy hosted the weekly women's Bible study and the waste trucks didn't dump on schedule. "So, we had to find an emergency service to come take care of it and it all worked out," Amy said. "Honestly, economically, I don't know if it saves money, but you can't put a price on your sanity."

With three children, five dogs, and three cats, it gets a little crazy at times, but Amy, who learned to drive the bus herself last year, sees it as quality time. "I like the tight quarters," she said, grinning. "But when the children are 15, I may not feel that way."

Harley, Tylie and Bodhi Sabbatini

The Davis Love III Family

Robin Love looked pretty darn good, if she did say so herself. Great pair of shorts, a cute T-shirt and sandals. The perfect outfit for her first trip to Daytona, right?

Not so much.

When Kyle Petty invited Robin and Davis to Daytona International Speedway, he failed to mention they would be his guests in the inner sanctum at Daytona — the pits. And he — and

everyone else — didn't tell them there was a dress code. But, as luck would have it, the wife of one of Kyle's crew members, who was used to such oversights, pulled Robin onto one of the crew tour buses and loaned her some jeans and boots.

"I looked at her and thought, 'Good Lord, how am I going to get myself into her jeans?'" Robin said, laughing. "I felt like the girl in that commercial when she's lying on the bed trying to zip her jeans. I was squatting, sucking in my stomach and when I finally got them zipped,

I didn't breathe for the next four hours."

She shakes her head. Davis and Kyle met at a Coca-Cola outing during the Masters in 1989. Robin has a photo from that event of her and Kyle, and they look almost like siblings. Robin's hair had that late '80s/early '90s perm and Kyle has black, wavy hair. "I took that picture to show him," she said. "It's amazing how much we look alike."

Davis eventually wound up driving a car around the track another time when Robin wasn't there. "I told him I couldn't be part of it," she said. "He called and said he had gotten up to about 120 miles an hour. In the end, I think he put a few dents in the car, but nothing bad, just boo-boos."

The friendship grew and, in 2003, Kyle asked if Robin and Davis would be part of the celebrity group for his annual Kyle Petty Charity Ride Across America. Schedules kept them from participating until 2005, when Robin and Davis joined the ride in Stanley, Idaho. Davis drove his Harley Davidson, with Robin riding behind him, and after the first five minutes of that ride, they were hooked.

"We drove from Sun Valley to Stanley to join them," Robin said. "You have on all the clothes you possibly can and you're still cold, but you don't notice. The scenery is breathtaking . . . you're in God's country."

The trip wound through North Dakota, South Dakota, and the Badlands, which always have a pink caste. "It's the most gorgeous, unfamiliar thing you have ever seen," Robin said. "The road goes so close to mountains, you can reach out and touch them. And Needles Highway has a tiny tunnel that leads to Mt. Rushmore and only motorcycles can get through it."

They rode for eight days, covered 3,000 miles, and ended at Victory Junction camp in Randleman, North Carolina. "All the kids who were able came out and cheered us on," Robin said. "It's just phenomenal what they've done for the kids." The camp was founded by Kyle and Pattie Petty in honor of their son, Adam, who died during a NASCAR practice run in 2000. A few months after the tragedy, Kyle and Pattie

Captain of the 2012 US Ryder Cup team, Davis Love III, and his wife, Robin, at the Ryder Cup Gala

partnered with Paul Newman to make Adam's vision for a camp for special needs children a reality.

The camp touched them so much that Robin and Davis donated money from the Davis Love Foundation to help build a nine-hole miniature golf course. Over the course of the next few years, supporting the camp turned into a family affair when daughter Lexie, then 20, spent a summer there as a camp counselor. As she was leaving that year, she asked if she could get a motorcycle and ride with them the next year. Davis said absolutely.

Davis IV, Alexia, Robin, and Davis Love III

"I wasn't too thrilled," Robin said. "I was thinking, why don't I ride in a car and let her ride behind Davis." Instead, she got her license and was on the Mackinac Bridge on a windy day with the ride. The only one who hasn't yet been on a ride is Dru, who wasn't old enough to drive at the time and was busy playing golf.

In addition to Davis, Robin, and the Pettys, celebrities who join the ride include NASCAR Hall of Fame driver Harry Gant, former NFL and University of Georgia running back Herschel Walker, and super model Niki Taylor. Robin was a huge Walker fan from his days at UGA, and one year when she and Davis weren't riding, she took a group of friends to a refueling stop in Brunswick, Georgia, so they could meet Walker. "It was a no-brainer; they all loved Herschel," Robin said. "As they watched everyone drive in, they said, 'You've never described this.

This is amazing.'"

Their second ride started in Coeur d'Alene, Idaho, and wound through Wyoming, over the pass into Glacier National Park and through Yellowstone. "We had to stop and let the deer and cattle pass in places," Robin said. "You'd see a bear off to the side and want to go watch it."

They've also driven Route 66, wound through the Blue Ridge Mountains and down the east coast starting in Bar Harbor, Maine. Every trip they made, the Loves had their bus follow the ride so they didn't have to haul luggage in and out of hotels.

"We didn't have to go unpack and repack each day," Robin said. "It is your house on wheels. You have your own linens, own towels, own shampoos . . . It was a luxury. During thunderstorms, a lot of people would wind up on the bus with us watching movies."

Robin and Davis haven't been able to ride the last few years because it has fallen during THE PLAYERS, a tournament Davis has won twice, but they hope to jump back on the ride soon. The past few years have been filled with everything Ryder Cup, since Davis was 2012 captain. They haven't been traveling as much and, therefore, sold the bus. Dru is in his freshman year at Alabama, while Lexie works for her parents' foundation and the McGladrey Classic.

They've had only one small mishap in five rides and it was at least amusing. "Davis got off the bike at a stop and thought he put the kickstand down," Robin said. "He didn't. He walked away and the bike and I went down. I was under the bike and he didn't notice until people yelled at him. I'm lying there thinking, 'Seriously, fifth year and you finally dropped me on the bike?'"

It's been quite a — pardon the pun — ride for Davis and Robin, who went on their first date as high school juniors. They drove 30 minutes to sit on a park bench and eat barbecue at Choo-Choos. As time went on, they became best friends and for the first three years of college, Davis dated one of her best friends. When they finally got together, she said, "He knew my heartaches, he knew my relationships with other boys. He was always my shoulder to cry on."

Once they started dating seriously, it was only a matter of time. He finished third in his first event as a pro — the Bahamas Classic — and they set the date. Almost 27 years later, he's in the World Golf Hall of Fame and they're still having a blast.

But one other moment bears mentioning. Their second date was to THE PLAYERS and it turned out to be another of Robin's fashion "oops" moments.

"I grew up watching Jack Nicklaus and I told Davis my dad would be very jealous," Robin said. "I was a wearing a cute, cute little sundress and flat sandals, and he asked 'Are you going to wear that?' He didn't think it was appropriate, but I told him I'd be fine. However, the course back then was hillier and there were more mounds. I didn't realize I was going to be crawling up hills and the sandals I was wearing had leather soles, so I kept slipping. I spent half my time that day on my rear end."

But, she looked cute doing it.

The Tim Finchem Family

Holly Bachand stood there dressed in a white blouse, a plaid skirt, white knee socks and — to complete the ensemble — a black riding hat. It was the 1980s and she was dressed for her job as tour guide, working inside the pristine grounds of Disney World's Magic Kingdom in Orlando.

"I have no idea why they had me wear that hat. But I gave information on Walt Disney, the park and its development, as well as a behind-the-scenes tour of the operations of the park," she says of her five-month internship. She smiles — all right, she laughs — at the memory now, the college senior living in a trailer on Seven Dwarfs Lane, and reporting to work each day to escort excited guests past Mickey, Donald, and the rest of the gang.

That was a little more than a year before she had her less-than-glamorous introduction to professional golf, an employment transition which allowed her to ditch the plaid skirt and riding hat.

That first job in golf came when she accepted a position as tournament assistant with the Chrysler Cup, a Presidents Cup-style tournament for Champions Tour players. Her office was in a trailer at TPC Avenel outside Washington, DC, necessary because the clubhouse construction wasn't finished. Her responsibilities were varied and included, among other things, transporting players. There were challenges involved in her position; among them, finding your way around the city of Washington, DC in the year 1986, before the time of GPS or Mapquest. "I was transporting a World Golf Hall of Fame member, Gene Littler, from the course to nearby National Airport. We got lost on the drive there. Well, I got lost. But I quickly righted myself," she says, shaking her head at the memory. "Thankfully, Littler was a great sport and simply grateful for the ride."

It was the memorable and firsthand experiences of her position as tournament assistant that started to develop Holly's love for the game of golf. But, it was a meeting she expected to be routine that would ultimately solidify the game of golf in her life forever.

Holly walked into her meeting with National Strategies and Marketing Group, the firm representing the TOUR's various sponsor relationships, and introduced herself to one of the founders. "Hello, Tim Finchem," the man replied. By the end of the meeting, the two had hit it off. A few days later, he invited her to dinner and a show. And just like that, Holly Bachand and Tim Finchem were a couple, her days in the Disney and Chrysler Cup trailers quickly becoming a thing of the past.

"Tim was a Washingtonian and he had many haunts to share with me," Holly says. One of those was the Old Ebbitt Grill for their first dinner together. Many more nights on the town followed.

Six months later, at the Harmon Presbyterian Church near the Congressional Country Club in Bethesda, Maryland, Holly married Tim inside the sanctuary on Persimmon Tree Lane. "It sounds really crazy to say it now, that we got married six months after we met," Holly said. "But we knew it was the right thing for us." And that's how Holly Bachand became Holly Finchem, and how golf became an integral part of her life.

Thirteen months later, Tim accepted the position of director of business affairs at the PGA TOUR in Ponte Vedra Beach, Florida. In 1990, he was named deputy commissioner and chief operating officer. When Deane Beman retired as commissioner in 1994, Tim became the TOUR's third commissioner, a position he still holds today.

With golf being such a major focus of their lives, it was only natural that Holly would soon give the sport a try herself. Holly, the golfer, stepped into the spotlight at the TOUR Wives Golf Classic in Arizona in

Holly and Tim Finchem

The Finchems: Spencer, Tim, Holly, Kelly, Carey, and Stephenie

1994, the PGA TOUR commissioner serving as her caddie.

"Cathi Triplett [Kirk's wife] invited me to participate. We had three kids, all under six, and I was feverishly trying to learn to at least get a swing," she says. "I knew the event was supposed to be low-key, and I was pleased to hear it was a scramble. But standing on the first tee, talk about nerves! I whiffed it on my first swing. That was not pretty." Fortunately, Holly's caddie helped her with her alignment, and she put the ball onto the fairway on her second swing. Quite a team.

That team raised three daughters. (Tim has a grown son from a previous marriage) However, they are now finding themselves empty-nesters. "Tim and I just passed our 25th wedding anniversary, and I realized our married life has been half of my lifetime. My home and my history is now firmly in Ponte Vedra Beach and much of it is with the PGA TOUR," Holly says. A certain amount of adjustment is taking place, with one daughter already a college graduate and two others currently enrolled.

Holly is now able to watch more golf in person than ever before, sometimes with her husband at her side. "We had the opportunity this past winter to hit the West Coast swing. While we were at the AT&T

[Pebble Beach National Pro-Am], I told Tim I wanted to get out there and see some of these magnificent holes live and in person, not just on television," she explains. "I said, 'Let's take an hour and go out and be in the gallery.'"

So they did. "It was the first time in quite a while that Tim had been on the ropes other than at one of the team-style events," she adds. "It was great. We walked a couple of holes at Pebble Beach and then situated ourselves at number seven, that beautiful little par-3. We experienced a tournament like a fan would, and marveled at the game and the competition like everybody else does."

Tim caddying for Holly during the TOUR Wives Golf Classic

"Traveling with Tim also provides opportunities for me to be more involved. During our trip to the Northern Trust Open and the Farmers Insurance Open, the TOUR partnered with Operation Shower." Operation Shower distributes baby gifts to pregnant women with military husbands deployed overseas. "Operation Shower is such a wonderful program, one that I've enjoyed being involved with. I love watching these women receive car seats, cribs, gift cards, and even vacations. The Operation Showers are a phenomenal new partnership with the TOUR that I can't say enough about."

Operation Shower is just one element of the TOUR's bigger-picture look at charitable outreach, and Holly remains amazed at the "Together, anything's possible" vision the PGA TOUR has — from what its tournaments do on a weekly basis to activities at TOUR headquarters, where TOUR employees have adopted needy families at Christmas time,

and volunteered at area schools and other community outreach projects.

For the past five years, Holly has been a reading tutor to students at a Jacksonville inner-city elementary school. "It's so rewarding to help kids who are behind in their reading skills yet so eager to learn. It's a privilege to witness the growth that is possible with a little one-on-one support," she says. One student's progress made an impact on Holly. "Richard is particularly memorable," Holly continues. "He had been held back from advancing to the first grade and was convinced he couldn't read, but with determination, he finally did. It was so exciting to see him move forward. I think about him all the time."

"This has been a great journey with Holly," says Commissioner Finchem. "There's nobody I would rather have by my side than her." Holly's frequent travel with her husband these days also allows her to serve in an official Finchem function as he often asks her to observe a speech and then serve as his critic. "Tim likes to ask me to grade him after the fact. I'm honest and straightforward," she says. "I don't know if everybody can be as honest as they might like to be with the person who's at the top of the organizational chart. I appreciate that he invites me to give him this feedback, and that he looks to me for an assessment of his delivery and message. Even after 18 years as commissioner, Tim is driven to always be at his best when representing the work of the PGA TOUR and its players. I admire that."

Tim and Holly model the same team approach that is echoed by so many TOUR players and their wives. It's quite possibly a part of why the TOUR has evolved into the family-friendly sport and profession that it is. As a team, their strengths complement one another, and their mutual support is a model and inspiration for others.

TOUR Wives Golf Classic – Kirk and Cathi Triplett, Curtis and Sarah Strange, Holly and Tim Finchem, Melanie and Phil Tataurangi

The Phil Mickelson Family

Imagine planning for a vacation when the only hint your spouse gives you about the getaway is to pack a bathing suit. Or a coat. The rest is a secret. Every other year, Amy and Phil Mickelson trade off. One plans the getaway for just the two of them, the other gets a surprise.

One year it might be climbing Mayan ruins, another year a quick ten-minute drive to a fabulous room with a view in Del Mar. Or a trip to the pyramids in Egypt. Or Laguna Beach for tacos and a movie.

It's the one thing they do for themselves every year to celebrate their anniversary — and pamper their better half. Amy calls it one of the best pieces of advice they ever got and it came from longtime friends, Terry Jastrow and Anne Archer, who have been married 34 years.

"They're such a high-profile couple and they're extremely in love and they make it work," Amy said. "It's unusual with two such demanding lives. We're all ears with advice from them."

"The concept is simple," Amy said, "and, honestly, lots of fun. One person takes the odd years, the other takes the even ones and you plan a trip completely with the other person in mind. The idea is to be very thoughtful," she said. "And the other person has the year off. You don't even need to get a card. You're just spoiled. It ends up to be most fun when it's your year to plan for the other person. You can get on the phone and talk to people, and start to think of all these little things and surprises."

It's not always easy to pick a date since the TOUR life means year-round travel and international events in the fall. But Phil and Amy have been married 17 years now and they've never skipped a year. Not even when Amy was pregnant with son Evan and on bed rest. Phil got permission that year to drive Amy ten minutes to Del Mar, which was huge because she was having such serious pre-term labor, she wasn't even supposed to be out of bed.

"He got a beautiful room with an ocean view and filled the room with flowers, candles, and a big basket of all the foods I was craving, which were wheat toast with butter, peanut butter, bananas and honey — which is like a pie," she said. "All we could really do was lie around and watch movies and play cards, but it just shows there are a lot of ways to be thoughtful without going to Egypt." Phil gave Amy the Egypt trip three years ago when she was on a break from undergoing breast cancer treatments, and Amy outdid herself with a trip for Phil to Chichen Itza.

But Amy's favorite? Their tenth anniversary getaway when Phil planned a surprise second wedding in Bora Bora. They had traveled so much internationally that year that Amy tried to cancel. She was burned out. Both of them were, but Phil wouldn't let her.

He snuck a dress from her closet so the tailor could use it as a model to alter the new wedding dress. He bought rings and rented a private hut where they could eat all their meals on the patio, and jump off the deck and swim.

And, of course, he ordered up a traditional Polynesian wedding ceremony where the woman waits on the sand and the man arrives in a boat.

"These little Polynesian men carry you to your bride — the man's feet aren't supposed to touch the sand," she said. "Phil's six foot three, and they're my size. Two boys are carrying him and his feet are dragging on the ground. I'm telling myself to breathe in and breathe out. I'm trying not to laugh and he's got this grin on his face. It's the sweetest, most romantic thing he's done, surprising me, and I'm dying laughing."

Over the years, they've had as many quiet, low-key trips as lavish

Phil and Amy

ones, always keeping in mind that it's all about the joy of giving to each other.

That joy spills over to their philanthropic outreach, which focuses on family.

Both Amy and Phil came from strong, tight-knit families and family always comes first. Any week they can plan for a family vacation with Amanda, Sophia, and Evan, that takes precedence over anything — even a big tournament. So when they see a way to reach out and help strengthen other families through youth and family initiatives, they do.

Amy admits their foundation efforts used to be very scattered. It did a lot of good work, but today, it has a narrower focus and bigger goals.

Two major outreaches from the Phil and Amy Mickelson Foundation are the Mickelson ExxonMobil Teachers Academy, an intense five days where 600 elementary teachers find innovative ways to teach math and science, and Start Smart, an annual shopping spree for needy students in the San Diego area.

Amy and Phil try to greet all the visitors at Start Smart, where each child receives a backpack of school supplies and is given a list of clothing items to pick from — jackets, sweaters, shirts and blouses, slacks and skirts, shoes, socks, and underwear. They consider themselves fortunate to be in a position to help and encourage others to give back, too. To date, they have helped over 11,000 children and families.

They also created Birdies for the Brave, a PGA TOUR military outreach program that is dedicated to supporting and meeting the needs of wounded US military and their families.

Not surprisingly, Phil's and Amy's commitment to giving has spread to their children, who not only help with Mom's and Dad's events, but also find ways to give on their own.

Sophia has set up her own charity — The ONE Charity. The slogan? It only takes one person to make a difference and that one person is you.

When she first decided to do something, Amy reminded her she

Phil and Amy, in Egypt

does give back by helping at foundation events. Sophia still wanted her own charity. When Amy offered to match her with a dollar for every dollar she raised, Sophia politely declined. She said, "You and Dad have your own foundation, and you should keep focusing on that. I want to do this all on my own."

She does chores to earn money for supplies. She makes jewelry, candles, duct tape crafts, paintings, and baked goods, and sells them at school and around the community. Her first year, she helped a shelter that supports homeless teen mothers and teaches them life skills.

"What I love is that she just does it," Amy said. "She doesn't overthink it. Her heart feels that tug and she does something about it." Her passion is infectious and she was even recently asked to speak at a powerful women's conference in Florida where she received the only standing ovation.

Sophia's passion has spilled over to her siblings, too. Older sister Amanda is interested in historical preservation, and initiatives to stop child slavery and trafficking. Evan is raising money for his charity — Cool Toys for Cool Kids which, of course, gives kids in need cool toys. And, like Sophia, they're doing it all on their own.

"At their age, giving should be for joy," Amy said. "You don't have to build houses or have a gala — it's just important to get outside yourself and think of people. Do what you can, and that's enough."

The last 20 years have been quite a ride. Phil and Amy have gone from dating at Arizona State to growing through major losses and sharing major victories, and last spring, celebrating Phil's induction into the World Golf Hall of Fame.

"For the first time in a long time, we stopped and thought about what golf has given us," Amy said. "We think about it sometimes, but we never really stopped to comprehend. Some of the things we've done we never thought existed. The places we've all seen just because of golf. The fascinating people we get to meet who give and inspire. There's so much to learn from them."

And, as all the Mickelsons will tell you, so many ways to give back.

Phil and Amy, at their Smart Start charity event

Photo by Dave Siccardi

Evan, Sophia, and Amanda, caddying for their dad during the Par 3 tournament at the Masters

CHANGING TIMES

Angie Pampling and friend

Early in the new millennium, the Association saw a shift in how it collaborated with and supported charities.

Members had always enjoyed interacting with those organizations that were a part of the PGA TOUR family, and specifically, those in the local communities that benefited from PGA TOUR tournaments. However, many times they were asked to simply tour various facilities to see the work that was done, rather than rolling up their sleeves and taking action.

A deliberate, yet subtle, transformation took hold when the members began actively seeking opportunities to get involved and make a difference. The Association's own donations had significantly impacted many charities, and while the funding was important, members knew volunteering their time would be just as impactful. They wanted to know that when they left a city, they left it a little better than when they arrived.

Community outreach and volunteerism quickly became part of the Association's culture. Festivals for children in the gardens at Children's Healthcare of Atlanta; barbecues at Target House; partnering with

the Association's friend Emeril Lagasse at St. Michael Special School for Mentally Challenged Children in New Orleans; packing food at the Greater Boston Food Bank; and building houses with Habitat for Humanity, are just a few of the many opportunities the Association has been involved with over the years. The more involved and hands-on the members could be, the more they enjoyed it.

That need to leave a footprint in the local communities is alive and well today. The PGA TOUR Wives Association is a voice to be heard. It is an example to others of the importance of lending a hand and the basis for what they believe in, which is captured in their motto:

Giving Time to Others
Giving Back to Communities
Giving Through Golf

Each time they go into a community, they touch a few hearts and leave a little piece of themselves behind. Giving comes in many forms and it is the passion that drives the members of the PGA TOUR Wives Association.

Since 1988, PGA TOUR Wives Association events have raised over $5 million for charities that help children and their families.

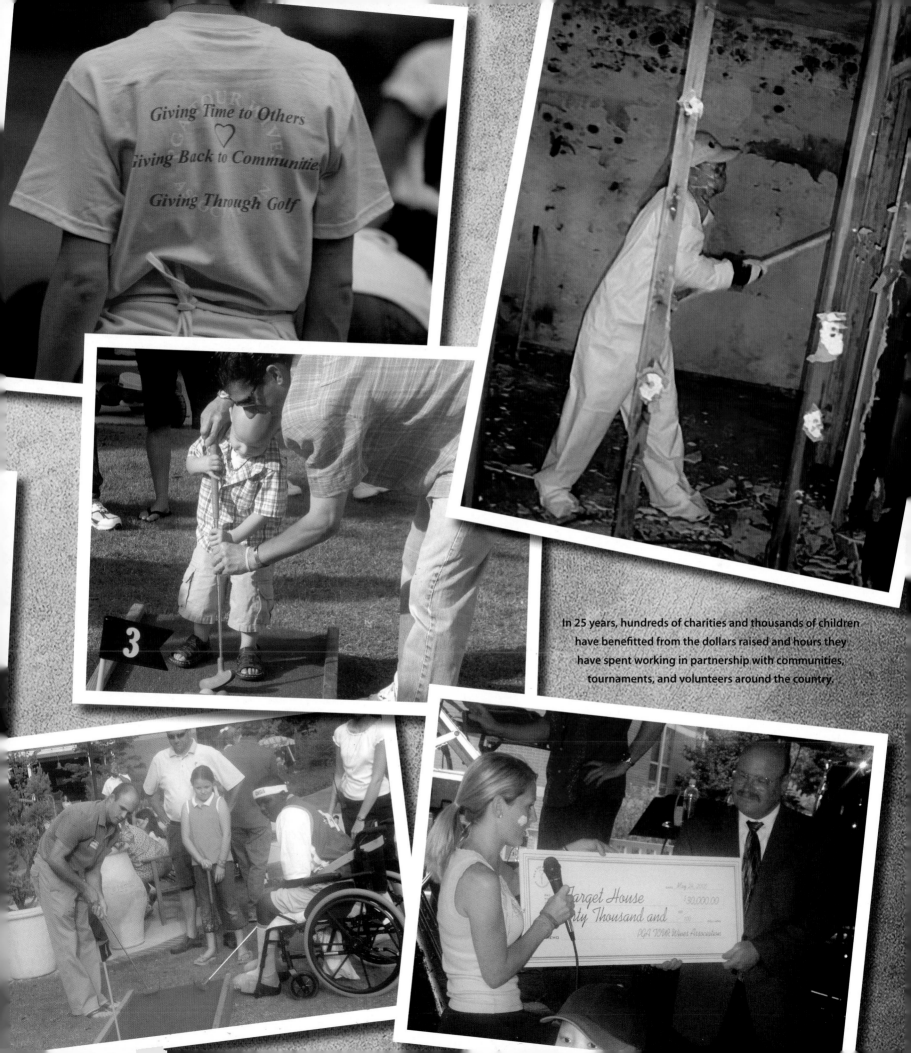

Giving Time to Others

Giving Back to Communities

Giving Through Golf

In 25 years, hundreds of charities and thousands of children
have benefitted from the dollars raised and hours they
have spent working in partnership with communities,
tournaments, and volunteers around the country.

CHARITABLE WORKS
2000-2006

2000

A Taste of the TOUR cookbook is published
TOUR Wives Golf Classic at the Phoenix Open
Golf Jam II at the TOUR Championship
Golf in the Garden at Children's Healthcare of Atlanta at the BellSouth Classic
Target House Family BBQ, St. Jude Children's Hospital at the FedEx St. Jude Classic
Silent auction at the Ozarks Open

2001

Fundraiser at the Canon Greater Hartford Open
Suds for Shelters - collected toiletries for local shelters
FORE HOPE breakfast event at the Memorial Tournament
Martha's Village and Kitchen at the Bob Hope Chrysler Classic
Golf in the Garden at Children's Healthcare of Atlanta at the BellSouth Classic
Michael's Special School for Mentally Challenged Children at the COMPAQ Classic of New Orleans
Jonsson Community School in conjunction with Christina's Smile at the Verizon Byron Nelson Classic
Orlando Day Nursery at the National Car Rental Golf Classic at Walt Disney World Resort
Charity auction at the NIKE Boise Open

2002

TOUR Wives Golf Classic at the Phoenix Open
FORE HOPE breakfast event at the Memorial Tournament
AstraZeneca presents: "Migraine Awareness Luncheon" at the Valero Texas Open
St. Vincent de Paul Village at the Buick Invitational
Martha's Village and Kitchen at the Bob Hope Chrysler Classic
Arnold Palmer Hospital visit at the Bay Hill Invitational
Golf in the Garden at Children's Healthcare of Atlanta at the BellSouth Classic
Children's Hospital of New Orleans at the COMPAQ Classic of New Orleans
Target House Family BBQ, St. Jude Children's Hospital at the FedEx St. Jude Classic
Winn-Dixie Hope Lodge Center at the Genuity Championship
Walk and Remember September 11th at the SEI Pennsylvania Classic
Whaley Children's Center at the Buick Open
Auction at the Nationwide Boise Open

2003

Kimberly Home "Baby Shower" at the Tampa Bay Classic presented by Buick

Martha's Village and Kitchen at the Bob Hope Chrysler Classic

Hubbard House in Orlando at the Bay Hill Invitational

Target House Family BBQ, St. Jude Children's Hospital at the FedEx St. Jude Classic

Golf in the Garden at Children's Healthcare of Atlanta at the BellSouth Classic

Easter Seals visit at the Buick Classic

J. Erik Jonsson Community School at the EDS Byron Nelson Championship

Hastings on Hudson School Literacy Program at the Buick Classic

Build a Bear Head Start program at the Valero Texas Open

Boys & Girls Club in Boston at the Deutsche Bank Championship

Auction at the Greater Hartford Open

"Lend a Hand" Golf Day in Orlando

FORE HOPE Breakfast at the Memorial Tournament

Wake Forest Boys & Girls Club at the SAS Carolina Classic

Boys & Girls Club of Tennessee Valley at the Knoxville Open

Ronald McDonald House of Springfield at the Price Cutter Charity Championship

Bringing Hope to Single Moms at the Utah Classic

2004

TOUR Wives Golf Classic at the Phoenix Open

Quilt Auction at the Deutsche Bank Championship

FORE HOPE breakfast at the Memorial Tournament

Miami's Lighthouse Center for the Blind at the Ford Championship at Doral

Arnold Palmer Hospital visit at the Bay Hill Invitational

Phoenix Children's Hospital at the FBR Open

Literacy in Westchester County Reading at the Buick Classic

Target House Family BBQ, St. Jude Children's Hospital at the FedEx St. Jude Classic

Adopt a Child for an evening at the Valero Texas Open

Greater Boston Food Bank at the Deutsche Bank Championship

Kimberly Home "Baby Shower" at the Chrysler Championship

Compass of Carolina at the BMW Charity Pro-Am at The Cliffs

Boys & Girls Club of Knoxville at the Knoxville Open

Kohl Children's Museum at the LaSalle Bank Open

Carnival Day and Kid's Clinic at the Lake Erie Charity Classic

Charitee for Charity Beanie Baby sales at multiple tournaments

Auction at the Price Cutter Charity Championship

2005

Auction at the EDS Byron Nelson Championship

"Giving Through Golf" Wristbands Fundraiser at multiple tournaments

Martha's Village and Kitchen at the Bob Hope Chrysler Classic

Habitat for Humanity at the 84 LUMBER Classic

Greater Boston Food Bank at the Deutsche Bank Championship

Phoenix Children's Hospital at the FBR Open

Golf in the Garden at Children's Healthcare of Atlanta at the BellSouth Classic

J. Erik Jonsson Community School at the EDS Byron Nelson Championship

Think Pink Gilda's Club of the Quad Cities at the John Deere Classic

Milwaukee Children's Hospital at the U.S. Bank Championship

Baptist Children's Hospital at the Ford Championship at Doral

Maria Fareri Children's Hospital visit at the Barclays Classic

Connecticut Children's Medical Center Book Drive at the Buick Championship

Target House Family BBQ, St. Jude Children's Hospital at the FedEx St. Jude Classic

Kimberly Home "Baby Shower" at the Chrysler Championship

Read Aloud program for the Drew Charter School at THE TOUR Championship presented by Coca-Cola

Respite Care of San Antonio Build a Bear program at the Valero Texas Open

Great Lakes Adaptive Sports Association (GLASA) at the LaSalle Bank Open

Boys & Girls Club of Tennessee Valley at the Knoxville Open

Virginia Home for Boys and Girls at the Henrico County Open

The Charles Lea Foundation at the BMW Charity Pro-Am at The Cliffs

Make a Wish Foundation of Northern West Virginia (Drive to a Billion campaign)
at the Pete Dye West Virginia Classic

Auction at the Price Cutter Charity Championship

2006

TOUR Wives Golf Classic at the FBR Open

Catholic Charities Operation Helping Hands, Hurricane Katrina Relief, Zurich Classic of New Orleans

Sunrise of Pasco County benefit and luncheon at the PODS Championship

Greater Boston Food Bank at the Deutsche Bank Championship

Children's Hospital and Health Center of San Diego at the Buick Invitational

Cook Children's Medical Center at the Bank of America Colonial

Baptist Children's Hospital at the Ford Championship at Doral

Golf in the Garden at Children's Healthcare of Atlanta at the BellSouth Classic

J. Erik Jonsson Community School at the EDS Byron Nelson Championship

Maria Fareri Children's Hospital visit at the Barclays Classic

Nicklaus Children's Hospital at The Honda Classic

Target House Family BBQ, St. Jude Children's Hospital at the FedEx St. Jude Classic

Fundraiser dinner and silent auction at the Shell Houston Open

Bauble, Beauty & The Blue Martini at the Arnold Palmer Invitational

Virginia Home for Boys and Girls at the Henrico County Open

Boys & Girls Club of Tennessee Valley at the Knoxville Open

Great Lakes Adaptive Sports Association (GLASA) at the LaSalle Bank Open

Heather and Charles with their children, Chase and Ansley

The Charles Howell III Family

Charles Howell III grew up just a couple of miles away from Augusta National Golf Club, which — as almost everyone knows — happens to be golf's Holy Grail.

Emphasis on almost.

Just getting a glimpse of Magnolia Lane when you're a kid is enough to send you to the practice tee for hours. So when Charles called the pro shop in December 1999 and asked if he could bring his girlfriend out for a look, he was pumped. He wanted her to see how special a place it was to him . . . to golf.

It was raining that day when they pulled into a fairly empty parking lot. "If this place is so popular," Heather Myers said, "then where are the cars?" She had no clue. "I think Charles must have thought, 'What did I get myself into?'"

He kinda did. Then again, he didn't. They had been dating four months and he knew she didn't realize just how exclusive this course was.

Heather didn't know a lick about golf, period. All the Myers' kids were raised on the basketball court. Their mom, Cherie, was the legendary high school coach at Okarche (Oklahoma) High School, and Heather played for Kingfisher High School. Heather could talk full-court presses, motion offense, and pick and rolls by the time she was in elementary school. But golf? She knew a few names and that was about it.

"I didn't know what a par or a birdie was when we started dating," she said. "I had no clue what the Masters was — had no clue about any of it. I knew nothing. I was so naïve."

Charles and Heather can't tell you when they started dating. It just happened. The first week of her freshman year at Oklahoma State, a friend of a friend was having a little party, so she went. Her friend wanted her to meet the golfer next door and so his roommates obliged.

"Charles is totally anti-social, anti-everything, so he wasn't at the party," Heather said. "We go next door and he's sitting on the couch in his boxers practicing his grip with his wedge."

She laughs that she should have run right then and there, but she didn't. A few months later, he was the top college golfer in the country, and they were sitting in the Augusta National parking lot.

"Lord only knows how we got together," she said. "The Lord just had a bigger plan. We never really went on a first date or anything. We really don't know how we ended up dating. We did have a class together — statistics. I did all the homework, he copied off me, then received a better grade on all the tests."

Today, Heather still laughs about her golf savvy. She knows the game, but don't ask her to get too technical. "I know the basics — the fade, the draw," she said. "I can follow about anything they say; I can't add to conversation. I can watch his swing and know it looks wrong, but I can't tell you why it's wrong. Someone asks me what club was that? I say 'a Mizuno?'"

Three-year-old Ansley may one-up her mother soon. Her favorite

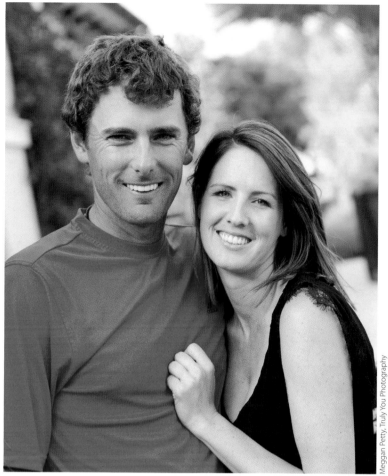
Charles and Heather

time of the day is late afternoon when she grabs her tiny set of pink golf clubs and heads to the Isleworth course with Charles. Last year, she was set to play in her first Masters Par-3, but it got rained out.

Heather has come a long way with golf since '99, but there is one last story she has to tell on herself. She and Charles were getting married in Hawaii the week after the 2001 U.S. Open and were talking about it in player dining at Southern Hills. An older gentleman in line with them started telling Heather how great the islands were and where to go.

"I go back to the table and say, 'Honey, whose dad is that? He's a really sweet man,'" Heather said. Charles grinned. "Honey, that's two-time U.S. Open winner, Hale Irwin, and he's in second place."

They just looked at each other and laughed.

The Steve Hulka Family

Steve and Mary Hulka, with their trailer

Steve Hulka, called simply "Hulk" on TOUR, was caddying and traveling, primarily by car, all over the country for years. But right after September 11, 2001, Steve was flying home to attend his aunt's funeral when he was introduced to the stress of airport travel. He was traveling light that day, carrying only a backpack, but still had to wait for over two and a half hours just to get through the security checkpoint at the Baltimore airport. As he waited anxiously during the screening process, he imagined how terrible it must be for TOUR players who, every week, fly to each tournament destination, sometimes traveling with enough luggage for weeks on the road. Then there are those players who also travel with their families and have additional luggage requirements.

As he thought about this, Hulka came up with an idea, an idea he hoped would ease the weekly travel for players and their families on TOUR. When he returned to work — at the time he was caddying for Pat Bates — he spent most of 2002 bouncing ideas off Pat and other PGA TOUR Players including Paul Stankowski, Ben Crane, and Jonathan Byrd, about a potential service to help PGA TOUR players streamline their weekly travel challenges from tournament to tournament.

The players welcomed the idea and encouraged him to create a truck-trailer business to haul golf clubs and suitcases, enabling players and their families to travel lighter. Hulka's Overland Player Express was born with the "H.O.P.E." that TOUR players would like the idea. It turns out they didn't just like, but loved it.

Now in their tenth year, Mary and Steve Hulka pack up their trailer with players' luggage and possessions every Sunday night during the PGA TOUR season. They drive straight to the next tournament, no matter how far away it is, and unload in the player parking lot on Monday. Once there, players meet the Hulkas to load their cars with their belongings to settle into wherever they may be calling home for the week.

The Hulkas drive 50,000 miles a year and are currently on their third trailer and third Chevy Silverado diesel truck.

Mary, showing how full their trailer is each week

The Tom Gillis Family

Jenny and Tom Gillis

Jenny and Tom Gillis, with their children, Aubrey and Trevor

TOUR family is . . . well, family! And what family would be complete without a little ribbing from your siblings? Jenny Gillis shares a story about practical jokes between friends.

"After the birth of our first child, Trevor, in 2005, our friend, Carl Pettersson, decided to play a joke on my husband, Tom. Tom's cell phone was programmed so that in order to delete a voicemail, you had to listen to each individual message before having the option to delete. Carl called repeatedly while Tom was on the course and filled his inbox completely. This of course, kept Tom busy for hours trying to clear all the voicemails. Though a tiny bit frustrated, Tom waited patiently for the right moment to 'repay the favor.'"

Returning home after many weeks on the road, Tom began to pay back Carl. First, a plumber arrived at the Pettersson's home to fix a massive leak . . . that didn't exist. Carl didn't think anything of it and assumed it was the wrong address. Later that night, 20 pizzas were delivered to their home. It didn't take Carl and wife, DeAnna, long to realize Tom was just getting started.

After an exhausting night with their infant daughter, the doorbell rang at 7:00 a.m. Twenty, five-gallon water bottles were being unloaded on their front porch. All DeAnna could yell was *"Gillllliiiisss!"*

It was just the beginning of a special friendship and more practical jokes to come with the Pettersson family.

The Chad Campbell Family

Chad and Amy, with their sons, Grayson, Dax, and Cannon

Amy Headington, Images of Grace Photography

"How could a kid ever have a second chance when he never had a first chance?"
— Chad Campbell

In 2006, Chad and Amy, a middle school teacher, had full-time custody of a former student of Amy's who could not stay out of the juvenile department and always found himself in trouble — at home, at school, and on the streets. They learned that his home environment was keeping him from having any chance of being successful.

"During his time with us, we saw a change in his behavior and his personal confidence," Amy said. "He experienced unconditional love and true acceptance for the first time in his life and, in return, he taught us how everyone deserves a second chance.

"Lewis opened our eyes to how many young people are in the same position he was in. Through this experience, Chad and I realized that we are the minority. Our life and reality are not most people's.

Chad Campbell, Lewis Taylor, and Amy Campbell

"Because of him, we teamed up with the nationally acclaimed non-profit, Heart of a Champion. Together we created a program called U-Turn, a specialized life skills program targeted at teens in the juvenile justice system. The program teaches teens the skills to make better choices and it assists and educates their parents or guardians on how they, too, can help their children navigate life experiences together.

"Since 2009, hundreds of students like Lewis have been given a second chance at life. Families have been given tools and resources to stop the destructive paths they are on, and make a U-turn. Most importantly, countless lives have been changed because of this program. Chad and I have found a greater purpose and a way to really make a difference in our community."

The Jeff Gove Family

Heather and Jeff, with their children, Jacob, Annie, and Hailey

Heather Gove narrates this tale of a case of mistaken identity.

"In 2003, Jeff and I traveled to Las Vegas for the tournament there. We were having a great week, staying at the Rio with our closest TOUR friends, Jess and Natalya Daley, and several other players. Unfortunately, Natalya got extremely ill that week while Jess and Jeff were at the golf course, and Natalya called me for help. I immediately called the tournament headquarters and informed them that Mr. Daley's wife was ill, and we were in need of a doctor. Within five minutes, one of the tournament volunteers called me back and said that a doctor was ready to see and treat her in 20 minutes, and a limousine would be down at the valet in the next five minutes to take us to the doctor.

"Thrilled with the incredible treatment from the tournament, I went and got Natalya and walked down to the valet. The limousine was waiting with cold drinks for us and we settled in for the drive to the doctor. We could not believe the luck and were both so relieved that she was able to see a doctor so far from home.

"About five minutes later, the driver lowered the window and said, "So, what time does John tee off today?" We both lost our breaths, looked at each other and realized they thought they were taking John Daly's wife, not rookie Jeff Daley's wife, to the doctor! I quickly blurted out, "He tees off at noon.

"To this day, we laugh at the treatment she got that day by mistake, we are very grateful for it anyway!"

Geoff and Juli Ogilvy, at the 2011 Presidents Cup Gala

The Geoff Ogilvy Family

Geoff Ogilvy no longer makes a sandwich, he creates one. None of this slap a little meat and cheese on bread. Instead, fill the extra space with lettuce and avocado and sprouts, and savor every bite.

Same with breakfast. The 2006 U.S. Open champion doesn't just scramble eggs. He tosses in spinach or mushrooms or salsa or cheese. Maybe all of the above.

Add a little quinoa salad on the side and . . .

After all these years, his wife Juli has to smile. She attended culinary school and worked for a master baker in the Phoenix area. She probably would have stayed there, too, had she not met Geoff, and transitioned into family and life on the PGA TOUR.

Juli cooks on the fly, taking a Barefoot Contessa recipe and making it her own. Geoff enjoys the art of cooking just as much as Juli and, according to their family, he's quite a master in the kitchen, as well. When Geoff and Juli were early into their marriage they made a deal. "Instead of asking each other every night, what do you want to eat, which turned into a 30-minute back and forth of 'I don't know, what do you want,' we said every other night, we'll take turns cooking. Rules are you can't ask the other person for any ideas, no complaints about what is served, and the cook doesn't have to clean," says Juli. "It was a great way for us to enjoy cooking for each other and to try new things. We've slipped a bit since having our third child, but we aim to get back on track with our

158

Juli and Geoff, with their children, Jasper, Harvey, and Phoebe

plan once our oldest starts school in the fall."

Juli has turned the whole family into healthy food foodies, but for her 35th birthday, Geoff gave her a bit of a decadent gift — a trip to French Laundry in the Napa Valley. "It was one of my bucket-list things," she said. "It's any foodie's dream just to see what it's all about. [Owner and chef] Thomas Keller is a genius. I felt a little like Cinderella, in a way."

Her only worry? She's now a pescaterian (fish only, no meats) and she didn't know how many dishes fit that lifestyle. "It turns out they're so great," she said. "They will make a menu up for you. You just tell them some things you'd like to try that have no meat and they add some things in. It was absolutely amazing."

Divine, really. But the food was only the appetizer. The staff there — Keller wasn't there — are golf fans and they just had the company golf outing the day before. "All they wanted to do was talk golf with Geoff," she said, "and I'm asking about the kitchen."

Despite her training in a bakery, Juli doesn't work from scratch much anymore, but is teaching her three children how to navigate the kitchen.

"I bake with my kids," she said. "It's a necessity to cook, but not to bake. I use so many mixes now, it makes it easy for the kids to help. As much as my kids love to cook with me, their favorite is actually cooking with Geoff's mom when we are in Australia. Both Geoff and I grew up with moms who made it a point to cook nearly every meal at home. It was a real treat for us to go out to a restaurant. It's a value that sometimes gets reversed with the traveling and TOUR lifestyle. We're often forced to eat so many meals out when we are on the road, the kids really see the beauty of being able to share a meal that we've all helped to create in our family kitchen. Cooking is one of those labors of love that really makes you slow down a bit and enjoy life. That's what I would say is possibly the biggest difference between life in Australia and life in the United States. In Australia, the people really enjoy a slower pace lifestyle. There they work so that they can enjoy a fun, fabulous life. I feel like in America, we often get caught up in working to live. We're fortunate that "work" for us is still something that Geoff really enjoys. But I'm also happy for our kids to see that a simpler way of life can also be fun and fulfilling."

Sean and Jackie O'Hair

The Sean O'Hair Family

You could call them tough times or simply challenging ones.

Living out of boxes. Traveling the country in an old black Ford F-150, then a motor home — just the two of them and their yellow Lab. Dinner usually meant lots of rice, beans and tortillas because it was cheap and filling. And the hotels? Some of them were very interesting.

Jackie O'Hair can laugh about it now, but back then sitting on the edge of a hotel bathtub and cooking dinner on a little two-burner stove perched on top of the toilet was a reality. An inch here or there and dinner would be down the drain — literally.

"At this one hotel, you couldn't plug in more than one thing at a time or everything would short circuit," she said. "The tub was the only place I could cook so nothing would turn off."

Jackie and Sean O'Hair were chasing the dream on mini-tours. Sean had turned pro at 17 and it hadn't been easy, but finding Jackie changed all that. They married young — she was 21 and just finishing school at Florida Atlantic University, and Sean was 20 — and together they started living their life.

He played and she caddied. It was just the two of them. Home was where the tournaments were and they played everywhere, from state

160

opens to regional mini-tours to some events on the now Web.com Tour. They were barely making ends meet.

"We didn't have anything," she said. "If we had weeks off, we'd go stay with my parents. I still remember when Sean won the Vermont Open in 2004, and he won something like $8,000 and we were psyched. We were set for the whole year."

Little did they know what was just around the corner. A year later, they were set for life.

Just before qualifying school in the fall of 2004, Jackie found out she was pregnant and her father, Steve Lucas, stepped in to carry Sean's bag. Sean has a great relationship with Steve who has become more than just a father-in-law. "Sean's always been able to talk to him, rely on him," Jackie said. "They hit it off from the beginning. It could have gone so many different ways, but it was meant to happen."

Sean had faltered down the stretch at the 2003 Q-school, but this time he made it, finishing fourth. Steve agreed to stay on the bag and they all went on the road.

That next year, Sean's rookie year on TOUR, was a game-changer for the couple. One minute they were splurging on one nice dinner, the next, Sean and Jackie were looking at their first house, daughter Molly, and Sean's first win — the 2005 John Deere Classic.

"It's crazy how it all panned out," Jackie said. "We were lucky to have a great little family dynamic. You think about how many talented players there are and what it takes to get out here, and the fact that all the stars aligned that year."

Jackie laughs. They started out as green as can be in professional golf. Now, they are the veterans on TOUR and are entering the next phase, trying to balance four children and Sean's career.

It can be tricky, but they're making it work — just like cooking in that hotel bathroom and not tripping the breaker. "We try to focus on the blessings we have," she said. "And you learn to never take anything for granted."

The O'Hair children: Trevor, Luke, Molly, and Grady

The Robert Garrigus Family

Ami and Robert with their son, R.J., at Wrigley Field

Many of the milestones for children in PGA TOUR families are associated with tournaments. Ami Garrigus shares one of theirs.

"In 2011, Robert qualified for the U.S. Open at Congressional Country Club through a qualifier in Ohio. We were so excited to take our son, RJ, to his very first U.S. Open. That week also fell during the week of Father's Day, Robert's first, so we knew it was going to be special.

"I carried RJ out to the course every day so he could be there for Robert's last few holes. On Saturday, I was walking around the 18th fairway trying to find a good spot for us to see one of Daddy's shots. It was a warm day, so I put RJ down in the grass near the fairway so he could cool off. The grass was so long that it was tickling RJ's leg, and the next thing I knew, RJ started crawling for the very first time, right towards the cart path. Up until that moment, RJ had been getting around by rolling or scooting, and we had begun to think he was going to skip crawling all together. In all of the excitement, I almost missed Robert's approach shot to the green. Robert shot a 68 that day! It was such a special day for our family — RJ had conquered a huge milestone, and Robert was playing exceptionally well in the U.S. Open.

"The next day we celebrated Robert's first Father's Day. Robert gave us a special gift and went on to tie for third in the U.S. Open, his best finish yet in a major, which earned him a berth into the 2012 Masters."

Small milestones definitely leave a big impact. What a special week all around for the Garrigus family and one that they will not soon forget.

Robert caddies for Ami during the TOUR Wives Golf Classic

The Jason Gore Family

Jason and Megan Gore

Megan and Jason, with their children, Jaxson and Olivia

Many golfers have hidden talents off the golf course. Megan Gore shares her husband's story.

"Music is very much a part of the Gore household. Guitars, drums, and pianos litter the house. Jason is the reason why; he loves music and it shows in our house, in our children and in our lives.

"When we were in college, Jason decided he wanted to learn to play guitar. He bought himself a guitar and learned to play by watching concert DVDs and following along with the musicians. While he won't admit it, he's got a great singing voice, and music comes very naturally to him. He's always got some type of music playing.

"Jason even travels with a guitar, and can frequently be seen striding through an airport with a Fender Strat on his back. His downtime while on the road is usually spent in his room playing through headphones. He takes his music with him on the golf course by carrying a guitar pick with his golf ball marker in his pocket, a constant reminder of his music.

"While Jason is at home, he plays with our friend and music teacher, Jason Iannarilli, who has helped Jason take his music even further. Recently, the two of them played acoustically together at a friend's wedding. Jason has also played onstage at the House of Blues with a friend's band. At home, it's a family affair as our children and I all join Jason for our own version of rock band, as the children love to play alongside of their dad."

Jason Gore is a man of many talents, whether he's holding a golf club or a guitar.

Arron and Angie Oberholser, with their sons, Ethan and Ryan

The Arron Oberholser Family

The last thing Angie Rizzo thought about was dating a golfer. She was playing full-time on the LPGA Tour and she couldn't see going out with a golfer, let alone marrying one. Never.

So when a friend suggested they play a round of golf with Arron Oberholser in 2004, she said, "Why not? You can never have too many friends in this game."

Two years later, they were juggling an engagement and two diverse schedules on two diverse tours. It got a bit easier when Arron won the AT&T Pebble Beach National Pro Am in February, 2006, and he could

make his schedule for the rest of the year, but even that was relative.

"The win meant he was in all the big events," Angie said. "I was used to playing, then coming home. Instead, I'd be on the road, go see him, or he would play two, then come watch me. We weren't home a lot. It was tough to balance, but we knew we had to do it to make it work."

LPGA Hall of Famer Juli Inkster gave Angie one piece of advice to keeping a two-career marriage strong. "She said never go more than two weeks apart," Angie said. "It was hard. We never had a tournament at the same time in the same state. Sometimes we were in the same time zone, but that was about it."

Regardless, she became one of his best swing coaches, and he became everyone's favorite visitor on the LPGA range. "He loved coming out to watch me and the girls," especially her close friends Angela Stanford, Carin Koch, Kristi McPherson, and Jenny Gleason. "We loved having him out there," Angie said. "Every time he gave one of them a lesson, it seemed like they would win."

In 2002, Angie was driving from Los Angeles back to Phoenix, and was rear-ended by a truck on I-10. She suffered injuries including severe whiplash, which took a toll on her neck and back. She retired when they got married, planning to travel with Arron and start a family.

Ironically, Arron's career has been plagued by wrist and back injuries. He sat out much of the last four years, undergoing four different surgeries on his hand. The blessing, Angie said, is he was home during the birth of both their children — Ethan and Ryan — and the start of their kids' toddler years.

"It's been a completely different lifestyle," she said. "He thought he was ready to come back in early 2012, but he wasn't. He's had so many surgeries in the last four years; he just wasn't strong enough to play week in and week out on TOUR yet."

Angie has had her hands full with all three boys, but still finds time to play a few state opens and corporate events. She is also tournament director for the PGA TOUR Wives Association's TOUR Wives Golf Classic, the Association's largest fundraiser. A few years ago, she and Shauna Matteson, who played college golf, were paired together in the tournament and ran away with it. Now Angie throws her time into organizing the event, and has been involved the last four times it has been played.

Angie is more laid back when she plays, which led to an interesting moment during the 2008 Minnesota State Open, when Arron caddied for her and didn't think she was giving it her best. "He threatened not to caddie if I didn't pull it together," she said. "I did. I won and he was pretty proud. It's a special bond."

So is the one he has with his grandfather Bill, who was there for his grandson's first Masters in 2006. Bill, then 85, put his chair down on the ninth hole of Augusta National's Par-3 course, took a seat, and waited all day to see Arron play and Angie caddie for him.

Bill wanted to take in the moment and they delivered. "He sat there the entire day waiting," Angie said. "And when Arron got there, he made a hole in one." It didn't end there. Arron went on to tie for 14th. Two

Arron plays the role of caddie for wife and tournament director, Angie, during the TOUR Wives Golf Classic

years later, he finished 25th. Then the injuries took a toll.

Angie and Arron are being cautious this time around. They've both tried to come back too early from their own injuries, and they've watched other players struggle too, some hurting themselves worse in the process.

The plan for Arron is to find the balance and get his career back on track; to play more Masters, more majors, and to play with his sons as they grow up.

Tim and Candice Clark with their son, Jack

The Tim Clark Family

It was supposed to be a lazy, sleep-in Sunday morning for Tim and Candice Clark. So, when they heard the loud rumble and felt the sliding glass door in their hotel room shaking at 5:30 a.m., they figured it was one of those legendary thunderstorms that occurred in Sun City, in the North West Province of South Africa.

Then, suddenly, the sliding glass door opened, both sets of hotel room curtains blew into their fifth-floor room, and they sat straight up in bed. It wasn't a thunderstorm.

Ten feet away, stood a five-foot tall male baboon who had one hand in their fruit dish, a mouthful of fruit, and both eyes on the Clarks. "He was just staring at us and eating," Candice said. "Then he walked out. It was insane."

And a little scary. Male baboons have two-inch-long teeth that can rip anything wide open. The pads of their hands are so large they can push against a locked door with the right leverage and open it. To make things crazier, they can scale a wall, which explains how the baboon got into the Clarks' fifth-floor room. "We were shouting and waving pillows in the air," she said. "Then he just walked out. Left."

Candice laughs now, but it was seriously scary at the time. Just like the time she and Ashley Appleby were on a drive in South Africa watching an elephant graze early one morning. "He flapped his ears and started running at the vehicle," she said. "The driver took off. I had a video camera with me. It was one of those moments that could be on 'When Vacations Attack.'"

But for every scary moment she's had in Tim's native South Africa, she can recount a zillion "wow" moments that are even more amazing and just as eye-opening. A mother lion carrying her cub across the road. A dung beetle moving — well — dung. Rocks glistening by the river that aren't rocks at all — they're baby hippos.

"It's kind of like you're watching *National Geographic*," she said, "and it's ten feet from you. You're looking at a tree and you think the wind is blowing the leaves. Then you see the two little eyes and the ears, and you realize it's a giraffe eating the trees. It's very surreal."

It's even more special that it's now part of her family heritage, which, she laughs, is a hodgepodge. Tim and his family are South African. Her mother is Swiss; her father is Canadian; she was born in Canada, but grew up in New Jersey and Arizona; and their son Jack is American. "By the time Jack was eight months old, he'd been around the world," she said. "We did an around-the-world ticket — Arizona to Australia to Africa to England, then back to Arizona."

They've been on TOUR now for ten years, and they try to get back to South Africa at least twice a year to see Tim's parents. It won't be long now until Jack starts telling his own wildlife stories, too.

It all seemed too exotic at first but, Candice said, you soon realize it's just a little different. Instead of dogs and cats roaming neighborhoods, think gray vervet monkeys carrying babies on their stomachs. Also think doors and windows locked tight. "You know how people in the northeast [U.S.] have raccoons that knock over garbage cans?" Candice said. "In South Africa, you can't leave the window or the doors unlocked, because if you do, the monkeys will come in and eat the bananas in the kitchen. They know how to open bread boxes, too."

"Tim's dad came home one day and a monkey was sitting in the living room. He had opened up a box of chocolates, and there were empty wrappers everywhere. When Tim's dad walked in, the monkey just ran out."

There are serious moments as well. In 2005, Tim won the Nelson

Jack, with the Clark's beloved family dog, Olive

Mandela Invitational, and he and Candice toured Carel du Toit School for the Hearing Impaired in Tygerberga, where Tim donated his earnings to a girl there who needed a cochlear implant.

"We got this letter and little book from her," Candice said. "It was sweet. She actually heard rain for the first time at ten years old. Can you imagine? We enjoy charity work, but that put it on a different level."

So was meeting Nelson Mandela — or Madiba, as they call him in South Africa. At the event, a group of children came in to sing just for him in his dialect, which is difficult to master. "It's an amazing feeling," she said. "There's an aura when he is around."

Candice has toured Robben Island, too, where the guides, all former political prisoners, walk visitors through the prison, the tiny cell where Mandela was held prisoner for 18 years and tell firsthand stories about Madiba.

Yes, South Africa is far from Scottsdale, the little oasis in the desert Candice and Tim call home, but it's home, too — just one that comes with those eye-popping stories, brilliant landscapes, and amazing wildlife.

One last fun fact about baboons . . . they love shiny objects. People must hide jewelry and anything metallic. Hotel staff even remind guests to put things in the drawers.

That night before going to bed in Sun City, Candice tossed her metallic gold purse down on the counter, which contained her ID and rand, the South African currency. The baboon never touched the purse, but Candice and Tim still laugh at what might have been — a baboon tossing rand everywhere. It would have been another great story, and it still might be one day.

167

The Will MacKenzie Family

Alli and Will MacKenzie, with their sons, Nash and Maverick

All players and families have their favorite stories to share. Here are two from Alli and Will MacKenzie.

Golf is for the Birds

One of Will and Alli's least favorite golf memories on TOUR occurred when Will was playing in San Diego. Will hit a beautiful shot that landed right in the middle of the fairway. Unfortunately for Will, a seagull liked his shot so much that it picked up the ball and flew off with it. Under the rules of golf, it was determined to be a "lost ball," and Will missed the cut by one shot.

Role Models

Many young golfers look to veteran players as role models on the golf course. Off the course, Alli and Will look to Sandy and Kenny Perry as a family role model. "Sandy and Kenny are the best! They have managed to have a successful golf career and still raised this amazing, close and fun family," said Alli. "We hope to do that with our lives; balance golf and career successes with strong family values and lots of love."

Will and Alli

The George McNeill Family

George and Ryan Lynn McNeil

Ryan McNeill describes her first date with George as being "like pulling teeth. He was so quiet and shy. I had to play 20 questions with him to make him talk. After that first encounter, it took him another month to talk me into a second date. Of course, he did and after that it was love."

Since those early days, George's shyness has receded, and he and Ryan have become much more adventurous. Ryan has tried her hand at the flying trapeze, and George earned his pilot's license. However, George wasn't the first in his family to love flying. His mother has flown planes, and his grandmother also had her pilot's license.

Ryan and George enjoy spending time fishing in the Florida Keys. It's a hobby that Ryan recalls discussing with President George H. W. Bush while at THE PLAYERS Championship. "It's one of my favorite memories while traveling with George on TOUR. We met President Bush. He had these clear, icy blue eyes, was toweringly tall, and sharp as a tack. Best of all, we had something in common. We both enjoy the same fishing spots on the west coast of Florida. Meeting the president is always a special occasion, but having the experience of talking about something so simple was especially nice."

It appears that the days of the super shy and reserved George may be over; it seems that Ryan has brought out the adventurous side of George and, together, they are enjoying life to its fullest.

Bryce and Kelley Molder, with their dogs

The Bryce Molder Family

The true test of character is how people respond to the challenges life throws their way. Bryce and Kelley Molder know plenty about character.

Bryce was born with Poland Syndrome, a rare birth defect that affects the chest muscle on one side of the body, and can cause webbing of the fingers on that same side. Bryce was born without a left pectoral muscle and an underdeveloped left hand, on which he has had two corrective surgeries. Bryce remembers the first surgery well: "I was six years old and scared. My parents promised me my own set of golf clubs if I was brave and cooperated with the surgery. That first set of clubs sparked my interest in golf.

"As a kid, I remember playing sports with friends and one team would be 'skins' and the other team would be 'shirts.' I never wanted to be on the 'skins' team, because I didn't want to take my shirt off and be seen differently. That pushed me to get more involved in golf. Despite my unique body, I could still be competitive. Golf gave me the confidence I lacked."

"In a way, Bryce's condition has been somewhat of a blessing," explains wife, Kelley. "There are kids who hear about Bryce and come out to the tournaments or send letters to tell him they have Poland Syndrome, too. They see Bryce out there making his dream come true and they realize they can do the same. It's fans like those who have pushed Bryce to persevere his way to a successful career."

When Kelley came into Bryce's life, she didn't know of challenges the Molder family had faced, and how she would eventually help them heal from their past. Bryce lost his sister, also named Kelli, very suddenly when he was fourteen. "I was playing in a junior golf tournament in Houston, and my family didn't show up on the last day to watch. I knew instantly something was wrong, because they never missed a shot. My parents had taken my sister, who was a year and a half older than me, to the hospital with a bad headache and flu-like symptoms. The next day, they couldn't wake her up. She had passed away from spinal meningitis."

Years later, Bryce met and married Kelley. "The day we got married, Bryce's parents said, 'We're so grateful we got our "Kelli" back,' said Kelley. Of course, Kelli will never be replaced; she'll always be a part of our lives. But I think having the same name is more than a strange coincidence. I think it was meant to be."

Bryce and Kelley are thankful for every day they have together, and know they are strong enough to handle any challenges that come their way.

Bryce and Kelley, enjoying Napa Valley

Ben and Heather Crane, with their children, Cassidy, Saylor, and Braden

The Ben Crane Family

Ben and Heather Crane are a perfect example of "opposites attract" and how two disparate halves combine to make one pretty formidable whole.

Heather is the financial whiz, the organizer and serious side of the pair — the buttoned-down, focused one, and the master of the to-do list. The one who puts the details together so they can operate.

Ben is the extrovert. He's passionate, gregarious, and never afraid to walk a little on the wild side. He's the creative one, on and off the course.

The one with a cult following for his wacky, self-deprecating videos, in which he stars wearing a helmet and spandex workout gear. He pokes fun at his slow play, pre-shot routine, workouts, and teamed up with Hunter Mahan, Rickie Fowler, and Bubba Watson to form the Golf Boys.

At first, Heather thought it was all a waste of time. Then she watched the first video and couldn't stop laughing. Now she grins when she talks about how many fans have reenacted the videos, which went viral on YouTube. "He just wanted people to know there was more to him than golf," she said. "Golf Boys took it to another level."

There's a method to his wackiness, too. Those younger fans he reaches by breaking golf's boring mold are also exposed to the Cranes' charitable efforts and their incredible passion to shed light on the battle against sex trafficking in Southeast Asia, as well as other issues.

Ben met Canadian singer Lamont Hiebert at the Bob Hope Classic. It wasn't long until the Ten Shekel Shirt front-man and co-founder of Love146, an international group dedicated to eradicating the sexploitation of children, invited Ben and Heather to join their board. The Cranes made their first trip to Southeast Asia in 2005 and, since then, they've helped raise more than $1 million for Love146.

Heather took friends Dowd Simpson and Athena Perez with her on another trip in 2010. She described their trip as "a constant combination of hope and despair." They toured the red-light districts, the safe houses, and the killing fields where Heather said trafficking is growing, too. "We mostly visited with those who are trying to empower people not to be so vulnerable to that kind of deception and oppression," she said.

"Trafficking thrives around and during large-scale events," Heather said, and her involvement in the Dallas community during the 2011 Super Bowl led her to another give-back. She now helps run a weekly women's Bible study in the Dallas jail. "When you walk in there, your life stops," Heather said. "You check everything, including your phone, at the door and for two hours, you are with women who want to change their lives, but they just don't have the tools to do it."

"In there, you're equal. The women don't know who you are, what neighborhood you live in, or what your background is. They may have abusive pasts and just need to be cared for and loved. It's a refreshing, raw time of sharing. You want to hear all their stories; you want to help them."

Ben, too, supports and often speaks at various outreaches representing College Golf Fellowship, Young Life and SEARCH ministries.

Heather and Ben were college sweethearts and one night he turned to her and said, 'Heather, you know it's possible I could make a lot of money one day playing golf.' She laughed. "I thought, 'What's he dreaming?' There was a side that believed in him, because I saw he had such a heart and he loved what he did so much." They married after Ben spent two years on what is now the Web.com Tour and, in 2003, he got his first win on the PGA TOUR at the BellSouth Classic.

The Cranes, spending the day together at the Fort Worth Zoo

"We started young," Heather said. "To some extent, [we were] a little shallow about it. We thought success meant you made a lot of money, and it meant you could buy nice things. We had no idea what was ahead of us."

Yes, they're very different people; a couple who makes sure people know that golf isn't boring, and that outreach comes in many forms — viral videos, a speech, or helping get one child or one woman out of a cruel life and into a safe house.

Heather plans to take her oldest daughter to Southeast Asia one day so she, too, can see the poverty and despair. "I want them to see the world, see the needs," she said. "I want them to see there's a lot of help needed out there and that our family cares enough to do it."

The Chris Tidland Family

Chris and Amy Tidland, with their children, Jackson and Bella, showing their love for Oklahoma State University

Early in their careers, many golfers had their wives or significant others caddie for them. Here's a story from Amy Tidland.

"The first time I caddied for Chris was during his debut as a professional golfer on the Hooters Tour. I didn't know all of the rules of golf, but felt confident enough that I could carry a bag and keep score. How hard could it really be?

On the tenth hole, Chris hit the ball out of bounds and had to hit a provisional. He thought he hit the provisional out of bounds as well, so he asked me for another ball. I grabbed another ball from my pocket and upon placing it in his hand. I said, "Hit it straight; we are going to run out of balls!" He was so mad at my comment that he smacked that ball right near the first one. Walking off the green after that disastrous hole, I asked him, "Was that an 8 or a 9?" I had to write down a score, for heaven's sake! That is before I knew how important the mental part of the game truly is."

The Vaughn Taylor Family

Katie O'Hardy Photography

Leot and Vaughn Taylor

Leot Taylor likes to tell this fish story about her husband, Vaughn. "My phone rang and all I could hear was Vaughn out of breath, saying, 'You won't believe it; I don't know what to do!' I immediately thought he had sunk the boat, something he has come close to doing before. But to my surprise, Vaughn pulled up to the dock with the largest striped bass of his life.

"Word soon got out and everyone was telling him he needed to get the fish officially weighed. He'd used the scale on the boat and then weighed it again back at home; the fish had lost 1.5 pounds within that hour.

"Time was of the essence. We had to find a digital scale that could print off a recorded weight. The Department of National Resources had closed for the day, so we needed to get creative.

"Immediately, we thought of a butcher or grocery store, but how were we going to take a dead fish into a public market? Not having a cooler large enough to hold this mammoth, we took a storage container, filled it with ice and off we went.

"At our local market, the meat and fish department employees are golf fans and agreed to help, as long as we wrapped the fish in garbage bags so other customers wouldn't be startled. We giddily pushed our shopping cart, with what looked like a dead body, into the market. Using their scale, we loaded the fish and gathered around . . . the scale flashed '0.00, 0.00' then 'error!' Vaughn's fish was too large for their scale.

"We repeated this process at two other markets. No one had a scale that could handle a fish this large. Sitting in our truck feeling defeated and worried more weight had been lost, we both contemplated who might have a scale large enough to handle the weight and print out a record of it. "FedEx," Vaughn screamed.

"Racing into the store, we dragged our makeshift cooler in and explained we needed to weigh something unusual and so not be alarmed. We pulled the fish out, placed it on the scale and overheard, 'This is a first.' To our excitement, the plan worked!

Vaughn, with the record breaking fish he caught

"At the DNR the next morning, we were informed Vaughn's fish had shattered the previous record for the Savannah River by over 13 pounds, weighing in at 56.2 pounds. Within 24 hours, I'd gone from having a 'disappointed golfer husband' after missing the cut, to 'an ecstatic fisher husband.' Sometimes when things don't seem to be going your way, maybe it's because better things are in motion. As we say in our house and on the course, '*Everything happens for a reason.*'"

Richelle and Aaron Baddeley, with their daughters, Jolee and Jewell

The Aaron Baddeley Family

When Aaron Baddeley, the son of former chief mechanic for driver Mario Andretti, sauntered into the restaurant in his form-fitting green bell bottoms and Euro-styled deep-v-neck shirt, Richelle thought, "Well, here comes Hollywood." It was 2003, and Richelle had come straight from her job as preschool center director to meet Aaron on a blind date. Richelle's preppy teacher attire was hardly a match to Aaron's Studio 54 getup, and by first looks, prospects for the night seemed bleak.

Even though the couple who set up the dinner and tagged along for the potentially awkward ride, Richelle had her own back-up plan for the

night. She asked her mother and some friends to eat dinner at the same restaurant, only a few tables away, just in case the date flopped and she needed an exit strategy. Richelle figured Aaron didn't know what her mom looked like anyway, so to him, she was just another customer.

Richelle says, "I'm sure that Aaron must have thought I had bladder issues, because I kept texting my mom to meet me in the bathroom, so we could chat! I remember telling my mom, 'Well, I think he's nice, but I honestly can't understand a word he's saying. I think it's English, but I just don't get it.'"

After dinner, the foursome went back to one of their houses to talk and extend the night without the hustle and bustle of the restaurant. Richelle begrudgingly agreed; however, that decision was the catalyst to a friendship neither Richelle nor Aaron had experienced before.

Richelle grew up with three sisters, Renee, Ricole, and Reanne, and is extremely close to her family. At the heart of their family is one common value, their faith in Jesus Christ. When Richelle and Aaron began spending time with and understanding one another, they found they were able to share about their life, their goals, and their beliefs in a sincere and connected fashion. What didn't come up much in their conversations, ironically, was golf. Richelle told Aaron, "You can talk about golf, but I'm not going to have much to add to the conversation . . . I am a great listener, though."

Richelle's exposure to the game of golf had primarily been founded in casual outings with her dad where she would drive the cart and attempt to keep his scorecard. She remembers thinking, "It appears easy . . . you pick a club, hit the ball, and try to get it in the hole." Her knowledge of golf may have been simple, but it didn't take her long to understand the difference between leisurely golf and golf as a career.

Richelle watched Aaron play in the 2004 Chrysler Classic of Tucson where he finished in second place. "I ran over and said, 'Can you believe those eight bogeys! Those were the best eight bogeys I've ever seen in my life!' Of course, with all the managers and other professionals around, you can imagine how embarrassed I was to find out it wasn't 'bogeys,' but 'birdies' that I was so happy about. And yeah, Aaron got some good-humored flack for a while about the

Another year and many tournaments later, Richelle and Aaron married. Since then, Richelle's learned quite a bit of golf lingo, and Aaron has become even more immersed into life with girls. Richelle credits Aaron's "No worries, mate" attitude with how he has managed to survive, literally, in a house full of estrogen.

Richelle and Aaron have an "open house" policy for friends and family, and encourage everyone, including Richelle's three sisters (all of whom live within a few miles) to stop by whenever Richelle and Aaron are in town. Especially on Sundays, you can bet the Baddeley family will all be barbecuing and spending time together. Aaron was definitely broken into the unique dynamic of girls as he grew up with his two sisters, Kate and Emma, and then joined Richelle's family of four girls. Taking on the role of father of girls was a different story. "He's absolutely the best dad to Jewell and Jolee. He comes home and just joins in whatever we're doing. Whether it's a dance party in pink tutus in the playroom or pretending to make cupcakes in the girls' kitchen, he's all about it. And thankfully, now, we have three brothers-in-law with whom he has become best friends."

Speaking of all those in-laws, their support for Aaron is unwavering. They have all flown to be present for every win that Aaron has had on TOUR. They, along with other die-hard friends and family, formed the "Badds Brigade" — nearly 100 members strong, complete with printed T-shirts and Australian chants. They turn out in packs to support Aaron, in particular during the Phoenix Open, and are usually identified by their "Aussie, Aussie, Aussie ... Oye, Oye, Oye!" chant. For the young man who left home at 17 to find his way on the PGA TOUR, Aaron has found not only a career, but also, and more importantly, a beautiful family and home.

Aaron and Richelle

The Ted Purdy Family

Arlene and Ted Purdy, with children, Andie and Sam, at the Big Dig event at the John Deere Classic

Whenever possible, players who have the opportunity to participate in a tournament will take advantage of the opportunity, no matter what it takes to do so. Here Arlene Purdy tells of a time that caught them by surprise.

"After play on Friday at Hilton Head, Ted was three shots off the cut line, so we were headed home. We flew from Hilton Head to Atlanta and as we were boarding our second leg of our flight to Phoenix, Ted got a call from his dad letting him know that he made the cut, right on the number. Ted did not believe him, so he called the TOUR, and they confirmed that Ted had, indeed, made the cut. The doors were getting ready to close on the plane, and when Ted stood up, the flight attendant was not thrilled with him.

"After pleading our case with the flight attendant, we all — Ted, myself and our baby boy — got off the plane. The last flight back to Hilton Head had already left, so our only option was to rent a car and drive back. It took six hours, but we arrived in the wee hours of the morning, just a couple of hours before Ted's tee time. He had to borrow clubs, clothes, and shoes from Mark Hensby, since all of our belongings were on the plane to Phoenix. We rounded up toiletries at Walgreens, and Ted ended up playing on virtually no sleep. Needless to say, it was not a great round of golf for him, but it just goes to show the dedication it takes to play this sport, not only by the players, but by the families that support them."

The Tag Ridings Family

Amy Headington, Images of Grace Photography

Brenda and Tag Ridings, with their children, Carter and Chloe

Sometimes the simplest things are the things people miss the most when they are away from home, like the joy of a home-cooked meal. Here, Brenda Ridings shares how they take a little bit of home on the road.

"When asked what our favorite tournament is, Tag and I are quick to reply, the John Deere Classic in Moline, Illinois. Moline is as close to my home in Iowa as we get during the season, so for the whole week, I get to spend time with my family and friends.

"We started a tradition at the tournament that has grown over the years. My parents have owned a small restaurant and catering business in Lidderdale, Iowa, for over 35 years. During our first year in Moline, we stayed at a Residence Inn, which had a grill available to those staying there. I called my parents and asked them to bring steaks and pork chops when they came so we could grill. We then invited other TOUR families to join us. That first year, there were about 15 of us and everyone pitched in, going to the local stores to get salads and drinks. My brother and dad grilled and we had a true home-cooked meal on the road.

"Since that first year, our tradition has grown and during our last outing, over 50 people joined us. With all of the food that was brought, we invited other guests staying at the Residence Inn to join in, as well. This event is like one large family get-together; the children get to play together, and my dad and brother still man the grill. Like every family spending time together around a home-cooked meal, it means fun, laughter, and relaxation with those who matter most."

Amanda and Jonathan Byrd, with their children, Jackson, Caroline, and Kate

The Jonathan Byrd Family

When asked what Jonathan's hobbies are when he is away from the course, Amanda had to think for a while, then responded, "Really just playing with our three kids and doing what they love to do at the moment."

"We live in such a great place for families. Davis Love has tried, since we moved to St. Simons over ten years ago, to convince Jonathan to take up hunting and fishing with him. Most recently, he tried to persuade him to try paddle boarding, but there is just so little time

when you have only one week off at home with three busy kids under six!

"Last spring we remodeled our playroom to include a stage. Both Jackson and Caroline love to play dress-up and have great imaginations. They often talk Jonathan and me into playing along as well. Even last year, when Jonathan was playing in China over Halloween, Jackson persuaded him to buy a pirate costume and made sure it was packed in his suitcase. He then made his daddy promise to wear it on Halloween

Amanda and Jonathan

recalls the time when Jonathan earned his first victory on the PGA TOUR. "I was walking in the gallery during the rainy final round of the 2002 Buick Challenge when Jonathan's tee shot on the par-5 seventh hole flew right into the trees and into the gallery. The ball hit me on the fly in the shoulder blade and knocked the wind right out of me. Jonathan wanted to see who he hit in the crowd, and see if they were okay, but everyone kept him away, telling him everything was fine and not to worry. He was playing well and they didn't want to concern him. He ended up getting a pretty good bounce, and went on and birdied that hole to win the tournament by a shot."

Time at home is so precious to the Byrds. They are thankful to have a weekly date night, have fun enjoying friends and the routine of school and where they live but, Amanda says, the real quality time comes on the road. They love to travel as a family. Amanda concluded, "We have countless memories of being together on the road. It can be a lot to pack up five people for a few weeks — but it's worth it every time!"

and, as proof, Jonathan I-chatted from halfway around the world, dressed as a pirate."

In the spring of 2012, Jonathan and Amanda welcomed a second little girl, just three days before the Masters. Caroline and Kate get their dad's undivided attention, too. "Jonathan grew up with an older brother and played sports all the time," she says. "Now he finds himself sitting for tea parties and even playing Barbies during his time off." Caroline has become quite the mischievous one since her sister was born. Amanda has found a credit card in the wine cooler, Jackson's baseball glove — oiled and ready for his first T-ball game, in the microwave, a dress Caroline refused to wear in the refrigerator and, most recently, her cell phone inside the cat carrier in the garage.

It's not all about the girls around their house. Jonathan does get to indulge in the sports that he grew up playing. Jackson is now involved in T-ball, soccer and, most recently, golf. If Jonathan is home for an extended period of time, he will even coach a few games. "He was so excited to give both Jackson and Caroline their first set of clubs this Christmas!" Amanda said.

Before the children came along, there was life on TOUR. Amanda

"ARRRRGGGHHHHH!" Jonathan joins in the fun of character play with Jackson and Caroline.

Diane and Luke Donald

The Luke Donald Family

She needed more than 40 characters, but Diane Donald summed herself up pretty well in her profile on Twitter:

"Proud Chicago girl, Greekie, Martha Stewart-in-training, part-time golf psychologist, full-time professional spectator, and of course, most importantly, a Mama."

She forgot journalist.

Diane laughs that she did indeed use that Northwestern journalism degree last April when she took to Twitter to break the news that her husband was not disqualified after a perplexing two-hour investigation at the 2012 Masters.

Did her husband, Luke, sign an incorrect scorecard in the opening round? Did he shoot 73 or 75? Did he birdie the fifth hole? Or bogey it? Scoring said one thing; Luke said another. The score board said 73; Luke said 75.

It took two hours to figure out the problem was a smudge on a faxed copy of his scorecard. It took seconds for Diane to let reporters at the Masters know her husband wasn't heading home.

"Just got off the phone with Luke, NOT disqualified. Thank goodness."

It was re-tweeted 462 times.

She laughs that, yes, she does have quite a following on the social media site, but not for the reason people might think. "They're only marginally interested in me," she said. "They're more interested in me in a Luke context."

Diane tweets pictures of daughters Ellie and Sophia, shots of her and Luke and, of course, changes in the world golf ranking. She tweeted her ticket to the Royal Box for the Wimbledon semifinals last summer, a note that it was so humid even Kate Middleton's hair frizzed the day before, photos from plane flights, and just whatever comes to mind. Luke has 20 times the tweeps his wife does and lets his sense of humor show through.

Most people haven't seen the really funny side of her husband. Who knew the Englishman, who looks so serious on the golf course, could be so funny? The hot dog dance. Cracking jokes from the podium, and pulling on a wig at a dinner filled with sports writers.

And, of course, tweeting.

"I think Twitter with Luke is a way for him to show more of his personality," Diane said. "The beauty of Twitter is that you can write something that's funny and witty, and you can make sure it's written the way you want."

Life in the Donald house is, as Diane says, fun. One minute Luke is dancing the hot dog dance along with Ellie, Mickey Mouse, Minnie Mouse, and Goofy; the next, he's pulling a practical joke on the phone; or doing an impression of someone — anyone — including Phil Mickelson, Matt Kuchar, Adam Scott, and Diane's mom.

"My mother has a funny way of how she puts food in the garbage," Diane said. "She gets a napkin and pushes it off the plate." Luke has her act down. And the players? It's all in good fun — who doesn't have a signature move? — and they love to watch him work. "At least once a day, he makes me laugh so hard," Diane said. "We laugh a lot in our house. Why be miserable when you have a choice. Be happy."

herself in a new world. "We were dating for six weeks," she said, "and he went through the final stage of Q-school. I didn't know that much about golf, but I knew this was important. He got his card and he never looked back." They married in 2007 on the Greek island of Santorini, and have known each other for over ten years. "That's more than a third of our lives," Diane said.

The family went through a gamut of emotions in 2011 when Luke lost his father, Colin, to a long illness a few days before Sophia was born. "Sophia," he said, "spread a little grace on the situation."

Luke has bounced in and out of the number one ranking in the world, but he's low-key. "He's similar to Roger Federer," Diane said, comparing him to the quiet, seven-time Wimbledon champ.

But there was nothing quiet about Luke when he stepped to the podium at the 2012 Golf Writers' Dinner to accept the 2011 Player of the Year award. He pulled on a wig and cracked jokes, some at his own expense. He had fun and the golf writers were surprised to see that side. "That's what he's really like," she said. "People came up to me and said, 'Who knew Luke was so funny?' I did. What do you think, I talk to a wall?"

For a little inspiration for his speech, he pulled a bit from Diane, and a little from funnyman David Feherty, who can make you laugh by just looking at him. "He's the most insanely funny person," she said of Feherty. "It's appalling how funny he is."

They're quite a pair. Luke's the focused one. Organized. Methodical. Intense. A list maker. Diane is more carefree, choosing to go with the flow. "It's good for me to be with someone who keeps me on track and it's good he's with someone that helps him lighten up," she said.

Their daughters are easygoing like Diane, but Ellie, who has stolen the spotlight more than a few times at trophy presentations, is more serious. "Sophia just wants to party all the time," she said grinning.

Luke and Diane Antonopoulos met the end of her freshman year in college. Back then, she wanted to be a doctor, but a C in organic chemistry took care of that. So, she switched to journalism. He was living in Evanston and playing golf.

They were friends, then it turned romantic, and Diane found

Armed with his speech, Luke practiced it just as hard as he does when he works on his game. "In England, speeches are a huge part of weddings," Diane said. "When you say, 'Oh, I went to a wedding,' the first thing people ask isn't about the wedding. They want to know how the speeches were. There's a lot of joking and making fun of the bride and groom. He did a speech at our wedding. He's really good at it." Diane was more nervous that night than anyone. "I was nervous; I couldn't even eat," she said. "He's like, 'That's why you practice and prepare.' Just like a golf tournament."

But back to the Masters.

No one knew exactly what was happening that day when Luke's score changed. Diane saw it on the scoreboard on her phone.

Luke and Diane, with daughters, Sophia and Elle

Technology did the rest when Luke's coach Pat Goss texted her. "I watched the round and knew what he shot," Diane said. "A half an hour later, it changed on my phone. I thought something must have happened."

So, she waited and when nothing changed, she called Luke. He said he had just been grilled by Augusta National members. Another phone call later, everything was fine.

It was the tweet of that day and maybe of the Masters.

Diane Donald, reporter. Luke Donald, funny man. Who knew?

The Ben Curtis Family

For those who play on TOUR, opportunities to participate in tournaments sometimes come when least expected. Candace Curtis tells this story.

"Ben earned his PGA TOUR card in December 2002 and he played in his first "major" — the British Open — in July 2003. Much to our delight, Ben won that tournament and I was with him to celebrate, as a couple, his first victory as a PGA TOUR player. It was a whirlwind experience! Ben went from no one knowing who he was to being a guest on the "Late Show with David Letterman," hitting wedge shots rooftop to rooftop

Ben and Candace celebrate Ben's victory at the 2003 British Open.

David Cannon/Getty Images Sport

during the telecast, to visiting the White House. Suddenly, everyone wanted to know everything about us.

Candace and Ben Curtis, with their children, Addison and Liam

"Ben's win at The Open Championship qualified him for what is now the World Golf Championship-Bridgestone Invitational in nearby Akron, Ohio. The tournament coincidentally happened to fall on the weekend of our wedding. There was no question that Ben would play in the tournament, despite the radio talk show hosts who conducted polls on whether or not he should play golf on his wedding day. Fortunately, Ben's tee times were late on Saturday. I called all of our guests and told them that the time of the ceremony would be delayed. The fans at the tournament knew what was going on so, when Ben finished his round, the gallery serenaded him with "Going to the Chapel." He even had a police escort from the course to the church so that he made it to the ceremony on time. This was a terrific example of the community getting behind a golfer and supporting him. The morning after our wedding, Ben reported to the course, on time, for his Sunday tee time. He was the first PGA TOUR player to get married during a tournament and ended up placing a very respectable 30th for the week."

The Charles Warren Family

Kelly and Charles Warren, with their children, Charlie and Riley

Charles Warren has a passion for Clemson and Clemson golf. As a collegiate player, he captured the 1997 NCAA Division I Men's Individual Golf Championship. "No Clemson golfer had previously won the title, and no one has won it since," says Charles's wife, Kelly.

Kelly and Charles met and dated during their last two years at Clemson. She remembers going out to support Charles during one of his collegiate events. "It was the first golf tournament I was able to go to and Charles shot an 80 that day." Coach Penley took the entire team aside and said, "That is the last time girlfriends will be allowed to come out to watch." Laughing, Kelly says, "Thankfully, that rule didn't stick around and Charles did win a few times with me there to witness them."

Charles being inducted into the Clemson Ring of Honor before a Tigers' football game

Since his time at Clemson, Charles has always felt strongly about giving back to the golf program, which shaped him and many other former Tigers who are now successful on the PGA TOUR. Charles chairs the Tiger Golf Gathering, which is a yearly reunion for the Clemson golf family as well as a fundraiser for the golf program. Along with a successful capital campaign, the Tiger Golf Gathering has raised over 3 million dollars since its inception in 2003. Because of Charles and several other Tiger golfers, they were able to build a state-of-the-art practice facility and range, in addition to a three-story clubhouse for the golf team.

Today Charles and Kelly are passing on the Clemson spirit to their children. On Saturdays, the whole family proudly wears their orange, packs their car with tailgating supplies, heads out to Death Valley, and gets ready to chant C-L-E-M-S-O-N T-I-G-E-R-S!

For the Warrens, Clemson will always have a special place in their hearts.

Katie and Johnson Wagner

The Johnson Wagner Family

Not long after the winning putt at the 2008 Shell Houston Open fell in the cup, Johnson Wagner started pumping his fists and jumping around on the 18th green.

He and wife Katie followed up with a long hug, a few kisses, and more than a few tears. Then it hit them. How in the heck were they going to get themselves, the dog, the RV, and all their stuff to Augusta?

Life moves fast on the PGA TOUR, just ask Johnson and Katie. One minute they're wondering if it's finally their week, the next they're holding a Waterford trophy, a two-year exemption, and an invitation to the Masters — which starts in four days. "We were pretty much shell-

Johnson and Katie, with their children, Marianne and Graham

shocked," Katie said.

It was the first year the Masters had reinstated the policy that a player could win the week prior to the tournament and still get in. And it happened — to them.

She asked agent Jimmy Johnston what they had to do. "Nothing," he said, "I got it covered." "Jimmy showed up out of nowhere like a ghost in the mist and arranged everything, even where we were supposed to park the RV," Katie said.

"We were on a chartered plane with him that night and Davis Love's driver was free that week and he offered for his driver to drive the bus back." Cinnamon, the dog, would be traveling over with Johnson's parents in their Airstream. And the plane ride? A charter which turned into a tempered celebration.

"Half of the plane ride was celebrating," she said. The other half was, 'Where are we going to stay tonight? Where are our parents going to stay? How is everyone going to get there?' It was a mad scramble to get everyone there."

Then a high school friend of Katie's got her email address, sent her a note, and said a friend had a house they could use. Her parents grabbed it

and her dad, an accountant, worked 36 hours straight — it was tax time, mind you — before they could head to Augusta. Siblings and spouses and aunts and uncles turned their schedules upside down and . . .

"It was a revolving door," Katie said. "Not everyone could get off for an entire week, but they could come for a few days. They even had to put beds on the floor, but no one complained. Everyone was happy to have a place to stay."

It was all smiles and beers in hand that week, starting with the night they landed. Katie fell asleep at 2:00 a.m.; Johnson, his caddie Steven Hale, and his agents stayed up until 4:00 a.m. Then, there were two days of mini celebrations each time a family member arrived.

"He rode this adrenalin high until Tuesday, then he crashed and regrouped," Katie said. "It was, 'I have to refocus now and play in the biggest golf tournament of my life right after I win my first tournament.'"

Katie had known Johnson since they were freshmen at Virginia Tech — back when just getting to any tour, let alone the PGA TOUR, was a dream. So, when she got a feeling that it might be his week in Houston, she held her breath.

"Johnson's not an uptight person by any means, but he had this kind of eerie calm about him that week," she said. "He had this focus I hadn't seen in him before. He was very peaceful."

They never talked about it, even on Saturday night, when he had led the first three rounds. And there was no talk Sunday morning either. "We were as casual as our nerves would have allowed us to be," she said. "It was right under the surface; somebody wanted to say something, but nobody did."

A week later, Johnson finished, tied for 36th in his first Masters.

"To see him finally reach this goal, this dream . . .," Katie said. "I've known him so long; I knew him when this really was the dream. To watch him take every step was incredible."

Just like the mad scramble to get everyone to Augusta, it all just fell into place.

Kim and Zach Johnson

The Zach Johnson Family

Remember that sweet moment behind the 18th green at Augusta National in 2007 when soon-to-be Masters champion Zach Johnson cradled his 11-week old son, Will, and kissed him on the forehead?

It almost didn't happen.

Kim Johnson didn't really consider the possibility of Zach winning until the 16th hole that Easter Sunday and, when she did, her mother stepped up. Will was in day care, which meant a trip outside the gates of the club to pick him up, and Kim's mom was the only person at the time who could do that.

"My mom, who's kind of timid and doesn't like to bother people, books it to the parking lot and asks for a police escort to get her through the traffic to day care," Kim said, chuckling. "When she got back, she was walking through the crowd, saying, 'I have Zach Johnson's baby.'"

Kim and Zach, with their sons, Will and Wyatt

"I had hugged Zach and he was walking off when my mom came up. He came back and the cameras captured that special moment. It might not matter to anyone else, but one day it will matter to Will."

That was just one of many behind-the-scenes stories that occurred that day. Zach certainly secured his place in Masters' history in 2007, but the Masters was already a part of Zach's and Kim's history.

A few weeks after they started dating, Kim got a phone call from Zach telling her he probably would not be available to do anything with her for the next few days. He went on to explain that the Masters was on television, and he would be giving his undivided attention to golf. He actually likened it to "Holy Week." They get a kick out of remembering that story and the irony of him winning it during the actual Holy Week of Easter.

The following year, he scored practice round tickets to the Masters, and attended with some buddies who were also playing mini tours at the time. They went for the day and did all the normal spectator stuff; ate their weight in egg salad sandwiches, asked for autographs, and bought lots of T-shirts from the merchandise tent. The cool part is one of the other mini tour players who attended was his good buddy Vaughn Taylor, who would end up being his playing partner on Sunday in 2007. "I have known Vaughn almost as long as I have known Zach," Kim said. "They

roomed together on the Hooters Tour, got their PGA TOUR cards the same year, and made their first Ryder Cup team together. It was such a sweet part of the day that Vaughn was the guy walking next to Zach on the 18th hole."

Kim remembered standing on the 18th hole as Zach and Vaughn hit their final shots. "Zach looks up at the scoreboard, then over at me, and just smiles and shrugs," Kim said. "In that moment, we were both thinking this might really happen." The next thing she knew, Zach had been whisked off to Butler Cabin and she was going to a reception in the clubhouse, in a raincoat and flip flops. "One thing I learned is if he is ever fortunate to win again, I will have a change of clothes in the car!"

Another lesson learned came the following day on their whirlwind media trip to New York City. "We obviously didn't plan on him winning the Masters, and we certainly didn't anticipate going to New York City. We did not have a garment bag to carry the jacket in, so we improvised and used a trash bag. We were walking into "[The Late Show with David] Letterman" and someone got a picture of Zach carrying the jacket in the trash bag, Kim said. "The next year, when Trevor [Immelman] won, Carminita said they left the clubhouse with the jacket in a garment bag with his name and 2008 stitched on it." Kim told her, "I think you have us to thank for that. Now winners get a garment bag to go with the green jacket so no one else puts theirs in a trash bag."

The most memorable moment of the whole day happened late at night when it was just Kim and Zach. "We were back in our motor home trying frantically to pack for the trip to New York and making plans for my mom to stay with our 11-week-old baby, and Zach just stops and looks up at me and says, 'Kim, what did I just do?' I looked back at him and said, 'I don't know, but I think it was really, really good.'"

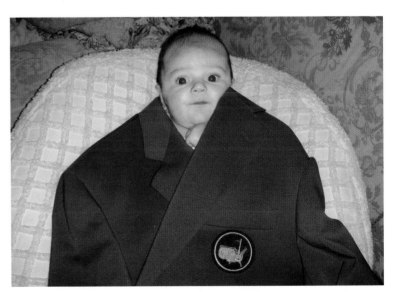

Wyatt, wearing Daddy's Green Jacket

Kate and Justin Rose, with their children, Charlotte and Leo

The Justin Rose Family

Kate Rose doesn't sit on the sidelines. She doesn't wait for someone else to come up with a suggestion. She shows up to meetings with a list of ideas, and she finds a way.

Kate knows there's no one answer to problems like poor nutrition or childhood obesity, but she does know that you can change things through education — one child, one classroom, one school at a time.

In Kate's meetings with teachers and administrators at one of the five Orlando, Florida, area schools the Kate and Justin Rose Foundation supports through Blessings in a Backpack and other initiatives, she doesn't suggest a boring, dry lesson. "We want to teach them from the inside out," she said. "What about a vegetable garden at school where they can learn about nurture and patience, then take home the produce to help feed their families? What about a rose garden reading area, where

192

Justin and Kate

they can go and relax, and take the new book they chose for themselves through our partnership with Book Trust? What about reusable water bottles the children can top off when they head home to keep them hydrated in the Florida heat?"

"Since we've become parents," Kate said. "We realized there is a massive correlation between good food and behavior. Justin's an athlete and I'm a former gymnast. We know your bodies and minds can't work if you're not fueling them properly."

"Justin can't turn up without the right energy and expect to play good golf for four hours and win. How can you expect children to turn up for school on Monday ready to learn when they haven't had a decent meal all weekend?"

Kate and Justin, born in England and South Africa respectively, have now settled full-time in the Orlando area, and have targeted five schools where they can help implement a mind-body-soul approach to nutrition.

"We can delve deeper into things with a small community," she said. "Instead of expanding one project like Blessings in a Backpack to 20 schools, our Foundation works closely with teachers at our five schools to establish solutions for their core needs. We will start with five schools, and that way we can dig deeper and try to make a real, tangible difference with those same kids. How else can we help? What other needs do they have? What other opportunities can we help provide?"

The key, she said, is educating them with fun things — with Justin talking about golf or sports in general. Even taking them on field trips, such as a day at the beach or golf tournament, or behind the scenes in a TV studio, or a trip to a college campus, that takes them out of the classroom and helps them apply what they have learned to the outside world. "We tell them we'll be outside for another hour and ask them what kind of snacks should they have on a hot day? Should they drink more water?"

Kate served on the PGA TOUR Wives Association board for four years and currently serves on the national Blessings in a Backpack board. As she has learned, some families don't actually have anywhere to cook. Others have more mouths to feed than their budgets allow, which leads to consuming fast food.

Kate, with Charlotte and Leo

"Many parents struggle," Kate said. "It's tricky. Times are tough and there's not always adequate support out there, or the education about where to go for help. "Nutrition is so crucially important," she said. "Obesity is such a problem in the developed world. Fast food is a very easy habit to slip into. The mother may have two jobs and it's easier to buy food than cook. She just doesn't have time to cook nutritious food all the time. No one likes eating fast food all the time, but no one's doing anything about it."

Kate and Justin are, a few schools at a time. Kate can see expanding to middle school where all too often, she said, teenagers slip through the cracks. She points to local programs that offer medical and psychiatric care to those students, and has already started partnership discussions with the people running them.

Justin, with son, Leo

As passionate as they are about their projects, they're equally focused on making sure their own children remain grounded, and understand how fortunate they are to be comfortable financially. It's working. At just three years old, their son, Leo, keeps asking them to "come help with the children."

"Ultimately, he's living in a bubble," she said. "It's our real life right now, but it's not real life for 99.9 percent of the county. He does need to know about it."

She paused.

"I really believe the more you're given, the more responsibility you have to give it back."

If you want to learn more about the Rose's foundation, visit their website: www.kjrosefoundation.org.

Jen and Ryan Palmer, with their children, Madelyn and Mason

The Ryan Palmer Family

Jen and Ryan Palmer are always on the go. Usually with pre-schoolers Mason and Madelyn in tow.

Rangers games. Cowboys games. Legoland. Roller coasters. The zoo. The aquarium. Golf tournaments. Airports. Skiing. "My kids are very active," Jen said. "If we're not doing something, they're asking where we're going."

Ryan is right there with them. They have so much fun, in fact, that Ryan and Jen go to amusement parks even when they're by themselves.

Palmer family, enjoying a Dallas Cowboys game

What do they do when they pause for a minute and chill out?

"You know how there are those husbands who have hobbies?" Jen said. "My husband likes to sit in front of the TV and watch television." Jen, on the other hand, makes time for a little classwork.

Once a year, she takes infection control and continuing education classes. Every two years, there's a CPR class. Every three years, it's a jurisprudence brushup.

Jen has a plan. As a licensed, but non-practicing dentist, she takes those classes to keep her license current so that in the not-too-distant future she can take mission trips and fix some smiles. She'd like to grow the Ryan Palmer Foundation, too. Maybe even find a way to work her dentistry practice into the outreach.

Ryan and Jen started dating just before their senior year at Texas A&M, and got married her senior year of dental school. He played on the then-Nationwide Tour in 2003 and Jen took her boards and landed a job as an associate dentist in Colleyville.

But all that changed when Ryan made the PGA TOUR in 2004 and she flew out to the AT&T Pebble Beach Pro-Am. "When I got home, he asked 'You think you might want to try this traveling for a while?'" Jen said. "I never went back to work."

That same year, their foundation, based in Ryan's hometown of Amarillo, was formed. Later, in 2010, the Foundation donated $100,000 to Northwest Texas Children's Hospital for a healing garden and two Palmer rooms — Palmer's Playhouse for younger kids and Palmer's Sports Zone filled with big screens and game consoles for older kids.

Jen, Ryan, and their Foundation now also work with Kids Matter International, an initiative through Kohl's, and they have provided 20,000 backpacks for low-income students. Ryan supports Birdies 4 Brighter Smiles by donating $50 for every birdie he makes and $100 for every eagle. In 2011, that added up to $15,000.

Once the kids are in school, they plan to branch out the foundation to the Dallas-Fort Worth area where Jen — thanks to those annual classes — will be ready to use her general dentistry degree again.

But one thing is sure. The Palmers won't be slowing down.

Matt and Sybi Kuchar in Hawaii

The Matt Kuchar Family

As a kid, Matt Kuchar wanted to be Boris Becker.

That pretty much explains why if he's not on the golf course, you might want to look on the tennis court. Matt would rather spend 45 minutes on the court with his wife and doubles partner, Sybi, than hit the fitness trailer. She'll hit with him, move him around the court, and give him all the workout he needs.

"He's good," Sybi said. "You can tell he was serious about the game at one point. He's got good strokes, good fundamentals. He enjoys

Celebrating Matt's win at The Barclays with their sons, Cameron and Carson

Matt scheduled a three-day trip for them to Nick Bollettieri's Tennis Academy, where they worked on their games six hours a day. A few weeks later, he tied for third at the Masters. A few weeks after that, he won THE PLAYERS Championship. If there is any connection between the two, they're not saying.

In the last year, Sybi and Matt have become formidable doubles opponents and their singles matches are too close to call. "We love to play together," Sybi said. "I have so many friends who say, 'I can't believe you and Matt play doubles. Don't y'all get in fights? It's not hard for you?'

"Now if I lose to Matt in singles, I can get frustrated, but as far as playing as a team, there's never a fight or cross words or frustrations. Matt's the only person I want to play doubles with."

Sybi and Matt didn't date in college. The golf team and tennis teams hung out, but they didn't date until after she'd broken her elbows and moved back home. Less than a year later, they were married and Matt was working his way toward the TOUR.

Looking back, Sybi is convinced that had Matt chosen tennis over golf, he would have played collegiately. Now, when Sybi's not around, he plays with Adam Scott, Sergio Garcia, or John Mallinger.

They have two young boys — Cameron was born on their fourth anniversary; Carson is two years younger. The boys have a backyard with a rope swing and a tree house, but you can find them on the court, too. They started out sitting courtside in their strollers. Now, they sit on the bench waiting for their turn to play.

"We'll let them hit for a while and wear them out," she said. "I hope they continue to like it and I hope they have fun with it."

As for the future? Sybi and Matt keep getting better, although one group wanted to split them up because they weren't a strong team. The Kuchars said, "Let's go one set and see." You know what happened. They won 6-4 and didn't get split up.

getting better."

Matt may be one of the world's best golfers, but he started out as a pretty good junior tennis player. He didn't transition to golf until his mother expanded their club membership to include it when he was 12. "That," Sybi said, "is when tennis fever turned into golf fever."

Sybi has never put her racquet down. She played at Georgia Tech, where they met, and later taught in San Francisco and played in a few professional events. But any hope of a professional career ended one day when she went out for a run and tripped on a cracked piece of sidewalk. She broke both elbows and spent six weeks with both arms immobilized.

A decade, a marriage, and two boys later, tennis is as much a part of their daily routine as golf. It's part guilty pleasure, part competition, part workout, and part just fun and alone time.

After finishing tied for tenth at the 2012 Transitions Championship,

DeAnna and Carl Pettersson

The Carl Pettersson Family

He was raised on pickled herring and tunnbrodsrulle, a Swedish snack which is a hot dog — no bun — with mashed potatoes on the side. His musical tastes ran toward Ah Ha, Ace of Base, and any other '80s group with a Swedish connection.

So how in the devil did Carl Pettersson morph from refined and

polished European who speaks multiple languages, into country fried steak-loving, vintage Johnny Cash-Hank Williams Sr. and Jr.— total old-style country son of the South? Let's just say he took to it faster than a hot knife slices through butter.

The gregarious Swede has been known to take the microphone

DeAnna and Carl, with their children, Chase and Carlie

for his own rendition of Lynard Skynyrd's "Simple Man" or bust into a country song. And his accent? It's a hodgepodge — a little Swedish, tinged with a bit of the oh-so proper King's English and a dash of North Carolina twang.

"He's sharp and witty," wife DeAnna said. "I've always enjoyed the dry and quick-witted humor that most Brits have and Carl certainly nails it." But as for those country roots he's put down? "I remember he'd start singing to a country song," she said, "and I'd say, you lived in England half your life. How do you know this?"

Carl was born in Sweden, grew up in London, and his father, an executive with Volvo, moved the family to Greensboro, North Carolina, when he was in high school. It was culture shock at first, but by the time he'd spent two years at Central Alabama Junior College, he was putting down southern roots.

When he got to NC State, he met DeAnna Ellis, a budding singer who could belt out southern gospel music and cook like nobody's business. She had never lived outside the state of North Carolina, but she learned to cook from one of the best — her grandmother.

DeAnna's country fried steak was always, hands down, the go-to request from Carl and his roommates. She would grab her pots and pans and groceries, and whip up the southern staple, complete with mashed potatoes and gravy.

Funny, but when she and Carl first met, DeAnna wondered how two people from opposite sides of the world could have things in common. More than a decade and two children later, DeAnna can laugh about how much they've really always had in common, even though they didn't know each other the first 21 years of their lives. They found some interesting threads to connect them — both had moved seven times growing up, both were close to their grandparents, and now they find they're more alike than they ever thought.

"Over the years, we found we really have a lot in common, most notably, the resilience to adapt to change," she said. "That's so important for the life out here. You don't know if you're going to miss the cut, or be on the brink of missing your card and not having a job next year. Or if you're going from the cutline to winning like Carl did [at the 2010 RBC Canadian Open]."

Carl had to make a nine-foot putt just to make the cut in Canada that year, then shot 60 — he lipped out a birdie on the 18th — in the third round. A closing 67 gave him his fourth TOUR win.

"There's just so much volatility in this career. The ability to adjust to all the changes is vital," DeAnna said. "Little did we know that our backgrounds of having to change schools, and adjust to all different situations, would help prepare us for the life we have out here."

Or that Carl's grandfather's nurturing — they spent winters in Spain so Carl could work on his game — would have such a profound impact years later? Or that the way her grandmother taught her to cook — "You start out by putting some Crisco in the pan, about this much" — would be the way to Carl and his roommates' hearts and inspire part of this 25th anniversary book?

Today, that country-fried steak meal is for special occasions only, and DeAnna had her late-grandmother's handwritten recipes bound into a cookbook for family and close friends.

She and Carl are still adapting. He became a US citizen in 2012, and she's using the "pinch-and-taste" method of her late grandmother, to create healthier meals.

As for the pickled herring, tunnbrodsrulle, and Ah Ha? Carl will still inhale the tunnbrodsrulle, but pass on the herring when he's in Sweden. But nothing beats a little fried chicken and biscuits, a cold beer, and maybe a sing-along to another seriously southern anthem, "Sweet Home Alabama."

199

Heather and John Rollins, in Napa

The John Rollins Family

Heather Rollins was just a girl when she went on her first bird hunt. She was the bird girl. She didn't even know what that was. It didn't take her long to realize that she was supposed to find the bird after it was shot. It took her less time to realize she wasn't a hunter.

Oh, she showed livestock in high school. Everyone in the tiny Texas town of Joaquin had some connection to a farm or ranch. The men all drove pickups and hunted and fished to put food on the tables. They sold livestock for a living or, in Heather's case, for college tuition.

So, when the former Future Farmers of America sweetheart met Virginia golfer John Rollins, she was thrilled. "He drove a sports car and didn't hunt," she said, "and I thought this is the most fabulous thing on the planet. This guy will even shop with me!"

She paused. "A couple of years go by and he's driving a four-door pickup and he hunts every opportunity he has." Depending on what season it is, John will grab a buddy and head to the deer lease. Or shoot hogs. Or turkeys. Or birds.

"They sucked him in," Heather said, and chuckled. "I feel like I've been punked."

Yes, she's kidding. Kind of. She's still trying to get used to the red stag head mounted in their lake house, but she loves the way he's embraced hunting.

"I despised hunting when I was young because it kept the men in our family away from us," she said. "Now I think it's great for John; it's a passion outside of golf."

The same goes for the Texas flag that's on his golf bag. He may be from Virginia, but he lives in Colleyville — about 200 miles up I-20, northwest of Joaquin — and says he's a Texan now. "We're small-town people living in a big-city world," Heather said.

John had never been to a rodeo until a few years ago when Heather took him to one at American Airlines Center in Dallas. It was much fancier than the East Texas rodeos Heather went to growing up, but he got the idea.

Like so many small-town Texas girls, Heather showed calves and chickens. It got her through college and into business where she eventually moved to Dallas and met John. "That part of my life has kept me very grounded," she said. "Being from a small town where everybody knows everybody, you appreciate things that are part of the value system."

In keeping with that, she made sure John knew the importance of hunting before he raised a bow or gun. "I told him to make sure he planned on doing something with the meat," she said. "Donate it or cook it. Those animals are for food." So, when the stag went down, they grilled venison burgers.

Hunting isn't all that's come into John's life. Heather got him to trade a can of beer for a glass of good wine. Now, they have a dream of retiring to Napa someday. It too, has that small-town feel.

As for four-year-old Georgia? She's into dance and gymnastics, and is too young to even to hold a bow, let alone be tapped as a bird girl. But that doesn't mean she doesn't hunt. "She is obsessed with the Deer Hunter game on iPad."

All Heather could do was chuckle and shake her head. Punked again.

The Rollins family: John, Heather, Georgia, and Bella

D. J. Trahan and Kristen Koldenhoven

D.J. Trahan takes his girlfriend, Kristen Koldenhoven, hunting for the first time.

During the off-season, D.J. Trahan and Kristen Koldenhoven don't head for the Bahamas or an exotic vacation location, but for D.J.'s farm and the closest deer stand. Here's their story.

"D.J.'s favorite time of year is hunting season. Hunting was a completely foreign concept to me when we first started dating. I had:

    a) Never shot a rifle

    b) Never owned any sort of camouflage clothing

    c) Never thought I would ever enjoy anything with a) or b) in it

"My first time out was a little like a hunting version of prom. We had just finished Thanksgiving dinner and D.J. told me to 'get ready.' I got a new outfit and I could not wait to take the tags off my new serious hunter gear. After I was satisfied with my 'hunter chic' look, I went out into the family room to meet D.J.. His parents had their cameras out and were taking pictures of us posing with the dogs outside on the porch. The whole thing was pretty exciting, right down to getting a gun instead of a corsage. D.J. sprayed me down with 'no-scent' and we were off.

"Clearly, I had no idea what was coming. Sitting for hours without moving and not talking was not what I had anticipated. After two-and-a-half hours of no action, we called it a night and came home empty-handed. Now, after a few hunting seasons, I have my own rifle, several items of camouflage clothing, and we sit together in a deer stand almost every time we go to the farm."

The Jimmy Walker Family

Erin and Jimmy Walker with their son, McClain

While the focus on the PGA TOUR is golf, the competition is not necessarily left on the fairway. Erin Walker explains how she and Jimmy channel their type-A personalities into other interests.

Although golf takes up most of their time, the Walkers still find ways to relax away from the golf course. For the past few years, Jimmy has taken up astrophotography, a specialized type of photography that entails recording images of astronomical objects and large areas of the night sky. This stellar activity gives him a way to wind down when he is at home. Being the true competitor that he is, he has become quite accomplished at his hobby, and is gaining recognition among other astrophotographers. He enjoys that they respect his photos because of his skill and not because of his day job.

Jimmy supports his wife, Erin, as she competes in the 2011 Colorado Summer Horse Show and wins the $2,500 NAL Adult Jumper Classic.

Erin's passion is hunter/jumper horse competitions that she has been involved in for over 15 years. She is currently ranked in the top 25 in the country for her division and she says her horses are the perfect outlet for her competitive spirit.

Both off and on the course, this family's competitive spirits are seen in the success they enjoy in their hobbies and in their lives.

Charley and Stacy Hoffman, with their daughter, Claire

The Charley Hoffman Family

They've seen U2 in Dublin, Amsterdam, Denver, Phoenix, Las Vegas, and Chicago. They saw Bon Jovi, The Fray, Toby Keith, and Lionel Richie all in the same week in 2012. Jack Johnson? That was in Canada. Green Day? They were seniors and pretty much their whole high school was there when Billie Joe Armstrong and the boys rocked San Diego.

Stacy and Charley Hoffman can work a crowd, a VIP area, or general admission seating. It doesn't matter, as long as they're there taking in the atmosphere and music. They've learned the ropes on how to find the best seats, how to slide up a little closer to the stage, and how to juggle an 18-month-old at a music festival.

Take last spring when they went to Jazz Fest in New Orleans. They love the event and go every year, but Stacy and Charley had never seen

Bruce Springsteen live, so they planned their day around The Boss's concert.

"We went down to Canal Street early and bought a couple of folding chairs. When we got to Jazz Fest, we picked out a spot and put our chairs down," Stacy said. They spent the next four hours weaving their way through the jazz and cultural performances with daughter, Claire, in tow. Claire is no rookie at music festivals, this was already her second Jazz Fest and she was just as excited as Charley and Stacy. "There are so many people from all over, all different ages, all different backgrounds, and everyone is there to enjoy the music. It's just fun to be part of the entire experience," Stacy said.

"Just before show time, Charley made a test run through the crowd to find their seats, then came running back to get Stacy and Claire. "We wound our way back to our seats, weaving through the people," she said. "After a few concerts, you learn the ropes and people respected that we put chairs down."

They rocked out, while Claire clapped and bounced on Charley's shoulders. Good times, and now one less group on their must-see musical bucket list.

Stacy and Charley have never been ones to sit around and lie low while on the road. They're always doing something — heading to a concert, a baseball game, a football game, an NBA game, or just out to see what the city they're in has to offer. Like the time when they were in Dublin, Ireland, after the U2 concert. The streets were filled with people and the pubs were slammed. They walked down the streets, taking it all in.

They've known each other since high school, when their circles of friends from Poway High School's class of 1995 overlapped. They saw each other after their freshman year in college, when a whole group went jet skiing and camping at the Yuma River. They kept running into each other when everyone was home for summer or holidays, but they didn't date until she was working in New York City and he was in Las Vegas. "It's kind of funny now," Stacy said. "We would say, 'I didn't know you knew so and so.' I always knew who Charley was. We both probably would have chuckled if you had told us we'd end up with each other."

Today, people tell them they look alike, they can finish each other's sentences, and say what the other person is thinking. And they each think they're funnier than the other one.

"One time we were all sitting at dinner and had a contest to see who was funnier," Stacy said. "Charley won but, to this day, I swear the only reason he won was he had more friends at the table. They didn't really know me yet, so it's a running joke that we need a re-vote."

They can be a little crazy, too. Take their wedding reception, when Charley changed out of his regular tux and into a powder blue one for the festivities. His groomsmen followed suit, only their reception tuxes were bright orange. Yes, they borrowed it from *Dumb and Dumber*. "In the midst of wedding planning, Charley said he wanted to wear a powder blue tuxedo. I immediately said no. Then, after some thought, I realized, well, I am wearing what I want to wear. Why not, as long as he didn't wear it to the church. So, then when we Googled 'powder blue tuxedos' the *Dumb and Dumber* outfits popped up," says Stacy. "We looked at each other and were like, 'We have to do it!' It was a huge hit and really set the mood for the evening." In fact, a few months after they were married, Stacy received a phone call from her mom who said, "Stacy we were flipping through the channels and that movie *Dumb and Dumber* was on and, oh my gosh, does Charley look like that guy." Stacy replied, "Now you know why it was so funny."

Before she was married, Stacy's career was in public relations. She spent nearly ten years working for agencies in San Francisco, New York City, and San Diego before traveling full time with Charley. Now, she's using that degree and experience in a dual role for the PGA TOUR Wives Association, as the group's secretary and vice president of communications and public relations. She also handles the work for the foundation she and Charley set up, the Charley Hoffman Foundation.

She's always working on something, even their high school reunions. "I did make Charley go to our ten-year reunion because I planned it," Stacy said. "I guess I'm getting ready to plan the 20th." Yes, always planning. For that, and for their next concert.

Charley and Stacy, at their wedding reception

The Fredrik Jacobson Family

For every TOUR player, the first goal of the week is to play well enough on Thursday and Friday to make the cut so that he can play Saturday and Sunday. If he isn't playing on the weekend, he's not getting paid. Freddie Jacobson shares this story about playing the weekend, against all odds.

"At the 2011 Byron Nelson, I had an early tee time on Friday morning. The weather was good, but I played poorly. At the end of my round, I was in 109th position, with only half of the field left to play before the cut. It was a no-brainer; there was no way I was going to move up from 109th to 70th or better. I booked a flight to Fort Lauderdale, Florida, in the afternoon and flew home. When I landed in Florida, I checked my phone. I had made the cut after all.

"A turn in the weather caused the afternoon tee times to play in 35-40 mile-an-hour winds. Now, I just had to figure out how to get back to Dallas before my 7:15 a.m. tee time the next morning. I called a local pilot I knew and got lucky; he agreed to fly me back. The whole family left at 4:30 a.m. from Stuart, Florida, and headed to Dallas. I made the tee time by seven minutes . . . against all odds."

Erika and Fredrik Jacobson, with their children, Emmie, Alice, and Max

The Boo Weekley Family

Boo and Karyn Weekley

When you say the name Boo Weekley, the image most people think of is that guy who rode his driver down the fairway at Valhalla Golf Club during the 2008 Ryder Cup. For residents of Santa Rosa County, Florida, however, the Weekley family is a big-hearted group with a passion for giving back to their hometown.

Boo and Karyn started an annual golf tournament to benefit Camp Compass in 2002. According to the organization's website, Camp Compass is a non-profit group devoted to helping "urban, disadvantaged, inner-city youth through the means of mentors who provide unique outdoor experiences." For a camo-clad Boo, providing kids with the experience of hunting and fishing is near and dear to his heart. "Taking these kids out to experience for the first time something I've done my whole life and often taken for granted, is a humbling experience. It's great to show them how I've always viewed firearms, as a tool for hunting, which may be something totally different than what they often see in the inner-city environments," said Boo.

The Weekleys are expanding their reach to the Sacred Heart Children's Hospital and Santa Rosa Kids House of Santa Rosa County, Florida. While Boo was busy working at Jackson, Mississippi, Karyn was playing "Mrs. Claus," delivering over 800 gifts to 53 kids at Sacred Heart. They are also helping to raise awareness for the Santa Rosa Kids House, "a child advocacy center which serves abused and neglected children in Santa Rosa County." Boo, who was overcome with emotion just thinking about the kids and how their work is impacting others, said "Seeing your own kids give to others is so humbling. It's an honor to give back to our community."

And giving back is at the heart of the Weekley family.

D. A. and Lori Points, with their daughter, Laila

The D. A. Points Family

To Laila Points, he's simply Mr. Bill.

He's the funny man who plays golf with her dad, comes to her birthday parties to eat cake and pizza, and brings her cool birthday presents, like the bag of windup toys that now goes everywhere with her.

Of course, one day she'll realize that he's not just Mr. Bill, but Bill Murray, one of the great comedic actors of our time. She'll understand, too, how sweet the moment was that Mr. Bill shared with her dad in 2011 at the AT&T Pebble Beach National Pro-Am.

Sometimes two players just hit it off. Blind pairings become great friendships. It happens weekly on the PGA TOUR during pro-ams, but that bond is usually between the players. This one, however, turned out to be a friendship for the whole family.

"That week," Lori said, "changed our lives."

Lori and D. A. had always talked about how much fun it would be to play with Murray, who starred in the Points's favorite movie, *Caddyshack*, and who also grew up in Illinois. That was a dream, until D. A. listened to a message that Tuesday night: "This is Bill Murray. I got your phone number from the police. Do you want to meet me at Cypress tomorrow to play?" Turns out the always unpredictable actor has one constant when he is in Pebble Beach; he plays Cypress Point every Wednesday before the tournament with a few special friends. That kicked off a huge week for D. A., who is now part of the tradition.

"They had such good chemistry," Lori said. "D. A.'s fun and social, and everything just clicked. I thought he'd be a little starstruck, but he kept it cool."

During the week, while everyone was giving Points condolences on being paired with Murray, who many perceive can be a distraction, Points was embracing a chance to play with, well, quite a character. "D. A. said 'Let's just have a good time. It's something I've always wanted to do,'" Lori said. "It turned out to be a blast. Bill knows golf very well. He knows what to do, what not to do, and what buttons not to push."

The proof came on the 72nd hole when D. A., who had taken the lead when he holed a 100-yard wedge shot for eagle at the par-5 14th, tapped in the winning putt for his first TOUR win — he and Murray won as a team.

"The whole thing with the wins . . . it's always when you least expect it," Lori said.

Ironically, one of Lori and D. A.'s life/career mantras comes from Bob Wiley, Murray's character in *What About Bob?* Bob was learning to cope with life by taking "baby steps." "We're always saying baby steps," Lori said. "Baby steps to the trophy, baby steps to . . ."

The next level.

Lori and D. A. had to fly out the night they won to get to Los Angeles, but they stopped at the Tap Room for wine, champagne, and burgers with Murray. "We woke up the next morning in LA and just looked at each other," Lori said. "Did that just happen? It didn't sink in for a couple of weeks."

When it did, all Lori and D. A. could do was smile.

Baby steps to a two-year exemption.

A great week with Mr. Bill.

Their Cinderella story.

Troy and Shauna Matteson

The Troy Matteson Family

The first time around, Shauna didn't give Troy Matteson a chance.

He was a sophomore on Austin's Anderson High School's boys golf team and she was a senior on the girls team. She was also a self-described geek with seriously permed hair and glasses.

"I felt comfortable playing golf and being around the guys and girls," Shauna said. "I knew Troy as a friend. Where most guys weren't paying attention to me, Troy did. But I didn't give him a chance."

She went off to the University of Arkansas-Little Rock and turned into a social butterfly. He led Anderson to two state titles and two medalist honors, then went to Georgia Tech. He majored in civil engineering, and wound up winning the 2002 NCAA title and the

Shauna and her daughter, Tori, at the lake

Byron Nelson Award in 2003.

But it was a moment between his sophomore and junior years that changed everything. He was back home during the summer when he was just looking for some fishing gear and walked into her parents' store in Austin's Barton Creek Mall — Austin Outfitters — and she was working.

He asked her out. This time she said yes.

For the next two years, they dated long distance. She worked in Austin; he finished school. Her parents sprung for a few plane tickets from time to time, but often Shauna and Troy had to make do with talking on the phone. "We could easily go three or four months without seeing each other," Shauna said.

They were married a month after he graduated in 2003, but on the way to their rehearsal dinner, they found out Troy had gotten into the field at the FedEx St. Jude Classic. He grabbed one of his buddies who had flown in for the wedding to caddie for him and, after the ceremony, they drove to Memphis.

"We were already going to be heading to Georgia to set up our apartment," she said. "It was just a little detour."

Troy shot 67 to make the cut and finished 76th, and it hasn't slowed down since. He spent two years on the Web.com Tour, winning twice and earning the money title. Then it was off to the PGA TOUR where, at the end of his rookie year, he reeled off five top tens — including a win at the Frys.com Open.

Fast-forward to today when Shauna can only chuckle. Ten years have flown by, their daughter is turning four and they still haven't taken a honeymoon.

"You travel all the time," she said. "So, when you're off, you want to be home."

Like so many players, they travel in an RV. It was a must because marrying Shauna meant inheriting her cat, Kyber, and after six months of staying in pet-friendly hotels, they were ready for the convenience of a rolling home.

When they're at home in Austin, where they have a little piece of land, their four-year-old daughter, Tori, who is the spitting image of her dad, loves to fish. When Troy heads out to feed the deer, she hops on the four-wheeler and goes along with him.

As for their honeymoon? Shauna thinks about it from time to time, but they've never even gotten to the point where they might book a hotel or tickets. Life is still moving too fast.

"Eventually I'll get my honeymoon," she said, chuckling. "But what do you call it after you've had kids?"

Troy teaching his daughter, Tori, how to fish

Mandy and Brandt Snedeker, with their daughter, Lily

The Brandt Snedeker Family

When Vince Gill slid into the back row at Mandy and Brandt Snedeker's wedding, no one thought too much about it. After all, Vince and Brandt were friends and golf buddies. Why wouldn't he be there? What they didn't know was that he had a special part in their night.

Mandy and Brandt had asked Vince to sing something for their first dance as husband and wife at the reception, but they kept it a secret — even from their families. So, you can imagine everyone's surprise when they took the floor and he started singing, "When Love Finds You."

"He has just an amazing voice," Mandy said. "We thought it

The Snedeker family

Brandt is one of those guys who is always smiling. He talks fast and draws people to him even faster. So, when he sits down with celebrity golfers like Vince Gill or Ray Romano, they can jabber away about anything — not just golf.

One year, Romano offered Mandy and Brandt a ride from Pebble Beach to Los Angeles in his G5. The weather was bad and neither Mandy nor Brandt like turbulence. Brandt gripped his handrest so hard on takeoff that he broke it. Once they were in the air, Romano and Andy Garcia were picking Brandt's brain. "They were like kids in a candy store," Mandy said. "It was just a general question and it turned into a 30-minute conversation." That can happen to Brandt just walking down the street.

They once talked about leaving Nashville for a more moderate climate where Brandt could work on his game year-round. They couldn't. Nashville just means too much to both of them.

This brings us to one last story, which might surprise you as much as Vince Gill surprised their wedding guests.

would be an intimate, special thing. We didn't want to pick one of the standard songs. When he walked out, I basically think everyone was flabbergasted. It's something we'll always treasure."

Vince holds his own charity event each year — The Vinny — and Brandt wouldn't miss it. One reason is Vince, the other is that it benefits junior golf programs throughout Tennessee. "Brandt is very passionate about The First Tee and junior golf programs," Mandy said.

Brandt is a Nashville boy to the core. He grew up working in his parents' pawn shop and he has never lived outside a five-mile radius of his parents' house — including during his college days at Vanderbilt. Mandy, on the other hand, is from Ohio, and still shakes her head at how they found each other. "No one from Ohio goes to Vanderbilt," she says, "but I did."

When Brandt was 13 and his brother, Haymes, was 18, their mother pulled out two gorgeous diamonds she had set aside. She asked them to pick one to give to their wives one day. "Brandt picked out this beautiful, clear diamond," Mandy said. "It was a heart shape and he picked it because he liked hearts. Of course, come time to propose to me, he knew I'd like anything he picked out, but I wouldn't pick a heart. So, he gave me another ring."

Brandt learned so much about jewelry working at his parents' shop. He can take one look at a gem and tell you what it's worth. Since the diamond was so perfect and special to Brandt, he had it set in a necklace and gave it to Mandy that Christmas. "I wear it all the time," she said. "It is one of my favorite pieces."

The Chris Stroud Family

Tiffany and Chris Stroud

Sometimes the challenge isn't making the cut, its getting to the tournament to play. Tiffany Stroud explains a time when they almost didn't make it.

"Chris had finished playing in the Memorial Tournament in Dublin, Ohio, and we headed to the airport to catch our flight to the U.S. Open qualifier in Memphis, Tennessee. We were at the airport waiting for our flight when we heard our last name being called over the loudspeaker to come to the desk. Airport personnel explained to us that the flight was oversold, and since we were one of the last to purchase our tickets, we would not have a seat. They then put us on a flight the next morning.

"Unfortunately, Chris had an early tee time for the qualifier the next morning and taking the morning flight wasn't an option. We searched other airlines, but found there were no other flights available that would get us there in time. Our only other option was to rent a car and drive.

"Getting the car, we started out. I drove and let him sleep as the nine-hour drive got us into Memphis at 4:00 a.m. We were both frustrated and tired, but had no other choice. Chris made it to the tournament qualifier and went on to make it into the field for the U.S. Open. Sometimes you just have to do whatever it takes, no matter how hard, how impossible, or how tired you may be. The end result is what matters, and Chris achieved his goal of playing in the U.S. Open."

Halle and Harper Stroud

The Kevin Streelman Family

Kevin and Courtney Streelman, with their beloved dog, Snoop

Fortunately for Kevin and Courtney Streelman, what happens in Vegas doesn't always stay in Vegas.

Seven years ago, Kevin was in Las Vegas for a bachelor party and Courtney, too, was there for a girls' weekend. Kevin and his buddy had an afternoon tee time and they were struggling to make it to the course. They had just enough time to grab a quick bite to eat at a restaurant in the New York New York casino. Courtney and her girlfriends sat down at a table next to them, and the groups shared conversation and phone numbers. Kevin and Courtney were the only ones who had their phones with them, so their numbers were exchanged. The two groups agreed to meet later, and Kevin and Courtney have been together ever since.

Kevin and Courtney consider themselves best friends. They love going to sporting events, jamming out (Kevin on the guitar and Courtney on the drums), listening to their record collection, and engaging in competitive games of cornhole or washers. They also love sharing time with their families and their 11-pound dog, Snoop.

Kevin and Courtney share a special bond and are a great team that supports each other. Courtney does that with her passion for Kevin's golf. She travels with Kevin and manages the business, financial, and support functions for him. She has also been known to caddie for Kevin at PGA TOUR events. In 2009, together they developed an iPhone App called Golf Like a Tour Pro. Kevin, in turn, supported Courtney in 2011 as she organized a fundraiser for the tornado victims in Tuscaloosa, Alabama.

Immediately after the tornados, Courtney went to Tuscaloosa and spent a week volunteering. When she returned home, Kevin could see that Courtney wanted to do more. Courtney, a native of Tuscaloosa whose parents still lived there, worked with other PGA TOUR players to help raise funds for relief efforts benefiting the community that she calls home.

The Streelman team is unstoppable. Lady Luck was shining on them both during that fateful trip to Vegas. That time, they took a gamble that turned into a lifetime win . . . what happens in Vegas sometimes leaves Vegas in the most positive ways imaginable.

Amber Watney, caddying for her husband, Nick, at the Masters Par 3 contest

The Nick Watney Family

It was the Monday after the 2010 Farmer's Insurance Open and Amber Uresti was on a mission: get the laundry done, get packed, clean the rented condo, and move up the California coast from San Diego to Pebble Beach.

Nick Watney kept asking his girlfriend to take a break and walk down to the beach with him. She wouldn't; there was too much to do. He even told her he saw a seal on the beach and she needed to see it. She laughed and told him they had been there for a week, and she hadn't seen any seals. Again, things to do.

Then she walked into the living room and Nick was on one knee.

"I'm so sorry," Amber said, "is this why you wanted to go to the beach?"

Amber grew up in a golf world. Her uncle, Omar, played golf at the University of Texas before he headed to the PGA TOUR. Her dad, Rusty, who played baseball at the University of Texas, started caddying on TOUR when Amber was ten. Her brother and sister both played golf, and her grandparents loved the sport.

Amber and Nick met, not so coincidentally, at the annual Uresti Family Fajita Cookout on Tuesday of the Valero Texas Open week. Her grandparents, Minnie and Lupe, started the tradition years ago in a backyard. When tournament officials saw how popular it was, they moved it to the course's driving range.

The whole family turns out to cook and serve the players. Amber usually helped serve and plate the food, but that year — 2005, which was Nick's rookie season — she didn't have to work. She just dropped by to say hi to the family, and as it turned out, to meet Nick.

"It was a strange meeting," she said. "Dad had already put in a good word about me to Nick and he had talked to me about him. I asked what does he do? Dad told me he's a golfer and I just said 'No, thank you.'"

But Nick and Rusty kept up their friendship, and eventually Nick and Amber started spending time together. Amber was living in New York and interning at *GQ* magazine. They would see each other when Nick played on the East Coast. "Dad just thought Nick was the nicest guy he ever met," Amber said. "He kept telling me that. And it was really different when we started dating. If I was talking on the phone with Nick, Dad would want to talk to him. All I thought was, 'I don't know about this.'"

But when the time came, there were no worries about getting Rusty's permission to marry Amber. The only difference of opinion Nick and Rusty have is over football. Nick loves Oklahoma, which

Nick and Amber Watney

means he doesn't like Texas. The Longhorn logo is all over the Urestis' houses, from shirts and hats to golf bags, and Nick would be thrilled to see it all disappear. The Red River Rivalry has taken on a whole other meaning with these two.

Rusty teases about caddying for his son-in-law some time down the road. However, as close as they are, that's probably not going to happen. "Nick's told me, if Dad ever caddied for him, he would have to watch his language," Amber said. With the added pressure on the golf course to make the right decision for the game and relationships, it might be a little difficult. "It would be funny. I know he would be out there saying 'Yes, sir' and 'No, sir' to my dad." Not exactly what you see in the relationship between player and caddie when on the course. But for Amber and Nick Watney, golf is a family affair, both on and off the golf course.

Hunter and Kandi Mahan

The Hunter Mahan Family

One minute she was on the sidelines at Texas Stadium; the next, Kandi Harris was flying over Iraq, riding sideways in the back seat of a Black Hawk that was taking fire and returning it.

That's not all. Kandi also parachuted out of an airplane in the arms of one of the Army's elite Golden Knights, stayed in one of Saddam Hussein's lavish palaces for a night, stood just a few feet from where mortars had killed people a few days before, and performed at a base in the Middle East that was under mortar fire.

And you thought the life of a Dallas Cowboys cheerleader was nothing but sideline dances, pom poms and glamour shots. Kandi spent three years practicing and working out from 5:30 in the afternoon until 11:00 at night. She spent two Christmases overseas, and has traveled to

Iraq, Kuwait, and Korea.

The only thing she didn't do? Catch Hunter Mahan's eye in the stands. While Kandi was cheering for America's team, Heather and John Rollins were sitting at the games with Hunter, a die-hard Cowboys' fan, teasing him that he should go out with one of the girls on the sidelines.

The year after Kandi quit cheering, she was exploring the idea of a semester overseas. Her sister Katie was getting married to SMU golf coach, Jason Enloe, and they both thought she should meet Hunter. So, they mentioned Kandi to him. "He called me and we went out two hours later," Kandi said. "By the third day, he said, 'Let's give this a real shot,' and six months later we were engaged."

"We met while I was on Christmas break and Hunter had two solid months off," Kandi said. "Now we don't get a week off. We were able to be together 24/7 and that's rare for golfers to have that time. I didn't realize how valuable time was because I didn't know the [golf] life. This probably wouldn't have worked out if we'd met when I was a cheerleader. We wouldn't have had the time."

Hunter and Kandi, in Thailand

Kandi grew up in Odessa, Texas, and went to Odessa Permian, the high school that inspired the book, movie, and TV series, *Friday Night Lights*. She was a Cowboys and Permian fan, started cheering in the third grade, added dance to the mix, and kept right on going when she went college to UT-Arlington. During her first two years at school, she danced for the Dallas Mavericks, then she made the Cowboys' squad and the team's elite show group, which allowed her to travel internationally.

Hunter, meanwhile, was a Cowboys fan even as a youngster in Orange, California. In the sixth grade, he wrote a poem about wanting to be the best golfer in the world, and included a Cowboys star and something about the team. It was just before the family moved to the Dallas area — McKinney — when he was 12. His mother saved it and had it framed for him for his 27th birthday.

Today, Kandi and Hunter have Cowboys season tickets, and he plays golf from time to time with Cowboys quarterback Tony Romo. While they're focused on golf, they take time to enjoy their downtime.

They've taken a page from Amy and Phil Mickelson, and are trading years and giving each other surprise anniversary trips. When they decided to try it on their first anniversary, Kandi wanted to be the first to plan the surprise.

"I wanted to set the bar high," she said. So, she took Hunter to New York City for dinner and a private cooking class with Mario Batali at Eataly. It turns out Batali is a huge fan of Hunter's.

"It blew us away," she said. "We didn't know what to expect. Mario came in from the set of "The Chew" with his orange Crocs on and we

chatted for a long time. He wanted to know about golf, and Hunter wanted to know about cooking and restaurants. After that, we picked what we wanted to make, and he cooked it and gave us tips."

The next day, they met him at another of his restaurants, Babbo, for lunch. Turns out, Mario would give anything to change lives with Hunter for the day and Hunter is hooked on food. He was already watching "Diners, Drive-Ins and Dives" and "The Chew," and now cooking is his hobby. Now it's not unusual for Hunter and Kandi to spend two and a half hours shopping at Central Market for the perfect foods and spices.

Kandi was ready for the next stage of her life when she and Hunter met. She told him all the stories about traveling during Operation Iraqi Freedom and Saddam's palace. "It was US headquarters, so we stayed there, but it was still furnished with his things," she said. "It was so lavish — all this gold and marble. It was one of the most extravagant palaces I've ever seen."

But the best moment, she said, was parachuting with the best in the world. "It was the most amazing feeling jumping out of the plane," she said. "I can't describe it. Free falling is an awesome shot of adrenalin."

She paused. It was strange to think Hunter wasn't in her life during that time.

"Even now, I think, did I really do that?" she said. "Was I a cheerleader?"

She was, indeed, and one with more than sideline stories to tell.

The Parker McLachlin Family

Parker and Kristy McLachlin, in Hawaii

Parker and Kristy McLachlin both have a strong Hawaiian heritage and embrace that heritage in their everyday lives.

Kristy's Hawaiian history dates back to when her great-grandfather worked on the sugar cane plantations while making his way from Japan to California. "Growing up in a household that loved the beach and surfing, Hawaii was our family's favorite vacation destination and we both have a special place in our hearts for the islands. I love the beaches, the food, the culture, and the way of life," said Kristy.

Parker and Kristy got married in Hawaii. When their daughter was born, they wanted her to have a piece of their heritage with her always. "We named her after a beach in Maui, which is Parker's favorite island," said Kristy. "Makena means 'abundance' in the Hawaiian language. Even though we are not living in Hawaii, we always try to keep *Mana Hawai'i,* the spirit of Hawaii, alive in our everyday lives."

Kristy and Parker, with their daughter, Makena

The John Merrick Family

John and Jody, with their son, Chase

There are many things in life that you just can't plan for. Among those is the blessing of the birth of children. Jody Merrick shares the story of how trying to plan the impossible can be tricky with a professional golf career on the line.

"In 2011, John had conditional status on the PGA TOUR, which means he got into a very limited number of events, especially at the beginning of the year. At the time, we were expecting our first baby, due in the summer. As luck would have it, John happened to be eligible for seven events in a row, which presented him a wonderful opportunity to move up in the ranks and, hopefully, gain full status. The downside was that my due date fell right in the middle of these seven events!

"To provide even more of a challenge, we live in California, and most of the events John was eligible for were in places that would be difficult to commute to and from. John played the first three of the seven events, finishing up at the John Deere Classic in Moline, Illinois. He managed to get a flight home that Sunday, making it to our house at 11:00 p.m.

"By midnight, we were at the hospital, beginning the induction process. The plan was that I would deliver by morning, and John would head back out Tuesday night. Of course, like most births, things didn't go quite as planned. After a C-section, John withdrew from the tournament that week in Mississippi, so that he could be there to help take care of me and our son, Chase. The following Sunday night, he left for three more weeks on the road. I couldn't bear to think of John going that long without seeing his newborn son, so I packed up the car and took Chase, and met John for his third week out in Reno. Despite the bad timing, it was quite a journey, but having John home for Chase's birth and his first week of life, to share that special time, will always be a memory that we cherish."

The Garrett Willis Family

Garrett and Jennifer Willis

"After meeting George Lopez at the Pebble Beach golf tournament one year, he invited Garrett and me to a taping of his show the following week in Los Angeles. At the time, the *George Lopez Show* was our favorite show on television, so we were really excited to go to a taping. We picked up our tickets at will call and then went to our seats," says wife Jennifer.

"George knew where we were sitting and had us come down to be with him while he was entertaining the crowd before the taping. He told the crowd how we had met the previous week at Pebble Beach and shared his love of golf with everyone. George took us backstage and, once taping began, we expected to go back to our seats and watch from there. Instead, George had us stand right by the cameras the entire time. He would come over and talk to us between each break and it was so interesting to learn about what goes on behind the scenes of these shows.

Jennifer and Garrett, with their son, Gage

"George was such a gracious host and we never expected that he would be so generous with his time while we were there. He sent us home with logoed T-shirts that we still wear, and lots of other *George Lopez Show* goodies. George and Garrett keep in touch, and when we run into him at Pebble Beach each year, he treats us like longtime friends. I am so thankful that golf provides us the opportunity to meet such great people and do such cool things off the course."

Camilo Villegas and Maria Ochoa

Camilo Villegas and his girlfriend, Maria Ochoa, during the Masters Par 3 Contest

For Camilo Villegas and girlfriend, Maria Ochoa, coastal Florida has its perks. Beautiful weather and convenience of travel while playing on TOUR are among the top. But, like most people, they feel there is simply no place like home. The comforts of familiarity, especially family, simply can't be duplicated anywhere else.

Staying connected to their home country of Colombia is important to Camilo and Maria. Because of their desire to give back, they created the Camilo Villegas Fund in Colombia. Through this fund, they invest in nonprofit organizations in Colombia that support childhood education and sports, specifically golf. "It is still a work in progress, but our main goal is to help as many kids and projects as we can," states Maria.

Camilo has always supported nonprofit and grassroots organizations in Colombia, including one organization called Circo Momo that teaches children who used to sell things on the stoplight corners to be circus acrobats. There is now a new circus organization featuring these children and they do shows for the city. Think Cirque du Soleil with amazing kids who went from poverty to finding a way to support themselves through the teachings of show and acrobatic directors.

Maria has also given years to the charitable work of the nonprofit organization, Give to Colombia. Give to Colombia is a "US-based nonprofit organization with 501(c)(3) status that creates, promotes and facilitates alliances between international donors and Colombian grassroots organizations." As part of her efforts with the organization, Maria has created an online boutique to share the products of talented Colombian designers with the world. The name for the boutique, Luv Cha, is very near and dear to her heart. Maria's dad, who passed away in 2010, was called "Cha" by her niece. Luv Cha is a never-ending tribute of love to her father.

For Camilo and Maria, there are many things they hold dear. But, high on their list of priorities are charity, hope, and love.

The Mark Wilson Family

You could say Amy Wilson was an accidental president.

She was. And yet she really wasn't.

One minute Amy was managing a new set of challenges with TOUR life on the road, the next — or at least it seemed like it — Dory Faxon suggested she run for the PGA TOUR Wives Association board. A year as vice president of fundraising later, Dory stepped down as president in 2008 and Amy stepped up.

Talk about the perfect handoff.

After spending five years as a change management consultant with Accenture and five years on TOUR, Amy was ready for the challenge; she applied the same skills she used when she was streamlining companies and . . . six years later, no one wants her to leave that office.

"I think because of my consulting background, when I came in, I wasn't afraid to ask questions," she said. "I would come in and interview everyone. 'What do you do? How do you do it? Where do you get your information? Why do you do it that way?' My job was to step back and look at the big picture and see how we could make it better."

She started with giving Sara Moores, the woman who had helped the wives form the Association and had been working with them for two decades, the title of executive director. Then she tweaked the governing structure and went to work on visibility.

"We were doing such good work, but we weren't getting recognition," she said. "We needed to do bigger things; things that made a bigger impact, bigger splash. We needed to make media aware of who we were and what we were doing.

"I think people thought we were a club. I don't think they understood we were going into communities and leaving our footprint, and making a difference in peoples' lives. We've raised a lot of money. Just thinking bigger, I looked at the events that we were putting so much time into and not that much money was being raised. We started getting smarter about our fundraising initiatives and bringing in bigger dollars."

Amy knew the plan would work just as surely as she knew — on their second date — she'd marry Mark. Today, the mother of three boys just keeps pushing to make the Association better. She's as comfortable in today's corporate world as she is with toddlers and travel.

She understands best practices, branding, and working with clients; she speaks the executive-suite language. It's the perfect blend since her job puts her in the spotlight working with the sponsors and corporations who invest in the PGA TOUR.

But the key to her success? No question, she said, it's Mark.

Mark and Amy Wilson

Mark and Amy Wilson, with their sons, Cole, Lane, and Graham

It's funny now, but when they were set up on a blind date, she was shaking her head. "He was still living at home with his parents," she said. "I was working full-time and traveling. Why would my friends set me up with someone who travels?"

Turns out it was the perfect match. They started dating just as Mark got his TOUR card, so they've gone through the entire journey together. It's been an evolution. "You change, your spouse changes, you change together," Amy said. "Your first year on TOUR, the last thing you do is play golf. It's all where is the course, where do you stay, where's the laundromat."

Their schedule used to be rigid. If Mark said they needed to leave for the course at 6:42 a.m., he meant it. They would leave three minutes late and . . . he wasn't happy.

"I learned those three minutes accounted for something," Amy said. "He would practice two hours before his round, two hours after. Fast-forward to today and if he practices 15 minutes, that's good some days. If we leave the house 20 minutes after he wanted, he's fine."

Of course, three boys under the age of six is an evolution itself —

just like her roles with the Association.

"[The Association] was started in 1988 by women who traveled 30 weeks a year," Amy said. "The majority of the focus on the road is on the golf, but a lot of them are traveling with children. It's a full-time job just traveling and maintaining your life back home too; just maintaining logistics."

Yet the women are always there for each other.

"The thing I love is that no matter what you face, someone's already gone through it," she said. "Whether its being a newlywed or first-time parents, or just knowing the best places to stay, best strollers for travel or whatever it is, someone is there to help you out. When you're young, you think you're the only one [learning and struggling]. You're not."

Amy worked full-time for the first two years she and Mark dated. Then, when they realized they were in love and heading towards marriage, she decided to travel with Mark. "I thought, if this is going to happen, I need to find out more about this life and golf," Amy said.

She opened a decorative glass and wood painting business, but as

226

she started getting to know the other wives and girlfriends, and began attending TOUR Wives events, there was less time for that. She was drawn to the projects and the commitment, and joined in 2006. She was equally fascinated by the fact that the TOUR gives back more to charity than all the other major professional sports organizations combined.

The TOUR Wives fuels Amy's business side. One of her proudest moments was working to gut the inside of some New Orleans homes destroyed by Hurricane Katrina. The group of wives involved wound up doing the work two crews would have done in two shifts.

Amy is always on the lookout for more opportunities for the Association, but she and Mark are also involved in their own initiatives as a couple. They support organizations such as the Evans Scholars Foundation, Midwest Athletes Against Childhood Cancer, and Blessings in a Backpack, and they just started the Wilson Delta Gamma Lectures in Values and Ethics at her alma mater, Indiana University. Jack Nicklaus was the inaugural speaker.

The Wilsons aren't the only busy couple juggling jobs and charitable efforts on the PGA TOUR, but they are one of the most visible.

Like everyone, they have days that test them. A flight is delayed; a rental house is infested with ants; one of the kids starts crying at wheels-up. But they also have days when a missed cut turns into a fabulous Saturday morning hiking Diamondhead or visiting Sea World.

"And," she said, "moments when you're invited to stand on the back of the green with President George H. W. Bush and Barbara. All the wives are there with Barbara and she's rubbing my (pregnant) belly. Moments like that are so wonderful."

At times, their obligations overlap early in tournament weeks. Mark's practice days are usually also the days Amy schedules meetings, charity events, and interviews. It turns out, that's where their partnership shines.

It's not uncommon for Mark to play with the boys in the morning, deliver them to day care and head to the range in the early afternoon. Amy finishes her meetings and picks them up. He knows the TOUR's traveling day care staff by name. And when Amy has an ultra-busy day, Mark irons both his and her clothes for the next day.

Amy, president of the PGA TOUR Wives Association, speaks at Walter Reed Hospital.

He's so adept at balancing. "Their friends swear if he's not the gold standard at partnerships, he's close. The same goes for Mark's and Amy's marriage. "You have to be best friends to make it work out here," she said. "There is no way I could do the president's job to this extent without his support.

"He's amazing . . . We always look at what his commitments are off the course and his tee times and work around it. He is so supportive."

Make that extremely supportive.

Before the last election, Amy suggested it might be time for her to step down. Lots going on. Mark said no. "You make a difference," he said. "If you think you can still make a difference, we're doing it again."

And — who knows? — maybe again.

25 YEARS OF FUNDRAISING

PGA TOUR WIVES GOLF CLASSIC

PGA TOUR WIVES ASSOCIATION

Fundraising is a necessary function of all not-for-profit organizations. For the PGA TOUR Wives Association, fundraising has taken on many variations over the years. While the TOUR Wives Golf Classic continues to be a mainstay for the Association, it is but one of many the group has enjoyed organizing over the years. A myriad of fun and successful events have enabled the Association to raise money to support its mission of helping children and their families. These events range from golf to bowling, food to wine, auctions of memorabilia to decorated shoes, disco dances to movie premieres, "green carpet" affairs to walks against domestic violence. Here is a visual walk down 25 years of the group's fundraising memory lane.

BLESSINGS IN A BACKPACK

It's a simple program, really, but one that is making a big impact. And all it takes is a backpack and a little food.

While many kids receive federally subsidized meals during the school week, they're often on their own on the weekends. As a result, many students go to school on Mondays in bad moods. They are also often sick.

Blessings in a Backpack allows the kids to arrive back at school on Monday morning with full stomachs and a greater ability to focus and learn. Its mission is to send schoolchildren home every weekend with non-perishable food they can eat on Saturday and Sunday.

Since its start, in 2007, the organization continues its incredible growth, having implemented its program in more than 437 schools in the United States and annually feeding in excess of 62,000 students each weekend during the school year. The success and impact of the program garnered the attention of *People* magazine, which named Blessings in a Backpack as its very first charity of the year in 2012, which was quite an accomplishment for a four-year-old organization that just wanted to feed kids.

It didn't take Mark and Amy Wilson long to get involved. The Wilsons heard about the program in 2008. "I was hooked. I think for a lot of people it's hard to embrace the concept that kids go home and there is little or nothing to eat. Often, the only food they get is at school," says Amy, president of the PGA TOUR Wives Association. "The last thing they need to worry about is if they're going to eat. School is hard enough, even when you have a full stomach," she adds. "So every Friday, the kids get this backpack full of food. It's wonderful."

"The thing we like so much about Blessings in a Backpack is that every dollar goes to buy food," says Mark Wilson, a full-time PGA TOUR player since 2003, with five career victories. "There are no administrative costs. We just buy food."

visiting with students, and holding fundraisers through their foundation. Proceeds benefit Blessings in a Backpack programs in the five schools they support.

"This program is very close to our hearts because I know Blessings in a Backpack fills a crucial void for children who might otherwise go hungry," says Justin, a four-time PGA TOUR winner, and multiple international victories. "I can't expect to play good golf if I'm not properly nourished, so how can we expect kids to go a full weekend without enough to eat and then be able to focus on learning the next school week."

The Wilsons and the Roses are just two of about a dozen player families that currently support the program in their own hometowns. The support of the Association and the individual TOUR families is appreciated by the Blessings organization.

"Our longstanding relationship with the PGA TOUR Wives Association has been crucial to our continued mission of feeding children, one backpack at a time," said Ramona Ustian, chairman of the board of directors for Blessings in a Backpack. "The correlation between hunger and a child's ability to learn makes this a problem we cannot ignore in our country. Not only has the PGA TOUR Wives Association impacted Blessings on a local level, they have graciously opened doors across the country to benefit Blessings in a global way."

Throughout the year, whether at the Sony Open in Hawaii, the Farmers Insurance Open, or the Waste Management Phoenix Open, the members of the PGA TOUR Wives Association will spend a day helping pack the backpacks and distribute them to students.

Blessings in a Backpack is structured so that it only costs $80 to feed a student during the weekends for an entire school year. Each Friday, volunteers and school officials distribute backpacks packed with kid-friendly food, which requires little or no preparation. Staples can include ramen noodles, macaroni and cheese, instant potatoes, soup with pop-top lids and snacks such as peanut butter crackers and granola bars.

Justin and Kate Rose have enthusiastically embraced the program, as well, doing a little bit of everything, including stuffing backpacks,

And how do the members know they are making a difference? Sometimes, a simple note says it all, like the ones they received from ten-year-old Cassy and from Adrian:

I have a brother and a sister. The food really helps my family and me . . . because my dad lost his job, and my aunt and cousin lives with me. But sometimes I go to get food, but sometimes we don't have food. Thank for the food. — Cassy

I have two sisters and one brother. I need food because we don't have that much money to buy food. My mom doesn't have a job. It helps us not be sick and is good for you. The food is good and help us grow. I like the food for my family. Thank you for the food you give us. — Adrian

That really says it all.

CHARITABLE WORKS
2007–present

2007

Hilton Head Regional Habitat for Humanity Women's Build at the Verizon Heritage Classic

Habitat for Humanity at the Zurich Classic of New Orleans

Habitat for Humanity at the U.S. Bank Championship

San Diego Rescue Mission at the Buick Invitational

"Gather and Gift" for Sunrise of Pasco County at the PODS Championship

Chip in for Recycling at the Frys Electronics Open

Great Lakes Adaptive Sports Association (GLASA) at the La Salle Bank Open

Pink Lady Golf Bag Raffle at THE PLAYERS Championship

TOUR Wives R-O-C-K at the Arnold Palmer Invitational

VIVA Las Vegas Beach Boys concert and fundraising event at the Frys.com Open

Family Works Center at the EDS Byron Nelson Championship

Christina's Smile Dental Clinic at the EDS Byron Nelson Championship

Golf in the Garden at Children's Healthcare of Atlanta at the AT&T Classic

The Children's Home at the Traveler's Championship

Target House Family BBQ, St. Jude Children's Hospital at the Stanford St. Jude Championship

St. Mary's Medical Center Nicklaus Children's Hospital visit at The Honda Classic

Victory Junction Gang Camp at the Wyndham Championship

Virginia Home for Boys and Girls at the Henrico County Open

Nationwide Children's Hospital visit at the Nationwide Children's Hospital Invitational

2008

TOUR Wives Golf Classic at the The Honda Classic

GustBuster Umbrella Seat fundraiser

Soirée Under the Spires, Kentucky Derby event at the Ryder Cup

San Diego Rescue Mission at the Buick Invitational

Mock Baby Shower for Sunrise of Pasco County at the PODS Championship

Habitat for Humanity Build at the Verizon Heritage Classic

Greater Boston Food Bank at the Deutsche Bank Championship

Levine Children's Hospital at the Wachovia Championship

J. Erik Jonsson Community School at the EDS Byron Nelson Championship

Winnie Palmer Hospital for Women & Babies and Arnold Palmer Hospital for Children
at the Arnold Palmer Invitational

Target House Family BBQ, St. Jude Children's Hospital at the Stanford St. Jude Championship

St. Michael Special School at the Zurich Classic of New Orleans

Operation Homefront at the Valero Texas Open

Library with Love, charity book and donation drive at the Rex Hospital Open

Auction at the Price Cutter Charity Championship

2009

TOUR Wives Golf Classic at The Honda Classic

Poolside Art Party at Arnold Palmer's Medical Center at the Arnold Palmer Invitational

AVON Foundation for Women - Walk the Course Against Domestic Violence,
Charlotte at the Wachovia Championship

These Kids Can Play – Paintfest! at THE PLAYERS Championship

Operation School Bell

Blanket Build for the Children's Hospital of Wisconsin and For Every Child at the U.S. Bank Championship

St. Michael Special School and St. Bernard Project at the Zurich Classic of New Orleans

Military Family BBQ at Walter Reed Army Hospital at the AT&T National

Snowball Express for Kids at the Crowne Plaza Invitational at Colonial

PINK OUT! at the Crowne Plaza Invitational

Whaley Children's Center at the Buick Open

Healthy Packs Program at the Deutsche Bank Championship

Back to School Packs, Evans Scholars at the BMW Championship

Taste of the TOUR Wine Tasting at the Travelers Championship

Fill the Cart with Fun! at the Nationwide Children's Hospital Invitational

Fischer House at Andrews Air Force Base at the Melwood Prince George's Country Club

Pink on the Links at the Fort Smith Classic presented by Stephens, INC.

Springfield Habitat for Humanity Women's Build at Price Cutter Charity Championship

Stuff the Backpacks at the Northeast Pennsylvania Classic

2010

Blessings in a Backpack at the Sony Open in Hawaii

Blessings in a Backpack at the Waste Management Phoenix Open

Target House Family BBQ, St. Jude Children's Hospital at the St. Jude Classic

St. Michael's Special School with Emeril Luncheon at the Zurich Classic of New Orleans

These Kids Can Play – Bookfest! at THE PLAYERS Championship

Story Time in the Kids Zone at the HP Byron Nelson Championship

Operation Literacy at THE PLAYERS Championship, HP Byron Nelson Championship and the Valero Texas Open

AVON Foundation for Women - Walk the Course Against Domestic Violence

at the Quail Hollow Championship

Youth Day at the Transitions Championship

Healthy Packs Program at the Deutsche Bank Championship

River Bend Mobile Food Pantry at the John Deere Classic

Greenbrier Farm at The Greenbrier Classic

Shake, Rattle & Bowl at The Honda Classic

A Green Carpet Affair at The Barclays

COCKTAILS FOR THE CUP presented by KETEL ONE at The TOUR Championship presented by Coca-Cola

Comfort of Home Baskets at the Nationwide at the Melwood Prince George's County Open

Fill the Cart with Fun! at the Nationwide Children's Hospital Invitational

2011

TOUR Wives Golf Classic at The Heritage

Blessings in a Backpack at the Sony Open in Hawaii

Blessings in a Backpack at the Waste Management Phoenix Open

Home of Hope at the Shell Houston Open

Blanket Build for The Hole in the Wall Gang Camp at the Travelers Championship

Ultrachic Fashion Show at the Bob Hope Classic

Beach Clean-Up at the Farmers Insurance Open

Transitions Youth Day at the Transitions Championship

These Kids Can Play – Wild Things! At THE PLAYERS Championship

AVON Foundation for Women - Walk the Course Against Domestic Violence at the Wells Fargo Championship

AVON Foundation for Women - Walk the Course Against Domestic Violence at the BMW Championship

St. Jude Children's Art Party at the FedEx St. Jude Classic

River Bend Mobile Food Pantry at the John Deere Classic

Healthy Packs Program at the Deutsche Bank Championship

Style Your Sole with TOMS Shoes at the AT&T Pebble Beach National Pro-Am

Little Hands Need Big Help at The Barclays

COCKTAILS FOR THE CUP presented by KETEL ONE at The TOUR Championship presented by Coca-Cola

Fisher House at the Nationwide Melwood Prince George's County Open

Fill the Cart with Fun! at the Nationwide Children's Hospital Invitational

2012

Blessings in a Backpack at the Sony Open in Hawaii

Blessings in a Backpack at the Farmers Insurance Open

Blessings in a Backpack at the Waste Management Phoenix Open

Transitions Youth Day at the Transitions Championship

Operation Shower at the Northern Trust Open

Ochsner Medical Center at the Zurich Classic of New Orleans

These Kids Can Hula! at THE PLAYERS Championship

Ronald McDonald House of Fort Worth at the Crowne Plaza Invitational at Colonial

St. Jude Children's Art Party at the FedEx St. Jude Classic

Relief Aid at The Greenbrier Classic

Vacation Day at Brenner Children's Hospital at the Wyndham Championship

Camp Abe Lincoln Gilda's Club at the John Deere Classic

Healthy Packs Program at the Deutsche Bank Championship

Goodie Two Shoes at the Justin Timberlake Shriners Hospitals for Children Open

Whiffle Ball Challenge benefiting Blessings in a Backpack at The McGladrey Classic

Style Your Sole with TOMS Shoes at the AT&T Pebble Beach National Pro-Am

COCKTAILS FOR THE CUP presented by KETEL ONE at The TOUR Championship presented by Coca-Cola

Fill the Cart with Fun! at the Nationwide Children's Hospital Invitational

The Louis Oosthuizen Family

Nel Mare and Louis, with their daughters, Sophia and Jana

Louis and Nel-Mare Oosthuizen both grew up as the children of farming families in South Africa. Today, they are traveling the world and experiencing things that Nel-Mare could never have imagined. But their hearts are still in South Africa, with the hay and the cattle and the John Deere tractor on their own farm.

Louis's dad, Piet, was a full-time farmer with a great athletic ability and a special affinity for tennis. When he wasn't tied up working the farm, he spent time with his sons hoping they would also fall in love with the sport. For Louis and his brother, however, it was golf, not tennis, that captured their attention. Louis began playing golf at the age of ten and quickly progressed into a talented junior player. Piet soon had another job that took almost as much time as farming; driving Louis to play in junior golf tournaments.

The trip to tournaments in Johannesburg took 14 hours. The demands of travel, golf, and finances were starting to take a toll on his family. Luckily, another South African golfer, Ernie Els, was paving the way for kids with talent and promise like Louis. At the age of 17, Louis enrolled in the Ernie Els & Fancourt Foundation (EEFF). While there, his game matured and the financial strains of the sport were lifted from his family. The EEFF paid for travel expenses and tournament entry fees, helped outfit students with golf gear and prepare them for a career in golf. Louis credits much of his success to his time at the EEFF and the mentoring from Ernie himself.

Nel-Mare also receives credit for Louis's success. Louis has been sure to mention how important his family is and how special it is having them together on this journey. Traveling with their children, Jana and Sophia, across the world is no easy feat, but they make it work because of how important it is for them to all be together.

To "pay it forward," Louis organized his own golf foundation in 2009, the Louis Oosthuizen Junior Golf Academy. The Academy was established to encourage and instruct juniors in all aspects of the game, as well as the discipline, etiquette, and sportsmanship that is a part of the game of golf. The foundation will support youth in the Mossel Bay area in South Africa.

As the Ernie Els & Fancourt Foundation did for him, Louis hopes he, and his foundation, can help promising young golfers reach their potential.

The John Mallinger Family

Mike Steelman Photography

John and January, at Pebble Beach

John, with Fred Couples

January Mallinger tells this story about "Security Guard Fred."

"Growing up, John idolized Fred Couples; he even had a life-sized, cardboard cutout of him. When John's dad was out of town, his mom would put the cardboard "Freddy" in the window to give the impression that there was a man at home.

"Shortly after John got his TOUR card, he had the pleasure of meeting Fred and having him as a golf mentor. Fred was very generous in helping John get adjusted to TOUR life. It was a dream come true for John to get to know the person he had tried to model his golf game after. John and Fred became friends and, not long after, we ran into Fred in San Diego while visiting John's family for Easter. We had dinner and drinks together one evening and ended up inviting Fred to the Mallinger's Easter dinner the following day. To our surprise and delight, Fred accepted the invitation.

"John's mom had prepared Easter baskets for everyone, including Fred. We had a great time, and Fred joined in the family football game with our nephews. During dinner, we all laughed as we reminisced about how cardboard Fred used to 'protect' the Mallinger family home when John's dad was away."

"Security guard," golf mentor, friend. John Mallinger found them all in his childhood idol.

Martin and Meagan Laird, on their wedding day

The Martin Laird Family

It was late when they checked into the hotel in Dallas, and the desk clerk apologized. Yes, they had booked a king-sized bed on an online discount website, but there wasn't one available. In fact, they had only one room left. Take it or leave it.

Meagan and Martin Laird took it. They had just gotten engaged, they were tired from traveling all day and Martin had to be at Las Colinas for the HP Byron Nelson Championship the next morning. They didn't have a car, so they'd make the best of what was left. Or so they thought.

It turned out, the only room available was a children's room with tiny twin beds with footboards, chalkboards, glow-in-the-dark stars on the ceiling, stuffed animals, a toilet specifically for potty-training age,

242

no iron or coffee pot, and only childproof electrical outlets. Martin made the best of it, trying to push the two beds together, but he's six feet three and she's five feet nine.

"Bless his heart," Meagan said. "He's trying to make the most of it, pushing the beds together but, because of the footboards, he didn't have much luck. And with light-up stars covering the entire ceiling and permanent night lights, the room never got even remotely dark."

"It was a cute room. If you had kids, it would be fantastic, but it had nothing [adults] could possibly need."

Not so amused at the time, Meagan laughs about it now. They were moved to a regular room the next day, but it was the last time they ever rolled the dice with booking a hotel on a discount website. It was one night, one miscommunication. And Lord, did they ever know about things getting lost in translation.

They met at Colorado State and he was a year older. The short version? Meagan said he never did ask her out. Martin said he did, but just not on a dinner date.

She had a huge crush on him and his Scottish brogue, and he would ask her to hang out with him and his friends. Her thought? "That's real nice," she said. "But I don't want to go on a date with your friends." Then when he went home to Scotland for Christmas break, she didn't hear from him. No texts, no calls, no emails. She was done, and eventually deleted his numbers from her phone.

Three years later, she had worked in the NFL for the Denver Broncos and then in the golf industry. He was playing professionally, living in Scottsdale. After a move to the desert, they ended up living in the same apartment complex. He finally asked her to dinner and, no, he didn't want to be just her friend.

"It turns out it's different in Scotland when you are younger. When they ask you out, it's not one-on-one for dinner," Meagan said. "It's going out with friends. That's asking you out."

"We obviously both speak the same language, but we were just from two different cultures when it came to dating."

Martin and Meagan

And the absence of texts and calls? Martin now jokes that it was too expensive to talk or text from overseas back then and he couldn't afford it.

People laugh when they hear the story, but it's so much a part of Martin's and Meagan's journey that it was a subject in Martin's speech at their wedding reception. And even then, he added one little part that had been buried — not just lost — in translation and made Meagan chuckle.

He started the speech by talking about them fancying each other and mentioning there were two sides to every story, but he refrained from launching into great detail. He reminded her it had nothing to do with her.

"One of the things that does definitely stand out is my inability to ask her out on a real date, which I have now learned involves dinner," he said. "It really came down to the fact that I was a student but, much more importantly, a Scottish student, and I didn't want to have to pay for two meals."

He paused. "Three-and-a-half years later, a different city, the same apartment complex, I finally took her out to dinner and here we are. If I had only known all I had to do was feed you."

Matt and Kelly Bettencourt, on their wedding day

The Matt Bettencourt Family

To say "it was the best of times, it was the worst of times" may seem cliché, but that pretty much sums up the first year of marriage and TOUR life for Kelly and Matt Bettencourt. Luckily, they came into it armed with a sense of humor and the perseverance to carry on.

The wedding was perfectly planned, from the wedding dress to the sit-down dinner reception, to the first dance, the flowers and the goodbye. Kelly and Matt couldn't have imagined that the vows they were about to take would become a reality so quickly. The ceremony was perfect. Then she and Matt stepped into the limo to go to the reception. He said he wasn't feeling well. A stomach thing.

"I told him, 'Don't be nervous, the serious part is over. We're going to go and have fun with our family and friends,'" Kelly explains. "Little did I know!"

An hour later, Kelly was on the floor of the men's locker room in her wedding dress at Thornblade Country Club, lying beside Matt as he was throwing up nonstop in a trashcan. He'd made it through the first dance, waved off dinner, navigated the speeches, and cut the cake — but only with frequent bathroom visits. Then he disappeared.

"'In sickness and in health' suddenly had new clarity for me," says Kelly, "but I guess you can't schedule a stomach virus. It's the last thing you think about happening on your wedding day. As I was visiting with our guests, my dad tapped me on the shoulder and told me Matt was getting worse. I cried when I saw just how sick he was and I knew then we wouldn't be going back to the reception. I also knew it was time to pull myself together and start taking care of my husband."

"We ended up with groomsman William McGirt and Matt's mom spending the night with us to make sure Matt was okay; he was just so sick. We laugh now; it was a special 'bonding' time. Several days later we learned that many of our friends had the same virus. Matt was just one of the first."

That was just one of the memorable and, in retrospect, comical events that took place that year, also Matt and Kelly's first year on the PGA TOUR. The expression "you can't make these things up" seemed to sum up their first year of married life together.

Kelly's first experience traveling with Matt on the PGA TOUR was to Hawaii a few months before the wedding. She hadn't yet learned that she needed to put toiletries in Ziploc bags. They leaked out and ruined half of her clothes.

Then they parked their personal car in the player parking lot at a tournament, but didn't have a proper parking pass. Matt missed the cut, went to get his car, only to find that it had been towed. "We made a rookie mistake," Kelly explains.

During another tournament that same year, Matt left his clubs and bag in his courtesy car at his hotel. During play, Matt always puts his wedding ring, cell phone, and wallet in his bag. Unfortunately, he left his clubs in the car, and when he and Kelly went to retrieve them, their car had been broken into and the bag, along with everything else, had been stolen. "I was upset about the wedding ring, not the clubs," Kelly said. "Sure, you can replace it, but it's not the one I gave him on our wedding day. Fortunately, through it all, we realized that being married was more than just the symbolic ring on your finger. It is something that goes

Matt and Kelly celebrate Matt's win at the 2010 Reno-Tahoe Open.

much deeper than that."

"We just laughed along the way — like 'Are you serious?'" Kelly said. "It was, 'Well, you'll never believe what happened now.' We got through it and it made us strong together. We can look back and laugh now. The funny thing is, I remember that first year more than the second year, and that's when we won for the first time on the PGA TOUR."

That positive attitude and resilience to laugh instead of cry is probably what changed their luck for the better. Matt turned things around on the golf course that year at the Memorial Tournament with a tie for fifth. "We started to figure out life on TOUR and the crazy events finally stopped," Kelly explains.

"When Matt wins his next event, we should redo our reception," Kelly said. "Get the band, the photographer, all the guests and have the party that, unfortunately, we didn't get to enjoy the first time around. We have so much more to celebrate now than we did then and have learned that, together, we can weather even the most challenging and crazy things life can throw at us!"

The Michael Letzig Family

Holly and Michael Letzig

Michael and Holly, on their wedding day

Michael and Louie, enjoying the lake

"Louie, our seven-year-old puppy, has a big personality. When we are home, Louie goes everywhere we go," says Holly Letzig. "We tried traveling with him; however, he was too spunky for airline rules and regulations, and quickly was put on the no-fly list. The lake is Louie's favorite place. He loves to jet ski, paddle board, and ride in the boat."

In 2009, Michael had Holly's engagement ring shipped to the locker room during the second round of the tournament because he wasn't available to pick it up in person. He kept the ring in his golf bag the entire round and asked his caddie to keep a very close eye on it, as it was a little more valuable that day. After making the cut, later that evening Michael proposed to Holly, and she said, "Yes!" Michael went on to finish tied for 12th for the tournament, and they were married months later on New Year's Eve.

The Justin Bolli Family

Justin and Amy Bolli

"On August 3, 2007, we went to dinner with my family to celebrate my birthday, and afterwards we all went to get a drink at the Westin Poinsett Hotel in Greenville, South Carolina," tells Justin Bolli's wife, Amy. "We decided to do a special drink that we nicknamed a 'Bolli Bomb.' The next week, Justin won the Nationwide Tour's Northeast Pennsylvania Classic and attributed his win, not to his skill, but joked and said it must have been the Bolli Bombs.

Amy and Justin, with their son, Brayden

"Fast-forward two years and again we are home on August 3, and we started joking that we needed to go back to the Westin so the guys could do another round of Bolli Bombs. Sure enough, we all went and sat in the exact same spots as two years before, at approximately the same time, and ordered the drinks, and talked about the likelihood of another win resulting from our Bolli Bombs. Against all odds, Justin won the next week at the Price Cutter Charity Championship in Springfield, Missouri.

"Two years later, we were all looking forward to returning for our biannual trip to the Westin Poinsett. You can imagine our disappointment when we realized that we were not going to be in town August 3. We tried to make up for it by going a few days later, but it just was not the same.

"We are looking forward to August 3, 2013, and our fingers are crossed that we will be at the Westin Poinsett Hotel with a Bolli Bomb in hand!"

Jason and Ellie Day

The Jason Day Family

He was 19 and not even old enough to sign for his room when they checked into their Las Vegas hotel. Luckily, she was 21.

Ellie Day laughs about it now, but being the older woman came in handy that day. "We had gone to the wrong check-in," she said. "They said, 'You're not old enough. Who is going be your guardian?' I said, 'I guess that's me.'"

Jason and Ellie still really look like kids. He was 17 when he turned pro and 19 when he started playing PGA TOUR events. Six years later, they're settled on a little piece of land in Ohio, in their forever house, and they're veterans on TOUR as well as first-time parents.

Ellie laughs about being kids when they came on TOUR, but they truly were. They met at Mavis Winkle's Irish Pub in Twinsburg, Ohio.

Ellie and Jason, with their dachshunds

She was a waitress at night and studying to be a hairdresser by day. Her eye was on New York. He was a 17-year-old professional golfer from Australia. His eye was on the TOUR. And Ellie.

"His caddie, Colin Swatton, was a regular at the restaurant and he would come through town bringing Jason," Ellie said. "I had a little secret crush on him."

Jason was a city boy and a golf prodigy. Ellie grew up in a small town where kids were in the Future Farmers of the America, line danced and the high school had a drive-your-tractor-to-school day. She knew nothing about golf. Heck, she didn't have a television or Internet in her apartment.

It took Jason a year to get Ellie's contact information, but persistence paid off. He stole Ellie's number from Swatton, who had gotten it from the bartender. Then he called her and made up a story about owing her dinner. "He was playing in a tournament in Cleveland and I drove over to watch him play," she said. "It was the first time I had seen golf." Jason won the event, the 2007 Legend Financial Group Classic. Ellie's reaction? "I said, 'Oh, great. Good job.' I had no grasp on what it meant."

She drove to Columbus the next week to watch him play in the Nationwide Children's Hospital Invitational, and they went on their first date. Six months later, with snow on the ground in Ohio, Jason flew her out to the Sony Open in Hawaii. "The temperature back home was minus-something and my parking lot was iced over," Ellie said. "We had so much fun in Hawaii; I cried the whole way back. When I returned home, I quit my job, and packed my bags. It was madness." They've been on the road together ever since.

Jason has turned into a country boy. He lines up clay pots to work on his aim. He has five acres and wants more. He has a few four-wheelers, too. And he and Ellie have started that big family she always wanted. They're established veterans of TOUR life. But even experienced travelers get thrown a curve every so often.

Jason and Ellie, like many TOUR players, made their home on the road truly a home on the road — an RV. They were on their bus at the 2010 John Deere Classic when they found out Jason got into the British Open at St. Andrews. They had no flight to Scotland and no housing either. On top of that, Ellie had not yet received her new passport. She was changing it to her married name, and it was still being processed. A whirlwind of calls and prayers later, she was on her way to Scotland. "It worked out, but that was just insane," Ellie grinned. That was only a couple of years ago. It seems longer.

"We have just kind of grown up out here," she said. "Now we feel like we've done it for 100 years."

The Cameron Percy Family

Cameron and Katie Percy, with their sons, Liam and Ashton

"It was 2005, and Cameron was playing on what was then the Nationwide Tour in Eugene, Oregon. I had just retired from caddying since we were expecting our first child, Liam," explains Katie Percy.

"On the ninth hole, a player hit his ball to the left among the trees, about 300 yards from the green. He pulled out his 3-wood to hook it around the trees, but there was no hook and no yell of 'Fore!'

"I was on the right side of the fairway under a tree, watching the green to see the end result of his shot. At the last second, out of the corner of my eye, I saw the ball flying directly at me and then whack! The noise of the ball hitting me was like a plank of wood striking the side of my head. I fell to the ground, more in shock than pain and, fortunately, I had not been knocked out.

"When Cameron saw me on the ground, he ran over to check on me. After the initial shock, I was okay, although I had a cut and a swollen ear. Thankfully, my sunglasses had taken most of the blow. My head was okay and luckily I didn't even get a headache.

"The player benefited from the errant shot when it ricocheted off my head and onto the fairway. He went on to birdie the hole. Cameron, however, missed the cut that day, but was able to take care of his pregnant and bruised wife."

The David Mathis Family

Chastity and David Mathis, with their son, Brady

Who says you can't win a golf tournament playing on a broken ankle? That's exactly what David Mathis did during a Canadian TOUR event, the Morelia Classic in Mexico in 2005. His wife, Chastity, tells the story.

"It happened during a weather delay in the middle of Friday's round. David was walking off the course and he stepped in a hole. At the time, David didn't know it was broken; he thought he had twisted or sprained his ankle. Since he was likely to make the cut and would be playing during the weekend, he figured out a way to play without putting pressure on his foot.

"David was playing great, even though he couldn't hit the ball very far. His short game was working particularly well for him. The distraction of playing with an injured ankle probably helped take his mind off of each shot because his focus was on simply trying to get through each round.

"During this time, I was working, and this particular weekend was hosting a seminar in Virginia Beach. On Sunday, David called from Mexico and said, 'Baby, I won!' I couldn't believe it! How could he have won playing on a hurt foot? When he got home, we went to the doctor to get his foot examined. To our surprise, we learned that he did, in fact, win a tournament with a broken ankle. David had to wear a medical boot and take a few weeks off from golf to allow his ankle to heal."

No pain, no gain? In this case, David Mathis showed that professional golfers can get beyond the pain to achieve their goals.

The Bill Lunde Family

Dana and Bill Lunde

Bill Lunde and Charley Hoffman have been best friends for as far back as they both can remember. Growing up, they lived just four houses down from one another and had a rule that they could not call each other to go outside and play before 7:00 a.m.

Growing up, Bill and Charley were always together and enjoyed playing golf with Bill's grandfather, Henry Lunde. Bill and Charley's parents both worked full-time jobs, so the boys spent most of their time at Bill's grandparents' house, which was just a few blocks away.

Charley Hoffman, Henry Lunde (Bill's grandfather), and Bill

To keep the boys entertained, Bill's grandfather took them to the golf course, where he taught them the game. The three of them would play after school and every day during summer breaks. Once the boys were able to play in junior golf events, Henry made sure he was available, not only to take them to the event, but also to volunteer as a walking scorer. As the boys grew up and went to college at the University of Nevada, Las Vegas, Henry continued to support them by attending their college events and keeping up with them in newspapers and golf magazines. Once Bill and Charley turned pro, Henry continued to support them through handwritten letters, congratulating them on their successes, encouraging them, and saying how proud he was.

Henry passed away in 2008 and did not see Bill make the PGA TOUR, but they know he still watches and encourages Bill from above.

The Aron Price Family

Aron and Lucy, on their wedding day in Sea Island, Georgia

Aron and Lucy, in front of the Sydney Opera House in Australia

In January 2011, Aron Price decided to do something that he hoped would merit him good karma for years to come. For golfers, the 17th hole at TPC Sawgrass is not only revered, but one of the most terrifying holes a golfer could ever play. For Aron, who had recently earned his PGA TOUR card, it was a hole he hoped to play often and well. So, in an effort to surround himself with good energy whenever he was on the hole, Aron decided it would be the location where he would ask his longtime girlfriend, Lucy, to marry him.

Aron is from Australia, but had become quite close to Lucy's family in St. Simons, Georgia. Her family was in on all of the engagement plans except where and when Aron planned to propose. Aron had asked Lucy's dad for her hand over Thanksgiving and Lucy's sister Kim helped design the engagement ring. When Aron invited Lucy and Kim to TPC Sawgrass to play a round of golf, since both Lucy and Kim played collegiate golf, neither sister had any idea what was to come on the 17th hole, other than a difficult shot.

Lucy remembers the day well. "We hit our balls on the green and I was getting ready to putt. Aron nudged me from behind and I thought he was just trying to annoy or distract me, but he didn't stop, so I turned around. There he was, on one knee with the ring in his hand. Of course, I said, 'Yes!' We didn't manage to finish the hole," she said laughing. "I'm very close to my sister; she's my best friend, so having Aron include her in the moment was really special to me."

Aron, who practices at the TPC Sawgrass course often, may not always get the score he wants on the 17th hole, but he'll always have the memory of winning the prize of his life there in 2011.

The Ricky Barnes Family

Suzanne and Ricky Barnes

Ricky and Suzanne, with their son, Brady

Ricky and Suzanne Barnes know a few things about the importance of physical fitness, nutrition and being a professional athlete. Before they married, Ricky's wife, Suzanne, enjoyed a career as a professional athlete on the AVP Pro Beach Volleyball circuit for seven years. She and her playing partner, Michelle Williams, had several top five finishes and became one of the most recognizable teams on the circuit. Suzanne still enjoys playing the sport, although her time for competitions has lessened since the birth of their son, Brady.

Ricky was familiar with professional sports even as a child. His dad, Bruce Barnes, is a former punter for the New England Patriots. The athletically gifted gene runs strong in the Barnes family as Ricky's older brother, Andy, was also a standout collegiate golfer at the University of Arizona.

Ricky and Suzanne have continued to keep sports and an active lifestyle a part of their everyday lives. They spend their time in the off-season skiing and snowboarding with family and friends. Together, they have spread their passion for fitness on to the next generation through the Ricky Barnes Foundation. The mission of the foundation is to "promote the physical and mental well-being of children through encouragement to develop an active lifestyle and make healthy choices to boost self-esteem and confidence." It's certainly a mission that is well modeled in Ricky and Suzanne.

Dustin Johnson and Amanda Caulder

Dustin Johnson, with his girlfriend, Amanda Caulder

Dustin, with his furry friend, Max

Being on the road for weeks at a time makes simple tasks, such as doing laundry, a bit of a challenge. Dustin Johnson's girlfriend, Amanda Caulder, shares one funny story.

"It was two years ago on a Sunday and we were in Santa Monica, California, for the Northern Trust Open. We had been on the road for a few weeks at this point and clean clothing was becoming scarce. Dustin only had a pair of white pants left to wear, which was fine except the only clean underwear he had was a colored pair. White pants and colored underwear were not going to work, so we washed white ones in the sink at the hotel that morning. We didn't have time to dry them, so on the way to the golf course I held them out the car window to dry. We must have been a sight to see, driving to the golf course! Dustin went on to finish third in the tournament, and we were both relieved he had on appropriate colored clothing with all the TV coverage he received."

Life on the road can be very challenging sometimes, but the funny moments are the ones that keep you going and the ones you remember throughout the years.

Audrey and Marc Leishman, with their son, Harvey

The Marc Leishman Family

Australian and American cultures clash in the nickname game. Here, Audrey Leishman talks about the discussions she and her husband, Australian Marc Leishman, had when choosing a name for their newborn.

"Aussies live by nicknames. You'd be hard-pressed to find a man in Australia called by his given name. Almost everyone in Marc's life calls him "Leish." Most of those who now call him Marc were introduced to him by me. When we were trying to decide on a name

for our son, Harvey, I had to really think about what it would be shortened to. Parker would be "Parks." Owen would be just "O." Harvey will be "Harv" or "Harvs." Aussies usually add either an o, y, or s to the end of a shortened name.

"One of the best stories I have about the way Aussies think of names is that one day when Marc and I were discussing names, and somehow Phil Mickelson came up. Marc swore to me his name was simply Phil. I said that it was most certainly Philip. We argued about this for a while, until Wikipedia solved it for us. Another Aussie in the room said that clearly Phil wasn't his nickname, because if it was, it would be "Mick-O." I reminded her that it didn't apply — this wasn't Australia — and it works differently here."

Marc and Audrey Leishman

Audrey and Marc, on their wedding day

The Blake Adams Family

Beth and Blake Adams, with their children, Libby and Jake

"Blake and I have always made it a point to involve our children with Blake's golf," explains Beth Adams. "Over the years, that has made for some pretty special moments. In 2009, while Blake was playing on the Nationwide Tour, Jake was only two years old and, to put it nicely, was a bit rambunctious and rowdy. After several occasions where he yelled, 'Hey, Daddy!' at some pretty inopportune times (once during a putt to win a tournament!), I decided that we needed to stand as far away from the greens as we could.

"As Blake was standing on the 18th green, he faced an impossible birdie putt of over 60 feet. Right before he putted, he looked up toward us and waved. Jake began flapping his arms up and down, and moved his legs back and forth. Blake smiled, shook his head, and proceeded to make the putt from across the green. Jake's little dance instantly became the 'Birdie Dance,' and our daughter, Libby, has since learned those special moves. We often find ourselves doing 'the Birdie Dance' in our kitchen, hotel room and, yes, even in public at the golf course."

The Graham DeLaet Family

Ruby and Graham DeLaet

In 2008 and 2009, Graham DeLaet stayed with a host family during a Canadian Tour event in Winnipeg, Manitoba, Canada. Before arriving, Graham's friend warned him that the host they would be staying with had an unusual morning ritual. At the time, Graham thought nothing of it, and figured the free housing was worth putting up with the host's morning routine.

When Graham and the other golfers arrived, the host was very accommodating and told them to make the place their own. He even bought steaks for them to barbecue and kept the refrigerator well-stocked. He had a big-screen TV installed the day the golfers arrived because he knew that they wouldn't be able to watch much television on his older, smaller model. Needless to say, he was a great host.

The host even provided a wake-up call service. Each evening, before the players would head to bed, the host would ask what time they needed to get up in the morning. The guys would tell him and then everybody went to bed.

The first morning there, Graham woke up to a very quiet bagpipe tune. Like a snooze button on an alarm clock, Graham rolled over and tried to go back to sleep. But the music continued to get closer and louder until eventually Graham was getting out of bed to a full-blown bagpipe melody. Each day, the wake-up call repeated until one of the players would get up to report they were awake. If you had a late tee time, you simply had to endure the early wake-up call and then try to go back to sleep. "When I asked Graham if he was at least a good bagpipe player, he just looked at me and said, 'Do bagpipes ever sound good?'" said his wife, Ruby.

Although Graham and the other golfers could have thought of more ideal ways to wake up in the morning, the bagpipes must have been good luck, because two golfers who had stayed there have won the tournament, including Graham in 2009!

Traveling on smaller tours and mini-tours provides opportunities to stay with host families and sometimes you just never know what you are going to find. Bagpipes were a very different touch, and this host provided a unique and interesting experience for all.

Rosalind and Charl Schwartzel

The Charl Schwartzel Family

It was the trip of a lifetime. Mozambique. The Serengeti. Six full weeks winding up, across and through Africa with a dozen or more couples, each driving their own SUV.

Rosalind and Charl Schwartzel, both native South Africans, drove six or seven hours a day to get to their next destination. They pitched their own tents most nights, set up their own showers and slept under the stars. They saw amazing vistas and incredible scenes on the 13,000-kilometer (almost 8,100-mile) trip.

"We saw the migration of the wildebeest; that was unbelievable," Rosalind said. "We saw lions, leopards, and many other animals; there were animals as far as you could see. They start out looking like little dots, then the closer you get . . ."

There was so much to see. It was the first time Rosalind had been in a tent. It was the first time she had camped, period. But there were areas where nothing was comfortable.

"Sometimes we stayed in a chalet, but a chalet in the middle of Africa isn't what you think," she said. "One night we stopped and it was so dirty inside, we tried to pitch a tent instead, but we couldn't. It wasn't safe. So we brought our stretchers (cots) inside the hotel room and slept. We must have looked very out of place with our stretchers in the hotel, but looking back on that night, it was really funny." And an adventure, nonetheless!

Charl's aunt and uncle were on the trip, as well; and, even though everyone was older, they knew Charl played golf. They didn't know it, but they were about to find how just how good he was.

Rosalind and Charl took the trip in the spring of 2009, which was the only time they could find in Charl's busy three-tour schedule. And the reason for that? He hadn't yet qualified for the Masters.

The trip was, she said, the ultimate. What followed two years later was the ultimate life-changer.

Charl played in his first Masters in 2010, then won it in 2011 for his first major and first PGA TOUR win. Now, their spring schedule is filled for the next few decades with trips to Augusta and a second caravan trip is on hold.

"That week, Charl was so relaxed," Rosalind said. "He was in a different world. What made that so good was that my mom and dad were there, and so were some of their friends from Illinois. I remember we stayed in this small, little house in Augusta where you could hear every noise."

It was a little too cozy at times, but it was perfect for them as the week unfolded. Charl came out of a stacked and chaotic pack of players on the back nine Sunday to become the first player to win the Masters by birdying the last four holes. And the asterisk? His win came 50 years to the day since South Africa's Gary Player became the first international player to win the Masters.

They didn't even have time to celebrate. They were on a plane to Atlanta that night with Rory McIlroy, then on to Malaysia for the week and another tournament. "It took a while for it to sink in for Charl," she said. "I think it only sank in when we arrived home the next week, and he could sit and take it all in and understand what he had just accomplished. Then it was crazy. Everyone wanted a piece of him."

Rosalind was working for her father when she and Charl first met.

And their first date? It didn't go as planned.

"He was on the way and phoned to tell me he had a flat tire," she said, chuckling. "My dad and I had to go help him change the tire. My dad was like, 'Nice start.'"

Strong finish. They've traveled the world for the past few years — literally. For those who live in South Africa, nothing is close except the local tours. It's a 16-hour flight from Johannesburg to Atlanta, 12 hours to Asia, and 11 hours to London. Their closest event is the European Tour's Omega Dubai Desert Classic, which is an eight-hour flight that Rosalind calls "a breeze."

"You can't actually go back home for just a week," she said. "You have to have two or three weeks. We can be out for ten weeks before we get home."

They maintain a flat in the UK, a home in South Africa, and now that Charl is playing more in the United States, they are looking for a place in Florida. It's the only way to balance the traveling.

Even when they're home, they're traveling — often by helicopter. Charl has licenses to pilot both airplanes and helicopters. To avoid Johannesburg traffic, he'll fly 20 minutes to his parents' house or an hour to their bush ranch. "He doesn't like to drive anymore," Rosalind said.

But he does plan to take another one of those six-week drives across Africa. One day. "We just wonder," Rosalind said, "When are we going to fit it in?"

The Michael Putnam Family

Michael and Kristina Putnam, with their son, Jantzen

Kristina Putnam found a way to encourage her husband while he plays golf, even when she's not at the course with him. Here is her story.

"When I started traveling with Michael in 2006, I began writing notes in Michael's yardage books. I would somehow either sneak his yardage book from his caddie while he was practicing on Tuesday or Wednesday or, if we were in the hotel room, I'd find it while he was showering or otherwise occupied, so he wouldn't notice me doing it. I wanted to do it to remind him that I'm thinking about him, to provide him encouragement and prayer for every hole. Sometimes it's just a little note or an 'I love you,' scribbled somewhere in the book, and I include a scripture verse, as well.

"Every week, we try to memorize a verse or two of scripture together. Sometimes I use the one we memorized in the book; other times I choose one depending on what kind of encouragement I feel he needs that week. When I have more time with the yardage book, I will write a verse on the first page, a little note somewhere in the middle, and something like 'I'm proud of you,' on the 18th page. I switch it up just to be fun and keep it interesting. It lets him know that I'm with him, even when I'm not."

"Be joyful always; pray continually; give thanks in all circumstances, for this is God's will for you in Christ Jesus." 1 Thessalonians 5:16-18

The Hunter Haas Family

Lorie and Hunter, with their children, Hayden and Piper

During the International Tournament in 2005, Hunter Haas received an invitation to a private dinner party to be hosted by CBS Sports producer Lance Barrow. It was in his locker, addressed to "Mr. Haas." Not having much success on TOUR yet, Hunter was a little surprised that he would be invited to dinner by such an important person, but he was very honored and excited to receive the invitation. When he arrived at the dinner, he saw Jim Nantz, Davis Love III, David Duval, Lanny Wadkins, and Jay Haas sitting at the table. What an incredible group of men to join for dinner, he thought.

But then Hunter noticed that there was not an empty chair at the table. He quickly realized that this invitation was meant for Jay Haas as he had occasionally received items in his locker that were meant for Jay and not him. He was very embarrassed, but the gentlemen at the table immediately asked him to pull up a chair and join them. He was very impressed by their graciousness and really enjoyed the evening.

He is now much more cautious about anything he receives addressed to "Mr. Haas."

Rickie Fowler

The training wheels came off his bike at age two. He was testing his nerve on a tiny BMX bike at three. A few years later, Rickie Fowler was jumping bikes and doing things kids twice his age wouldn't dare try, and his sister, Taylor, who is two years younger, was following her brother's lead.

Yep, training wheels off at two.

If you ever wondered where Rickie got his need for speed or passion for pushing a few envelopes from time to time, look no further than the Fowler house.

BMX. Motorcycles. Racing. Everything moves fast at the Fowler compound. His mother, Lynn, raced mountain bikes, and her husband, Rod, a motorcycle racer, won the Baja 1000 with Team Yamaha in

Rickie with his sister, Taylor

well. She's now a senior at Cal State Fullerton, and usually plays in the number one or two spot on the women's golf team.

Rickie and Taylor now share a bond not just as siblings; they're close friends. They support each other in golf and in life.

Rickie and Taylor also share a fondness for a special recipe from the Fowler kitchen. In high school, they began making oatmeal chocolate chip cookies. It's a delicate balance, not too many chocolate chips, not too much oatmeal, no cinnamon, and no one makes them quite like Taylor.

"When Rickie got his first house, there was one requirement," Lynn said. "Make sure we have a blender so Taylor can make cookies."

1986 — two years before Rickie was born. The two-wheelers were a start, but Rickie and Taylor also grew up camping on weekends, and that's where they learned about motorcycles and off-road vehicles.

Both kids competed in motocross, but in different events. Rickie was an expert at tricks, jumps, and what Lynn calls "crazy stuff," while Taylor raced. "They weren't in the same world growing up, but both are amazing athletes and competed every day of their lives," Lynn said. "That was the structure of the family."

Even though they were zipping around on bicycles and motorcycles while other kids were learning how to run, Lynn and Rod were never worried. "BMX and motocross are done in a safe and controlled environment," she said. "There's a comfort zone and when you know the kids have talent to hang, you don't get as nervous."

Lynn said about her children, "They were born to ride and do extreme sports, but most of all to compete." Turns out, they were also born to golf.

Rickie, who picked up the game at two, is in his fourth year on the PGA TOUR. Taylor played softball and competed in team penning — a rodeo event — with Lynn. "My daughter was more free-spirited and didn't want to play such a 'boring' sport as golf," Lynn said. Taylor eventually came around to the game of golf, picking up the sport as a junior in high school. Turns out it's a sport that she excels at, as

Rickie and Taylor, making oatmeal chocolate chip cookies

The Justin Hicks Family

Justin with his son, Owen

Kathryn and Justin Hicks

Justin Hicks spent his life chasing and achieving his dream of becoming a professional golfer. After he and Kathryn married, that dream changed to one of starting a family. After several years, they began the adoption process and, in the spring of 2010, were lucky to be quickly selected by a family. Unfortunately, the family decided to keep the baby.

In 2011, after years of working at local golf clubs and playing on the then-Nationwide Tour, Justin became a rookie on the PGA TOUR. He was very excited about playing in the AT&T Pebble Beach National Pro-Am and understood how his performance early in the season would determine the rest of his year.

Monday of tournament week, Kathryn received a call from their adoption attorney with promising news; the Hicks had been selected again. The baby was born the previous day, and Justin and Kathryn could meet the couple and take the baby home from the hospital the following day. This all happened so fast that Kathryn barely got to take in all the excitement as she was frantically trying to contact Justin. Since he was on the course, in the middle of a practice round, it was extremely difficult to get hold of him. They finally spoke and Kathryn shared the news. Justin was ecstatic.

Thankfully, the birth family agreed to the placement, despite the fact Kathryn was the only one able to pick up the baby, as Justin would not be able to meet them until the following week. On Tuesday, Kathryn met their son and brought him home from the hospital in a borrowed car seat. The couple had discussed names prior to the first adoption, so they had a couple in mind. They settled on Owen through phone conversations and "face-time" that week. The Hicks thanked their friends and families who helped provide baby Owen everything he needed for his first few days at home, while his daddy was clear across the country eagerly waiting to return to fulfill his dream of being a father.

A dream that together they had filled.

The Jeff Klauk Family

Shauna and Jeff, with their children, Jackson and Bridget

Jeff and the kids, clowning around at home

Jeff and Shanna Klauk are dealing with life day-by-day. Jeff has always been around the golf course, as his father, Fred, was long-time superintendent at TPC Sawgrass. Jeff started his career over a decade ago and earned his way to the PGA TOUR via what is now the Web.com Tour.

While Jeff was on the course, wife Shanna was a part of his team. Shanna herself is a talented golfer, and an All-American and two-time Division II individual champion. She understands the focus it takes to make it at the level Jeff plays. And when it was necessary, Shanna took on caddie responsibilities. But life changed for the Klauks in 2006 when Jeff had the first of many seizures; the cause was unknown. But with Shanna and his family's support, Jeff continued to follow his dream.

The seizures, however, continued. Jeff started having nocturnal grand mal seizures that progressed to complex seizures. While the grand mals were somewhat controlled with medications, the complex seizures were not. After many months and many different anti-seizure meds, Jeff decided to stop playing golf in June 2011.

In 2012, Jeff had an EMU and an inter-cranium surgery where 120 electrodes were placed on his brain to try to locate the scarred brain tissue causing the seizures. He spent 18 days in the hospital. During his stay, Jeff received encouraging letters from friends, family, and players on TOUR.

Shanna says that throughout this ordeal, the family has looked at the positive side of it; Jeff has been able to stay home and watch the children grow. They love having their father with them. Jackson is fully aware of what's going on. Bridget just loves dancing for her dad.

Shanna said, "Jeff and I have been blessed with so many good friends and family to support and help us. Jeff can no longer drive and they are there to help. Jeff misses playing golf and I miss watching Jeff play; it was always one of my most favorite things to do. I have been on the golf course with him since we were 18. Jeff wants to be back out there playing the game he loves but, for now, we are honoring our marriage vows and sticking together, through sickness and health."

The Alex Rocha Family

Alex and Jennifer Rocha, with their son, Rafael

All over the world, some of the most beautiful and scenic places are golf courses. For those who love nature, seeing it at its manicured finest is a feast for the eyes and senses. Jennifer Rocha shares an experience that began with heart-stopping beauty and ended with heart-stopping panic.

"I absolutely love walking around golf courses. Experiencing nature, seeing landscapes, observing indigenous plants and animals; for me, these are some of the most enjoyable aspects of traveling on TOUR.

"One of my most vivid memories is from the 2004 Costa Rica Open. I was enjoying an early morning walk around the course following Alex's group when I heard a strange buzzing sound. I noticed the sound, but quickly dismissed it and continued to enjoy the beautiful surroundings. All of a sudden, Alex and his playing partners dropped flat on the ground and started yelling at me. I was looking at them and wondering what in the world they were doing and trying to figure out what they were saying to me.

"Then it became clear. They were yelling 'Bees! Get down!' My heart was pounding! I dropped to the ground, thinking duck and cover. Swarms of killer bees were flying above our heads; that was the buzzing I had heard moments earlier. A few minutes later, they were gone. We all managed to escape unscathed, but it was a much closer call than any of us care to relive."

You never know what you will encounter on a walk around the course. Mother Nature can provide her finest, and her most dangerous, at any given time.

The William McGirt Family

William and Sarah McGirt, at the 2012 RBC Canadian Open

Sarah and William

The opportunity to learn from those who are more experienced is something many of us are blessed to have. Sarah McGirt, like many others, walks the course, providing quiet support while her husband, William, plays.

In 2011, The Barclays experienced a unique weather situation. Tournament week started with an earthquake that rocked the East Coast and was followed by Hurricane Irene barreling up the eastern seaboard. Sarah shares this story.

"William started the 2011 FedExCup Playoffs at The Barclays in 125th place. Only the top 100 would advance to the next tournament. After making the cut, we arrived at the golf course Saturday to learn that the tournament would be shortened to a 54-hole event because of the hurricane, allowing everyone to seek shelter before the brunt of the storm hit. All scoreboards, some bleachers, and anything that could get damaged in high winds had been removed from the course.

"Saturday's round seemed to pass quickly. William and his playing partners, Padraig Harrington and Charley Hoffman, were all playing well. Soon, we were on the 17th hole. William hit his tee shot down the middle of the 17th fairway to the cheers of the spectators. But with no leaderboards, he didn't know his position in the field and that he needed to birdie one of the last two holes to advance into the Top 100.

"Fortunately, I was walking with Caroline Harrington, who had been through similar experiences. She explained it was very important that William know where he stood, and that I needed to tell him. I was hesitant because I was uncertain if knowing would put more pressure on him. With her encouragement, I signaled to William '1-0-1' so that he and his caddie knew he was outside the Top 100 and needed to birdie the 17th or 18th hole. William birdied the hole and advanced to the Deutsche Bank Championship the following week.

"At the scoring trailer, William and his caddie thanked me. They said they needed to know their position and my signal helped them focus. I am so grateful to have women to rely on who have experiences on TOUR and can provide me with good advice when I'm faced with new situations. Sometimes, you need the wisdom of others in the game of life and even in the game of golf."

The Chris Kirk Family

Tahnee and Chris Kirk, with their son, Sawyer

Bad luck, good luck, best luck! Tahnee Kirk explains the three stages of luck . . . according to her husband, Chris.

"In 2009, right after Chris and I got married, Chris went through the qualifying tournament for the PGA TOUR. I wasn't working at the time, so I was able to travel with Chris to support him through the different stages. But, things weren't going well. Even though I wanted to be there for him, he banned me from watching because he decided I was bad luck. Apparently, the stress from the qualifying tournament can make people just a little crazy.

"Right before the final round, Chris decided I could go watch him play. That day, he ended up having his best round and making it onto what is now the Web.com Tour. Since that day, he hasn't banned me from going to any tournaments.

"Our luck has clearly changed and most of our special occasions are celebrated on the road. Two of Chris's wins have fallen during special times of our lives. One of his Web.com Tour wins happened on our first-year anniversary, and his first PGA TOUR win happened the night after we found out we were expecting our first child.

"Our bad luck turned into good luck and we look forward to celebrating more of those special times during our travels together on TOUR."

The Jim Herman Family

Jim and Carolyn Herman, with their daughter, Abby

Professional golfers are independent contractors, and most have never worked a job where they had to report to a boss. They could not define terms such as status meeting, a deliverable or project workflow. Then there is Jim Herman. Not only did he have a boss prior to his career on the PGA TOUR, he had the ultimate boss — Donald Trump.

Mr. Trump is the definition of work hard, play hard. He taught Jim priceless lessons regarding the business side of golf, and Jim taught him a thing or two about golf. Jim enjoyed playing rounds of golf with celebrities such as Samuel L. Jackson, Tom Brady, George Lopez, and Terry Lundgren (CEO of Macy's), as well as meeting many other powerful figures, such as Mayor Rudy Giuliani.

Jim's goal has always been to play on the PGA TOUR, and working for Donald Trump was a perfect opportunity at the perfect time in his professional journey. One day Mr. Trump came in to the pro shop and said, "Pro, what are you doing in my shop folding shirts and selling socks? You belong on TOUR!" He was a major source of encouragement for Jim and wife, Carolyn. They received calls of congratulations after earning what was then his Nationwide TOUR card in 2008 and PGA TOUR card in 2011.

Donald Trump knows quality and opportunity when he sees it. Jim may be one of the few that left the Trump organization without the famous exit, "You're fired!" Instead, he left the ultimate boss to become his own boss.

Jason and Amanda Dufner illustrate their divided house – Jason attended Auburn University, while Amanda attended The University of Alabama.

The Jason Dufner Family

The week before a wedding, the bride is dealing with hundreds of last-minute details, right?

The seating arrangements have to be tweaked. The wedding planner has a quick question or two. She's praying her mom can take care of this or that.

Amanda Dufner juggled it all from a New Orleans hotel room last year while Jason, her husband-to-be, was practicing at the Zurich Classic and wondering if this was the week. He was three for three in top ten finishes at the Zurich Classic and, well, he was still searching for his first TOUR win.

The Tommy Gainey Family

Photo by Heidi Graves

Erin and Tommy Gainey, with their son, Thomas

By far, Tommy "Two Gloves" Gainey has to be the University of South Carolina Gamecocks' biggest fan. Tommy, a South Carolinian, grew up in Bishopville, South Carolina, about an hour outside of Columbia. As a child, he cheered for the Gamecocks and watched every football game.

Tommy did not attend the University of South Carolina, but studied industrial maintenance at Central Carolina Tech. Soon after Tech, he worked for A. O. Smith, a manufacturer of residential and commercial water heaters. Tommy would spend all day working on water heaters, and all afternoon on the golf course working on his game. There were times when he would go straight from work, in his work clothes, to the driving range. After working there for a year and a half, he decided to commit to his dream of playing golf full-time and quit his job. Two years later, his parents' health became a factor, and Tommy set aside his dream to play professional golf to go back to work and aid his family. Tommy spent a year moving furniture before being rehired by A. O. Smith. Then in 2005, he found himself on Golf Channel's "The Big Break IV: USA vs. Europe." Tommy earned his PGA TOUR card in 2008 and A. O. is now a big sponsor of Tommy's. Through it all, though, Tommy never stopped supporting his Gamecocks.

Although Tommy never attended or played golf for USC, he is making up for it now. Whenever possible, he attends golf practices and recently joined the Gamecock Club. The Gaineys have season tickets to USC football games and have started taking Tommy's son, Thomas, to the games. Tommy was made an honorary letterman for the golf team in 2011, and shows his support by carrying a Carolina Gamecock golf bag, with a "Cocky" mascot head cover for his driver and "Go Gamecock" tees in his bag. His support doesn't stop there, and he can be seen on Sundays wearing his black and garnet.

While Tommy lives and breathes for USC, his younger brother pulls for the in-state rivals, Clemson Tigers. Tommy's wife, Erin, grew up a Georgia Bulldog fan, which is another huge rivalry for the Gamecocks, but will cheer for USC to support Tommy. Looks like it's a house divided for the Gaineys during football season but, for Tommy, there's really only one true winner.

The Bobby Gates Family

Lauren and Bobby Gates

Bobby and Lauren are huge foodies. They love to try new restaurants along with a great bottle of wine while traveling. Here's one story Lauren shares.

"When Bobby gained his Nationwide TOUR card in 2010, he asked me to caddie for him in New Zealand and Australia. After each round during the week of New Zealand, we would walk to Queenstown and enjoy the local cuisine. During one of our daily visits, we came across a wine-tasting shop. Bobby, having heard of the Penfolds Grange bottle of wine, wanted to try an ounce for $30. I told him he was crazy! Not thinking, I promised him that if he won the tournament, I would buy him the bottle.

"Bobby was leading after the first round and he jokingly reminded me of our bet. He stayed in the lead after each round and ended up winning the tournament. Right after his winning putt sank, his first comment to me was, 'How about that bottle of wine?' A bet is a bet, but I managed to postpone the purchase of the very expensive bottle of wine.

"When we decided to get married, I found a bottle of Penfolds Grange and surprised him with it the night before our wedding and paid off the bet.

Now the question is, when should we drink it?"

The Daniel Summerhays Family

Daniel and Emily Summerhays, with their sons, Patton, Jack, and Will, at the Big Dig at the John Deere Classic

People frequently have the misconception that all people who play golf for a living stay in expensive hotels and live a very glamorous life. But, as Emily Summerhays shares, sometimes golfers have to take the road less traveled to reach the dawn of new opportunity.

"In January 2009, after the birth of our second baby, we traveled to Phoenix so that Danny could get out of the snow and get some practice in. Danny had conditional status on the Nationwide Tour and we were essentially broke . . . I mean no money at all. We booked a room in a hotel that was dirt cheap, intending to stay for three weeks. To this day, that was the only time I ever had to go out and purchase cleaning supplies to clean the hotel room we were renting, from top to bottom, so my family could stay there. By the end of two weeks, almost the entire family was sick, a low point for our family.

"Danny's season started off pretty bleak as well, but quickly turned around in one tournament when he was the last man to get into the field for an event that he ended up almost winning. That second place finish turned his season around and eventually secured him his PGA TOUR card. Sometimes it truly is the darkest before the dawn."

The Kevin Kisner Family

Brittany and Kevin Kisner

When one person in a relationship is a professional athlete, a competitive nature is expected. When both parties embody that spirit, it can sometimes be a delicate dance of fuel and fire. Brittany Kisner shares a story of just such an event.

"Kevin and I are both super-competitive. He grew up playing all sports and I grew up playing tennis. One day, we decided to play mixed doubles with another couple in our hometown of Aiken, South Carolina. It was quite an experience," she said.

"Our friends are such a sweet couple; the kind that laughed and encouraged each other with every shot. Meanwhile, Kevin and I were literally yelling at one another, 'I can't believe you missed that!' or 'That's my side of the court!' While we eventually won the match, we walked off the court not speaking to each other.

"It wasn't too long before everyone was laughing about the day's events. We realized our competitive natures were getting the better of us and getting in the way of enjoying time with our friends. We knew then that Kevin's competitiveness would be best kept on the golf course between Kevin and his fellow players, instead of between the two of us on the tennis court."

The Michael Thompson Family

Rachel and Michael Thompson

Tulane University in New Orleans is where Michael began his college golf career and also met his future wife, Rachel, who was a member of Tulane's women's soccer team. In August 2005, Hurricane Katrina ripped through the Gulf Coast, causing massive flooding and destruction. New Orleans was completely devastated and parts of Tulane's campus were under eight to ten feet of water.

Forced to evacuate ahead of the storm, the men's golf team drove to Houston, Texas, taking up residence in a teammate's parents' home for ten days. Rachel and the women's soccer team, along with the Tulane football team, evacuated the day before Katrina came onshore, riding in buses to Jackson State University in Jackson, Mississippi. The entire group spent ten days sleeping on the floor of one of the campus gymnasiums.

With all the destruction, Tulane administrators determined the school would be closed for the semester. They worked with other schools in Texas and Louisiana to arrange suitable venues to host Tulane's athletics. The men's golf team spent the semester taking classes and playing at Southern Methodist University in Dallas, while Texas A& M University became the temporary home for the women's soccer team.

In December, Tulane announced they would re-open for the spring semester. However, due to financial constraints, Tulane was forced to cut several athletic teams, including men's golf and women's soccer. Keeping alive his dream of becoming a professional golfer, Michael transferred to the University of Alabama to complete his college career. Rachel, however, stayed at Tulane and became a student athletic trainer for the football team. This generated an interest in health care and the human body, eventually leading her to obtain a doctorate in physical therapy.

Rachel and Michael look back on those days, when Katrina caused so much death and devastation in the Gulf, knowing that their experiences during those times helped shaped their futures into what they are today.

Webb and Dowd Simpson

The Webb Simpson Family

Dowd Keith laughed when her best friend told her that she would meet her husband at Wake Forest University. Later, at her best friend's debutante ball, Dowd met Sam Simpson. Sam was instantly charmed by Dowd and, upon learning she would be a sophomore at Wake Forest, asked if she would agree to meet his son, who would be a freshman playing on the WFU golf team, and show him around the campus. Sam even offered her $100, to which Dowd replied, "If he's as cute as you, I'll do it for free."

When school started, Webb Simpson saw Dowd at a fraternity party, but didn't have the courage to say anything to her, although he thought she might be the girl his father had told him about. The following day,

Webb and Dowd, at Wake Forest University

Moments after Webb proposed to Dowd at the John Deere Classic

Dowd met Webb and remembers standing in his dorm room, her best friend by her side, with Webb straddling the back of a chair trying to look cool. Of that first meeting, Dowd says, "It's funny what you remember about moments like that. I don't remember what we talked about, but I remember his room, what I was wearing, and what I did. He was trying to be cool, so I just started going through his drawers and cabinets, ate some of his mints . . . just kind of messing with him." After they left and were walking across campus, Dowd's friend asked what she thought about Webb, asking if Dowd thought he might be her future husband. Dowd responded, "I don't know, we'll see."

A week later, Dowd was performing in an on-campus theater production. Webb came to watch Dowd and, before the show, handed her a handful of his dorm room mints.

They went on their first date in January and dated throughout college, breaking it off when Dowd graduated. They both felt they needed time to set their priorities and center on their faith. Dowd recalls, "During that year, there was no hope of us getting back together. It was the hope of what the Lord had in store for us today and developing that relationship as individuals."

Webb finished his studies at Wake Forest, and Dowd worked for a production company in Atlanta and then moved to Los Angeles. Nearly a year passed, without their talking to each other before Webb called Dowd, asking to take her to dinner. Dowd said, "I realized this is the same man I fell in love with, just so much better. Over the course of dinner and dessert, I knew I'd found the man I wanted to spend my life with — again."

A theater major, Dowd says there are many parallels between acting and golf, and that those parallels also brought them closer. "You have to be in the moment. You can't think ahead. You can't think about the mistakes you made."

Dowd and Webb leaving the church, after being pronounced husband and wife

Four years after graduating from Wake Forest, Webb Simpson won his first major — the 2012 U.S. Open at the Olympic Club. He finished before the final group, posting the low score, while he and Dowd waited with cameras watching them. When it was official, their 'I can't believe it' reactions were as sweet as how they first met.

Wondering about that $100 Sam Simpson offered Dowd to show Webb around the Wake Forest campus? He paid up and they went to a steakhouse in Winston-Salem. As for the story, they'll be telling it into their old age. "We love our story and we love sharing it with people," Dowd said. "It never gets old."

PLAYER DINNERS

While traveling on TOUR, player families look forward to a home-cooked meal. Many times, players will host other families at their homes, and make it an evening of fun and relaxation. That's when you see the family recipes make an appearance.

As the Association prepared for the publication of this book, many families prepared the special recipes they submitted for the book and served them at these gatherings. Here are pictures of those times spent away from the course with friends and family.

A TASTE OF THE TOUR
A LOOK BACK

SPLENDID SALAD

Submitted by:
Amanda Byrd

up, and the impact the Association has made on charities around the country.

We, however, felt that we needed to pay homage to that first publication and to the people who asked for the next volume. So, we asked our families for recipes that they love and make for their own families and included them in this book. We hope you enjoy making and eating these as much as you enjoyed those in our first book.

In 2000, the PGA TOUR Wives Association, in collaboration with the PGA TOUR Partners Club, produced and published its first book, *A Taste of the TOUR*. This book, a cookbook, contained recipes and short stories from our player families.

During that process, all of us involved swore we would never publish another book. But over the years, we've had many calls from people asking when our next edition would come out. Not only had the recipes been warmly received, but people enjoyed reading the short stories about our lives.

When we started talking about our 25th anniversary and how we could commemorate the occasion, we decided it was time to produce the next edition of the book to coincide with our celebration. But to our surprise, during the development phases, the book evolved from a cookbook to a story about our Association, the families that make it

Teeing Up

BEVERAGES

APPETIZERS AND DIPS

SOUPS

SALADS

BREADS AND MUFFINS

MULLED WINE

Liz and Bob Estes
Serves 4-6

Williams-Sonoma™ Mulling Spices
1 bottle red wine (Cabernet is best)
3 orange peels
3 tablespoons honey
1 bay leaf
Vanilla cognac

In a saucepan, toast spices for 3 minutes. When fragrant, add wine, orange peels, honey, and bay leaf.

Simmer for 30 minutes. Then add vanilla cognac to taste before serving.

Appetizers and Dips

DAVE'S FALL-OFF-THE-BONE WINGS

Alli and Will MacKenzie
Serves 4-6

24 chicken wings
1 bottle of Blue Front BBQ Sauce™
(regular or spicy, depending on preference)
1 bottle of Don Shula's BBQ Sauce™

Preheat oven to 300°F. Cut and wash chicken. Place wings in a pan lined with foil. Smother wings with both BBQ sauces so there is a solid layer spread over every wing. Cover the pan with foil and put it in the oven for an hour and a half.

Remove from oven and drain grease. Re-apply BBQ sauce until wings are again smothered. Put back into the oven for at least another hour and a half.

For more fall-off-the-bone goodness, leave in the oven longer, and reduce heat to 200–250°F.

GUACAMOLE DIP

Anita and Omar Uresti
Serves 4-6

3 avocados
1 small tomato
2 tablespoons onion
1 tablespoon lemon juice
3 leaves cilantro
1 tablespoon sea salt

Cut the avocado down the middle. Using a large knife, "hammer" it into the seed, then pull the knife out. The seed should pop out with it. Spoon out the avocado into a bowl.

Chop the tomato, cilantro, and onions fairly fine. The tomato is more for color. Add all ingredients to the bowl. Fresh lemon juice is best for a fresh taste, but it also helps the guacamole keep its bright green color. Mash the mixture together, but not too much; lumpy looks traditional. Add the salt and stir.

Save one of the seeds from one of the avocados and put it back into the dip until ready to serve. Serve with really thick tortilla chips.

PEPPERONCINI DIP WITH PITA TRIANGLES

Kelley and Bryce Molder
Serves 6-8

4–6 round pita pockets
Olive oil
Salt and pepper, to taste
8 ounces cream cheese, softened
¼ cup grated parmesan cheese
½ cup sour cream
1 10-ounce jar pepperoncinis
Pepperoncini juice, to taste

PITA TRIANGLES:
Separate each round pita pocket into two flat sides. Stack on top of each other and cut like a pizza into 6 triangles. Brush each triangle with olive oil, then sprinkle with salt and pepper. Place on a baking sheet. Bake at 350°F for 5 minutes or until crunchy and golden brown.

FOR THE PEPPERONCINI DIP:
Blend cream cheese, parmesan cheese, sour cream, pepperoncinis, and a ¼ cup pepperoncini juice in a food processor until mixed. Add more juice for a stronger taste, as desired. Serve with pita triangles.

Deviled Eggs

Kelly and Matt Bettencourt
Serves 5-7

5 hard-boiled eggs, peeled
1½ tablespoons Dijon mustard
1½ tablespoons mayonnaise
5 pimento-stuffed green olives, halved
1 teaspoon Cajun seasoning
Salt and pepper, to taste

Cut eggs in half lengthwise. Remove yolks. Mash yolks and stir in mustard and mayonnaise until desired consistency. Add salt and pepper to taste. Carefully spoon mixture into eggs.

Garnish with the olives and sprinkle with Cajun seasoning.

Black Bean and Corn Dip

Julie and Bill Haas
Serves 6-8

1 can sweet corn, drained
1 can black beans, rinsed and drained
1 cup Vidalia onions, diced
1 cup feta cheese, crumbled
¼ cup extra virgin olive oil
¼ cup apple cider vinegar
¼ cup sugar

Mix oil, sugar, and vinegar together. Add corn, beans, onions, and feta cheese. Mix all ingredients together and let sit in the refrigerator for an hour before serving. Serve with tortilla chips.

Stuffed Mushrooms

DeAnna and Carl Pettersson
Makes 4 dozen

2 packages button mushrooms
1 pound spicy sausage
1 pound cream cheese

Wash and remove the stems from the mushrooms. Brown sausage in a skillet, then drain grease. Mix in cream cheese and combine well. Carefully spoon the mixture into mushrooms.

Bake in oven at 375°F for 20 minutes or until lightly brown.

Christmas Chex® Mix

Kim and Zach Johnson
Serves 24

14 ounces Rice Chex®
14 ounces Corn Chex®
1½ pounds mixed nuts
1 pound pretzels
1 10½-ounce bag SunChips®, original
1 cup oil
1 cup butter, melted
2½ tablespoons Worcestershire sauce
1 tablespoon garlic salt
1 tablespoon seasoned salt

Mix all ingredients together in a large pan, and bake at 250°F for 2 hours, stirring every 15 minutes. Serve warm or at room temperature.

Buffalo-Style Sliders

Jennifer and Ryan Palmer
Serves 10 sliders

2 pounds lean ground beef
Blue cheese crumbles
Frank's® RedHot® Buffalo Wings Sauce
King's® Hawaiian Sweet Rolls
Salt and pepper

Using approximately 3 ounces of ground beef, form patties and add salt and pepper to season. On a grill, cook the beef to desired temperature. Medium is best.

Place patties in sweet rolls and top each patty with sauce and blue cheese crumbles.

Pesto Parmesan Cheese Ball

Amber and Nick Watney
Serves 16

2 8-ounce packages Philadelphia® Cream Cheese
1 3.5-ounce container Buitoni® Pesto with Basil Sauce
1 3-ounce container Buitoni® Freshly Shredded Parmesan Cheese
1 2.25-ounce package of almonds, shaved
Original or Wheat Entertainer® Crackers

In a bowl, combine cream cheese, pesto, and Parmesan. Mix well. Form two balls using all of the mixture.

Spread almonds onto a plate and roll each cheese ball in them until evenly coated. Serve with crackers.

PROSCIUTTO AND MOZZARELLA CROSTINI

Katie and Johnson Wagner
Serves 4-6

5 or 6 slices prosciutto, paper thin

1 ball fresh mozzarella cheese, sliced about ¼-inch thick

4 tablespoons butter, melted

Half a loaf of ciabatta bread, sliced

Preheat oven to 400°F. Place the bread slices in one layer on a cookie sheet. Bake for 2–3 minutes, being very careful not to burn them.

While the bread is toasting, pull the prosciutto apart to just smaller than the bread slices. When slightly brown, take the slices out and flip them. Using a spoon, drizzle with melted butter and return them to the oven for another 2–3 minutes.

Remove bread and top with a slice of cheese. Place back in the oven for 1–2 minutes until cheese melts slightly. Remove bread and top with prosciutto.

Put the crostini back in the oven for about 30 seconds to heat prosciutto, if desired.

CORN CHOWDER

Rachel and Michael Thompson
Serves 4-6

2 large baking potatoes, peeled and diced
2 cups boiling salted water
(or enough to cover potatoes)
1 bay leaf
¼ teaspoon sage
½ teaspoon cumin
3 tablespoons butter
1 onion, chopped
3 tablespoons flour
1¼ cups half & half
1 can whole kernel corn
1 can creamed corn
¼ cup chopped parsley
3 tablespoons chives or green onions, chopped
Salt and pepper, to taste
1½ cups cheddar cheese, shredded
French or sourdough bread loaf

Mix potatoes, water, bay leaf, sage, and cumin in a large pot and bring to a boil. Boil gently until potatoes are tender, about 10 minutes.

In a pan, melt butter and sauté onion until translucent. Add flour. Mix until flour is completely dissolved and there are no clumps. Add half & half and mix well.

Add the onion mixture to the potato mixture in the large pot. Add the whole corn, creamed corn, parsley, chives or green onions, salt and pepper. Simmer for 10 minutes, but be sure not to boil. Stir occasionally.

Add cheddar cheese and melt completely. Serve with French or sourdough bread for dipping and top with extra cheddar cheese if desired.

GREEK AVGOLEMONO CHICKEN SOUP

Dina and Steve Flesch
Serves 6-8

1 whole chicken
2 cups of white rice
6–7 eggs
1½–2 cups of lemon juice, bottled or fresh squeezed

Put the chicken in a large pot and cover it completely with water. Bring to a low simmer. When chicken is cooked through, remove, and let it cool. Remove chicken from bones, dice or shred it as desired then set aside.

Strain the reserve broth. Put the strained broth back on the stove, bring it to a boil, and add rice. Lower the heat (don't continue to boil). Stir and cook rice *al dente*.

While the rice is cooking, whisk the eggs continuously until frothy, add lemon juice to egg mixture and whisk very well again. Add egg and lemon juice mixture to broth when rice is *al dente*. Let soup come to a boil, stirring for a minute, then remove from heat. Pour a bowl and add the desired amount of chicken to each individual bowl. Refrigerate the soup and chicken separately.

VARIATION: ADD MORE LEMON/EGG MIXTURE, DEPENDING ON HOW STRONG OF A FLAVOR IS DESIRED. FOR A THICKER SOUP, ADD MORE RICE.

Lasagna Soup

Erin and Jimmy Walker
Serves 8

4 pounds ground beef
1 small yellow onion, diced
1 garlic clove, minced
1 teaspoon garlic powder
8 14½-ounce cans beef broth
4 14½-ounce cans diced tomatoes
1 tablespoon dried Italian seasoning
5 cups uncooked Mafalda pasta or corkscrew pasta
1 cup grated Parmesan cheese, divided

Season beef with garlic powder and brown the beef, along with the onion and garlic. Drain and then add the broth, tomatoes, and Italian seasoning. Bring to a boil.

Stir in pasta and cook over medium heat for about 10 minutes or until pasta is done. Stir in half the Parmesan cheese. Let guests sprinkle remaining cheese on top of the soup, if they desire.

This recipe can be made a day ahead of time, but do not add the pasta until right before serving.

VARIATION: FOR A SLIGHTLY SPICIER RECIPE, TRY ADDING 1 TABLESPOON OF TONY CHACHERE'S® ORIGINAL CREOLE SEASONING.

Taco Soup

Michelle and Chris Riley
Serves 4-6

1 pound ground beef
1 medium onion, diced
1 can of kernel corn, undrained
1 can Ro*Tel® Diced Tomatoes & Green Chilies
1 can pinto beans
1 can tomato soup
1 can chicken broth
1 packet taco seasoning

In a pan, sauté ground beef and onion. Once browned, drain ground beef and onion mixture in a fine mesh strainer and set aside.

In a large pot, combine all other ingredients. Add ground beef mixture and simmer for 30 minutes. Top with cheese and green onions, if desired.

BUTTERNUT SQUASH AND PUMPKIN BISQUE

Chastity and David Mathis

Serves 8-10

2 tablespoons butter, unsalted

1 onion, diced

1 clove of garlic, minced

3 pounds butternut squash — peeled, seeded, and cut into 1½-inch chunks

1 15-ounce can pumpkin purée

5 cups low sodium chicken broth

2 sprigs thyme

1 cup half & half

Nutmeg — freshly grated, if desired

Crème fraîche

Salt and pepper

Melt butter in large Dutch oven, over medium heat. Add the onions and cook until softened. Add garlic and sauté until fragrant. Stir in squash, broth, thyme, and nutmeg.

Bring to a simmer and cook until squash is tender. Remove thyme sprigs. Purée soup with a hand mixer or blender until smooth (in batches, if necessary).

Stir in pumpkin and half & half. Bring to a simmer and remove from heat. Season with salt and pepper, to taste. Garnish with nutmeg and *crème fraîche*.

SEAFOOD BISQUE

Karyn and Boo Weekley
Serves 8

2 cans cream of mushroom soup

2 cans cream of potato soup

2 cans whole kernel corn (do not drain)

1 stick salted butter

1 8-ounce block cream cheese, melted
(do not use low-fat)

1 quart half & half (do not use low fat)

5 whole green onions, chopped

2 tablespoons Cajun seasoning

1 pound fresh medium-sized shrimp – peeled,
deveined, and cut into small pieces.

1 pound fresh lump crabmeat, picked free of shells.

In a large Crock-Pot®, set on medium-high, add cream of mushroom soup, cream of potato soup, whole kernel corn, melted cream cheese, and Cajun seasoning. Whisk together, adding the half & half slowly. Cover and let it cook until seafood is ready to be added.

In a large non-stick skillet, add butter and onions. Sauté onions until wilted. Add shrimp and crabmeat to the butter and onions. Cook on medium heat, turning occasionally until shrimp turns light pink. It is very important to not over-cook the shrimp in the skillet because it still has an hour of cooking left.

After the seafood is cooked, add it to the soup mixture. Mix well, cover, and simmer on low heat for an hour. Stirring occasionally will help the bisque not stick. Serve with crackers or toasted French bread.

BEET SOUP

Jenny and Tom Gillis
Serves 4-6

3–5 red beets, peeled and cut into cubes

1 Hannah sweet potato or Japanese sweet potato, peeled and cut into cubes

1 box vegetable broth

1 cup carrots, diced

2 sprigs thyme

1 tablespoon coconut oil
(should have no odor of coconut and be able to be cooked at high heat)

½ yellow onion, diced

1½ teaspoons garlic

Salt and pepper

Sauté onion and garlic in coconut oil until onions are translucent. Add all other ingredients. Bring to a boil and simmer for 1 hour. Purée to desired texture.

VARIATION: FOR A SPECIAL TREAT, ADD DICED CHICKEN AND A LITTLE COCONUT MILK.

MEATBALL SOUP

Heather and Jeff Gove
Serves 8-10

3 tablespoons olive oil

½ cup yellow onion, chopped

¼ cup celery, chopped

2 cloves garlic, chopped

1 14-ounce can crushed tomatoes or 2 cans Italian tomatoes

1 4-ounce can tomato paste

2–3 14-ounce cans reduced-sodium beef broth

1 teaspoon Italian seasoning

1 bag Armour® meatballs (32-count)

3 ½ cups baby spinach leaves

2 tablespoons chopped fresh basil leaves or dried basil

½ cup small pasta shapes

In a soup pot, add olive oil and bring to medium/high heat. Add the onion and celery, stirring with a wooden spoon until all of the vegetables are soft, about 3–4 minutes. Add the garlic and cook for 1 minute. Add the tomatoes (including the juice), beef broth, tomato paste and Italian seasoning. Stir until all is combined. Bring to a low boil then simmer for 15 minutes.

Slowly add the meatballs to the simmering broth. Gently stir them so they do not break apart. Simmer for another 20 minutes until the meatballs are cooked through.

Add the pasta and spinach to the soup, stir well, and cook for an additional 15 minutes or until the pasta is *al dente*. Stir in basil and serve. Garnish with Parmesan cheese, if desired.

Lentil Soup

Dory and Brad Faxon
Serves 6-8

1 500 gram bag of red or green lentils
2 tablespoons olive oil
1 yellow onion, diced
2 celery stalks, diced
3 large carrots, diced
1 sweet potato, diced
1–2 boxes of broth, vegetable or chicken
½ teaspoon salt
½ teaspoon celery salt
1 teaspoon garlic powder
1 cup baby spinach
Crushed red pepper and Parmesan cheese, if desired

In a soup pan, sauté olive oil, onions, celery, and carrots until tender. Add lentils, broth, and sweet potatoes and bring to a boil. If liquid boils off, add more.

After 30 minutes, add salt, celery salt and garlic powder. Continue to simmer. When vegetables are tender, add baby spinach then serve. Add crushed red pepper and Parmesan cheese, if desired.

Homemade Tomato Soup

Meagan and Martin Laird
Serves 6-8

2 sticks celery, chopped
2 carrots, peeled and chopped
1 large yellow onion, chopped
3 slices of bacon – cut up into pieces
2 tablespoons butter
1 tablespoon flour*
3 pounds tomatoes, quartered
4 cups vegetable stock (use stock cubes, not boxes)

Sauté celery, carrots, onion, and bacon in butter for 5 minutes. Sprinkle in flour and stir. Add the tomatoes and the stock. Cook gently for 30 minutes.

Purée soup in blender. Add salt and pepper to taste, if desired. Garnish with fresh basil and serve.

VARIATION: USE GLUTEN-FREE FLOUR TO MAKE SOUP GLUTEN-FREE FRIENDLY.

TURKEY CHILI WITH KALE

Amanda and Justin Leonard

Serves 6-8

1 tablespoon extra virgin olive oil

1 yellow onion, finely chopped

3 garlic cloves, minced

1½ pounds ground turkey or chicken

1 teaspoon dried oregano

2 tablespoons chili powder

1 teaspoon ground cumin

¼ teaspoon ground cinnamon

½ teaspoon cayenne pepper

1 teaspoon salt

2½ cups low-sodium fat-free chicken broth

1 cup dark beer

2 tablespoons tomato paste

1 can (15-ounce) kidney beans, drained

1 can (15-ounce) black beans, drained

1 can (16-ounce) diced tomatoes with mild green chiles

1 cup colored bell pepper, seeded and sliced

1 small zucchini or yellow summer squash, sliced into half-rounds

1 cup kale, steamed and chopped or torn into bite-sized pieces

1 carrot, cut into small pieces

½ cup chopped fresh cilantro

1–2 tablespoons fresh lime juice, optional

In a 4–6 quart sauté pan, heat the oil over medium heat. Add the onion and garlic and sauté until translucent (about 5 minutes). Add the turkey and cook until browned, for 5–6 minutes.

Add the oregano, chili powder, cumin, cinnamon, cayenne pepper, and salt and sauté for 2 minutes. Pour in the broth and beer. Stir in the tomato paste. Add the kidney beans, black beans, tomatoes, bell peppers, zucchini or squash, kale, and carrot.

Bring to simmer, reduce heat to low, cover, and cook 30 minutes, stirring occasionally. Add the cilantro and lime juice, if using.

VARIATIONS: IF USING A SLOW COOKER, PRE-BROWN AND DRAIN THE MEAT, ADD ALL INGREDIENTS TO THE SLOW COOKER, AND COOK ABOUT 4 HOURS ON HIGH OR 8 HOURS ON LOW. FOR SPICIER CHILI, SIMPLY ADD MORE CHILI PEPPER OR CAYENNE PEPPER.

TLC Cheese Soup

Shauna and Troy Matteson
Serves 8-10

1 medium sweet onion, chopped
1 cup long grain rice
1 red bell pepper, chopped
1 large potato, chopped
2 tablespoons butter
1 cup milk
1½ boxes chicken broth
⅓ block of 16-ounce Velveeta® cheese
1 large handful of chopped cilantro
1 package boneless chicken breasts
Salt and pepper for seasoning
Olive oil
½ package shredded carrots (5 ounces)

Cook the chicken in a frying pan with 2 tablespoons olive oil. Cook until chicken is done, and put it aside to use in the soup at a later time. Use a large stock pot and add chicken broth. Bring to a boil and add in a chopped medium onion. Add rice, potato, red bell pepper, milk, cilantro, and butter.

While the mixture is coming to a boil, start chopping or shredding pre-cooked chicken then add the cooked chicken to the soup. Throw in the shredded carrots and mix in the cilantro last.

Cube the Velveeta cheese and add slowly, stirring after every couple of cubes. Bring all of this mixture to a boil then reduce the heat to medium low for about an hour. Stir every once in a while and add as much salt and pepper as desired.

Velvet Red Pepper Soup

Selena and Frank Nobilo
Serves 6

4 red bell peppers, sliced
3 carrots, peeled and sliced
3 shallots, peeled and sliced
2 cloves garlic, sliced
1 pear, peeled and quartered, or can of quartered pears in its own juice
1 tablespoon olive oil
4 teaspoons butter
2 cups chicken stock
½ tablespoon old crushed dried red pepper flakes
Pinch of cayenne pepper
Kosher salt to taste
1–1½ cups half & half
Fresh Italian parsley

Heat the olive oil and butter in a saucepan, and sauté the sliced vegetables and pears over medium/low heat until tender, approximately 8–10 minutes. Add the chicken stock, red pepper flakes, cayenne pepper, and salt. Bring to a boil and simmer, covered, for 25–30 minutes. Purée the soup in a food processor a little at a time (or use immersion blender, which is much easier and less messy). If making the soup ahead of time, place it in the refrigerator overnight or freeze it.

When ready to serve, add 1–1½ cups of half & half (depending on the thickness desired) and reheat on low heat. Add the Italian parsley and serve.

Salads

BROCCOLI NUT SALAD

Holly and Michael Letzig
Serves 8-10

2 broccoli heads
(florets only, cut into small bites)
1 cup salted peanuts
1 cup plump raisins or dried cranberries
10–12 slices cooked and crumbled bacon
2 green onions, chopped
2 tablespoons sugar
2 tablespoons white vinegar
1 cup mayonnaise

Mix the broccoli, peanuts, raisins/cranberries, bacon, and green onions together in a large bowl. In a separate smaller bowl, mix the sugar, white vinegar, and mayonnaise together. Keep both mixtures refrigerated after preparation.

Just before serving, stir the mayonnaise ingredients into the broccoli mix until well incorporated. Serve immediately.

HEAVENLY HASH

Kristina and Michael Putnam
Serves 8-10

1 package of mini marshmallows
1 16-ounce container sour cream
2 large cans pineapple chunks
5 small cans mandarin oranges

Empty the package of marshmallows into a large mixing bowl. Add sour cream and mix until all marshmallows are evenly coated. Drain pineapple and mix into marshmallows. Drain oranges then carefully stir into the marshmallows. Cover, and refrigerate overnight.

Sautéed Shrimp Salad

Cynthia and Michael Allen
Serves 6–8

1 head Boston Bibb lettuce, cleaned

1 pound medium shrimp, (uncooked and peeled)

Old Bay® seasoning

Extra virgin olive oil

Salt

2 tablespoons butter

1 tablespoon olive oil

1 ripe avocado, sliced into chunks

1 can artichoke hearts (not in oil), drained and chopped

Romano-Parmesan shredded cheese

Spread clean lettuce on platter, drizzle with extra virgin olive oil, and sprinkle with salt. Toss together, then top with avocado and artichokes.

Lay raw shrimp on a plate and sprinkle them with Old Bay" seasoning. Melt butter and 1 tablespoon olive oil in the skillet. Stir-fry shrimp until done. Pour shrimp over salad and sprinkle with cheese.

Laura's Perfect Salad

Heather and Ben Crane
Serves 4-6

1–2 tablespoons rice vinegar

4–5 tablespoons walnut oil

1 shallot, finely diced

1 clove garlic, pressed

1 teaspoon honey

1 dab horseradish

1 teaspoon Dijon mustard

Salt and pepper, to taste

Lettuce — red leaf or Boston head

¼–½ avocado per person

⅛ cup pecans per person

1 tablespoon dried blueberries per person

Mix together salad dressing ingredients. Use a small food processor and add the oil last, letting it drip through the little holes in the top. This helps it stay "emulsified." Add avocados, pecans, and dried blueberries to lettuce. Works best to wet hands and mix the lettuce by hand with dressing.

Variation: Add sliced, marinated chicken on top to make this a main entrée. Marinate chicken in *Fischer & Wieser's*® Roasted Blackberry Chipotle Sauce as it adds a nice flavor combination with the salad.

Lunde Salad

Dana and Bill Lunde
Serves 4

2–3 cups baby spring mix
¼ cup Gorgonzola cheese, crumbled
¼ cup dried cranberries
¼ cup roasted almonds, slices
3–4 tablespoons creamy balsamic vinaigrette dressing
½ cup red onion, sliced

Rinse spring mix and shake off excess water. Add all ingredients to a large salad bowl. Mix thoroughly, and serve.

Buffalo Chicken Salad

January and John Mallinger
Serves 4

4 boneless, skinless chicken breasts
1 head iceberg lettuce
1 tomato, chopped
1 red onion, sliced
½ cup carrots, shredded
¼ cup ranch dressing
2 tablespoons buffalo sauce
(add more for extra spice)
2 tablespoons olive oil
Salt and pepper, to taste

Rub chicken breasts with olive oil, then sprinkle with salt and pepper, to taste. Grill chicken breasts over medium-high heat until cooked through, approximately 6 minutes per side. Cut each breast into thin slices.

Chop iceberg lettuce and toss with tomato, carrot, ranch dressing, and buffalo sauce. Divide evenly into 4 servings and top each with red onion and a sliced chicken breast.

ORIENTAL NOODLE AND COLESLAW SALAD

Maria and Raymond Floyd

Serves 6-8

2 16-ounce packages coleslaw

4 packages Ramen noodles, oriental flavor, including seasoning

1½ cups almonds, slivered

2 5.5-ounce bags sunflower seeds

6 tablespoons sesame seeds

1 cup oil

½ cup rice vinegar

4–6 tablespoons sugar

Salt and pepper

For dressing, combine oil, rice vinegar, sugar, Ramen seasoning (small packet inside the Ramen package), and salt and pepper. Whisk thoroughly and set aside.

Break up noodles while still in the package and pour into a bowl. Toast almonds, sunflower and sesame seeds, and add to noodles. Toss together coleslaw and dressing. Let set for about 45 minutes to let the noodles soak up the dressing.

QUINOA SALAD

Juli and Geoff Ogilvy

Serves 6-8

1 cup quinoa, any color

1¾ cups cold water or vegetable broth

1 small red onion, diced

8 ounces feta cheese

1 can lentils, drained and rinsed

1 cup dried cranberries

1 cup olive oil

Juice of 2–3 lemons

1 teaspoon sherry vinegar

Salt and pepper

Cholula® or favorite hot sauce

Fresh chives

SALAD:

Rinse quinoa thoroughly in a sieve and drain well. Place quinoa in saucepan and cover with cold water or broth. Bring to a boil and reduce heat to low, simmer until all liquid is absorbed (about 10–12 minutes). Combine the quinoa, onion, lentils, feta, and cranberries.

FOR THE DRESSING:

Combine all ingredients and use a hand-held immersion blender. If an immersion blender is unavailable, cut up the chives first, then add all ingredients in a jar and shake vigorously.

If serving cold, once quinoa is cooked, place on a baking tray and place in refrigerator until cool, about 30 minutes. Once quinoa has cooled, combine quinoa, onion, lentils, feta, and cranberries.

WARM GOAT CHEESE SALAD

Julie and Tim Petrovic

Serves 4

2½ cups spinach leaves

2½ cups romaine lettuce

1½ cups dried tomatoes

1 cup crushed cranberries

1 cup grape or cherry tomatoes

1 cup tortilla strips
(can be found in salad section at store)

8 ounces goat cheese

Favorite salad dressing – red wine or strawberry vinaigrette tastes great with this salad.

Preheat oven to 350°F. Line a baking sheet with tin foil. With a spoon, scoop out some of the goat cheese and roll it in palms to form a ball about 1-inch in size. Roll goat cheese in crushed pecans and place on baking sheet. Repeat this process until 16–20 balls are formed. Bake in oven for 5–7 minutes.

While the goat cheese is baking, wash and cut salad leaves. Divide among 4 plates. Divide cranberries and tomatoes between plates. Just before removing goat cheese from oven, drizzle salad with dressing. With a spatula, place 4–5 goat cheese balls on each salad. Cheese will be hot and gooey. Top with tortilla strips.

BEAN SALAD

Kit and Arnold Palmer
Serves 6

1 cup sugar

7 ounces vinegar

½ cup salad oil*

½ teaspoon salt

½ teaspoon pepper

3–4 16-ounce cans green beans (drained)

1 5-ounce can sliced water chestnuts

1 red onion, sliced

1 4-ounce package crumbled blue cheese

Combine the sugar, vinegar, oil, salt, and pepper in a saucepan. Bring to a boil. Pour over the beans, water chestnuts and onion. Mix in the blue cheese crumbles. Chill.

*Salad oil is another term for a light tasting vegetable oil.

Breads and Muffins

Blueberry Oatmeal Muffins

Jennifer and Garrett Willis

Makes 12 muffins

2¼ cups plus 2 teaspoons all-purpose flour
¾ cups rolled oats
1 tablespoon baking powder
¼ teaspoon sea salt or kosher salt
¾ teaspoon cinnamon
¼ teaspoon nutmeg
1 cup buttermilk
2 large eggs, lightly beaten
1 cup sugar
6 tablespoons olive oil
1½ cups blueberries
1 tablespoon granulated sugar

Preheat oven to 375°F. Line a 12-muffin tin with paper liners.

Combine 2¼ cups of flour, rolled oats, baking powder, salt, cinnamon, and nutmeg into a large bowl. Whisk to blend thoroughly. In a medium bowl, combine buttermilk, eggs, sugar, and oil. Whisk until combined. Pour liquid mixture into bowl with dry ingredients. Whisk until just incorporated (do not over-mix). Toss in blueberries with remaining 2 teaspoons of flour then fold into batter.

Spoon equal amounts into lined muffin cups. Sprinkle with sugar and bake for 25–30 minutes, until a wooden toothpick inserted into center of muffins comes out clean.

Barbeque Bread

Diane and Frank Lickliter II

Serves 4–6

½ cup salted butter
¼ cup yellow mustard
1-inch squares of Swiss cheese
1 cup scallions, diced
Dash of Worcestershire sauce
2 baguettes of French or sourdough bread

Preheat the oven to 400°F. Combine butter, mustard, scallions, and Worcestershire sauce in bowl. Slice bread, but not all the way through. Between each slice, place the mixture and a square of Swiss cheese. Wrap bread in foil.

Bake at 400°F for 25 minutes. Slice top of foil and serve hot.

SOURDOUGH ROLLS

Amanda and Jonathan Byrd
Makes 1 dozen or more rolls

½ cup sour cream
1 stick of butter – melted (may use a little less)
1 cup self-rising flour

Combine butter and sour cream then add the flour. In a small muffin pan, scoop in mixture (not the traditional size muffin pan).

Bake at 425°F for 15 minutes or 350°F for 25 minutes. Take out sooner, if they begin to brown.

BEER CHEESE BREAD

Amy and Chris DiMarco
Serves 6-8

1 loaf French bread
1 pound cream cheese
1 pound Velveeta® cheese
½ cup beer
Garlic salt to taste

Mix all ingredients, except the French bread, in a blender until soft and creamy. Then dig out the middle of the French bread and break into little pieces.

Fill in the French bread with the cheese mixture and surround the loaf with the remaining pieces or place them on top, if desired.

Toast in the oven at 400°F for 8–10 minutes. Let set a few minutes before cutting and serving.

MORNING GLORY MUFFINS

Vivienne and Gary Player
Makes 12 muffins

1½ cups brown sugar
2¼ cups flour
1 tablespoon ground cinnamon
2 tablespoons baking powder
½ teaspoon salt
½ cup shredded coconut
½ cup raisins
2 cups grated carrots
1 apple, shredded
8 ounces crushed pineapple
½ cup pecan nuts
3 eggs
1 cup vegetable oil
1 teaspoon vanilla essence

Preheat oven to 350°F. In a bowl, combine the fruit, carrots, and nuts. In a separate bowl, whisk eggs with oil and vanilla. Pour this mixture into the bowl with the remaining dry ingredients. Blend well. Spoon mixture into cupcake tins lined with muffin paper. Fill each cup to the brim.

Bake for 35 minutes until toothpick comes out clean. Enjoy with cream cheese and honey.

WARM PECAN ROLLS

Amy and Mark Wilson
Makes 32 rolls

5 tablespoons butter

1 cup brown sugar

½ cup pecans, chopped

2 8-ounce containers
Pillsbury® Crescent Rolls

4 tablespoons butter, softened

¼ cup sugar

2 teaspoons cinnamon

¼ cup water

Preheat oven to 375°F. In a 9x13-inch pan, melt the 5 tablespoons of butter in the heated oven. Stir brown sugar, water, and pecans into the melted butter.

Separate crescent rolls into 4 rectangles, seal perforations, and spread the remaining 4 tablespoons of softened butter over dough. In a separate dish, combine sugar and cinnamon. Sprinkle over dough.

Start on short side of rectangle and roll up in each piece. Cut each roll into 4 equal slices to make 32 rolled pieces in all. Take the pan with brown sugar, water, pecans, and butter, and place the rolls cut side down on top of mixture.

Bake 20–25 minutes. To remove rolls, invert pan on to serving platter and drizzle remaining juice over the top. Serve immediately.

Breakfast Ideas

Entrées

Side Dishes

JASON'S FAMOUS FRENCH TOAST

Megan and Jason Gore
Serves 4–6

1 loaf of King's Hawaiian Bread™ sliced into 1-inch-thick slices

6 large eggs, beaten

¼ cup milk

Dash of vanilla extract

Dash of cinnamon

Combine eggs, milk, cinnamon, and vanilla in a shallow bowl. Dredge each piece of Hawaiian bread in the egg mixture, making sure to cover both sides equally.

Spray a skillet with nonstick cooking spray and heat over medium heat. Cook each piece of French toast over medium heat, turning once, until each side is golden brown. Serve piping hot with powdered sugar and syrup.

STUFFED FRENCH TOAST

Susan Barrett, on behalf of her son, Kevin Stadler
Serves 6–8

Challah or brioche bread – one loaf unsliced; more if feeding a crowd

Mascarpone cheese – 4 to 8 ounces

Jam: any flavor will do
(raspberry red chile is highly recommended)

6 large eggs

½ teaspoon cinnamon

¼ cup all-purpose flour

½ cup half & half

8 ounces fresh raspberries

1 tablespoon vanilla

2 tablespoons butter

Preheat oven to 300°F. After purchasing the bread (or making it), let it sit for 2 days so it isn't too soft. Slice bread into 2-inch slices. Allow one slice per person. This is rich.

Turn the bread upside down and using a paring knife, cut a "pocket" into the slice for stuffing. Set aside.

Mix the mascarpone cheese and jam to desired taste. Fifty percent of each is a good ratio. Using a teaspoon, stuff the mixture into the bread. Usually 2 tablespoons is enough. DO NOT OVERSTUFF.

In a blender, mix the eggs, flour, vanilla, cinnamon, and half & half until mixed well. Pour into a shallow pan. Soak stuffed bread in the egg mixture until very soft. While this is soaking, heat frying pan and butter until hot, but not smoking. Watch the butter so it doesn't burn. Cook French toast until browned but not completely done, then finish in the oven. Usually 5 minutes is sufficient.

While the toast is puffing up to deliciousness in the oven, put remaining jam (without cheese) in a small saucepan and let melt to the consistency of syrup. Place French Toast on warm plate, pour syrup over the top and finish with fresh raspberries. Serve with bacon or sausage.

CHOCOLATE CHIP PANCAKES

Arlene and Ted Purdy
Serves 3–4 kids

2 cups Carbons® Pancake Mix
(or orginal Bisquick®)

1 cup milk

2 eggs

1 cup chocolate chips

Clover Farmstead Organic
European-Style Butter with Sea Salt
(to grease the griddle)

Heat griddle or skillet over medium-high heat or electric griddle to 375°F. Grease with the Clover butter (surface is ready when a few drops of water sprinkled on it dance and disappear).

In a bowl, combine pancake mix, milk, and eggs until blended. Pour slightly less than ¼ cup of batter onto hot griddle. Add chocolate chips on top (as many as desired). Cook until edges are dry. Turn; cook until golden.

BEN'S BUTTERMILK PANCAKES

Candace and Ben Curtis
Makes 12 pancakes

INSTANT PANCAKE MIX:

Combine the following ingredients in a
Ziploc™ bag:

6 cups all-purpose flour

1½ teaspoons baking soda

3 teaspoons baking powder

1 tablespoon kosher salt

2 tablespoons sugar

*This instant pancake mix will last up to 3 months.

TO MAKE PANCAKES:

2 eggs separated, using both whites and yolks

2 cups buttermilk

4 tablespoons melted butter

2 cups instant pancake mix (see above)

1 stick butter

2 cups fresh blueberries, if desired

Heat an electric griddle or frying pan to 350°F. Heat oven to 200°F. Whisk together the egg whites and the buttermilk in a small bowl. In another bowl, whisk the egg yolks with the melted butter.

Combine the buttermilk mixture with the egg yolk mixture in a large mixing bowl and whisk together until thoroughly combined. Pour the liquid ingredients on top of the pancake mix. Using a whisk, mix the batter just enough to bring it together. Don't try to work the lumps out.

Check to see that the griddle is hot by placing a few drops of water onto the griddle. The griddle is ready if the water dances across the surface. Lightly butter the griddle then wipe off thoroughly with a paper towel so that no butter is visible.

Gently ladle the pancake batter onto the griddle and sprinkle on the fruit if desired. When bubbles begin to set around the edges of the pancake and the griddle side of the cake is golden, gently flip the pancakes. Continue to cook 2–3 minutes or until the pancake is set. Warm extra pancakes in oven if needed.

SWEDISH PANCAKES

Erika and Fredrik Jacobson
Serves 4

3 eggs
2½ cups milk
1¼ cups flour
1 tablespoon sugar
½ teaspoon salt
2 tablespoons melted butter
½ teaspoon Swedish vanilla sugar

In a blender or by hand, combine all ingredients till smooth. Heat a 10-inch non-stick skillet over medium heat until very hot. Lightly butter the skillet and pour ½ cup of the batter into it. Swirl the pan with batter to expand a thin layer.

Cook until bubbles form and the pancake is golden brown on the bottom, about 1½ minutes. Flip pancake and continue to cook for at least one more minute. Remove from frying pan.

Top with strawberry jam or sugar and squeezed lemon. The kids love it when they are rolled, like crepes. Other toppings to include could be ice cream, whipped cream, or chocolate.

GRANDPA CHARLEY'S PANCAKE AND WAFFLE BATTER

Stacy and Charley Hoffman
Serves 4

2 eggs
⅓ cup vegetable oil
1¼ cup milk
¾ cup instant oatmeal or old fashioned oats
1 tablespoon doubling baking soda
1 tablespoon sugar
1 teaspoon baking soda
½ teaspoon salt

*Optional ingredients: Chocolate chips,
heavy whipping cream and powdered sugar

In a bowl, beat eggs with hand-held or electric mixer until light and frothy. Slowly add the oil. Then slowly add the milk and continue to mix. In a separate bowl, mix all dry ingredients, and then add to the bowl of wet ingredients.

For Pancakes:

Once desired amount of batter is poured onto skillet, add the chocolate chips by placing them on top of each pancake. Flip when ready.

For Waffles:

Pour batter directly into waffle iron.

For Whipped Cream:

Pour one container of whipping cream into a bowl and add ½ cup of powdered sugar. Beat with an electric mixer until thickened. Continue to add powdered sugar to desired sweetness.

Entrées

Sun-Dried Tomato Ravioli

Laura and Briny Baird

Serves 4

1 package boneless,
skinless chicken tenderloins

20-ounce package Buitoni®
Four Cheese Ravioli

2 teaspoons garlic, minced

2 teaspoons California Sun-Dry® Garlic
with Sun-Dried Tomatoes

½ jar California Sun-Dry® Sun-Dried Julienne
Cut Tomatoes with Herbs

Parmesan cheese (optional)

¾ bag fresh spinach or broccoli

Cook ravioli according to package. In a large sauté pan, heat 1 tablespoon of the oil from the julienne tomatoes jar. Add minced garlic and sun-dried tomato garlic. Slightly brown the garlic, then add chicken. Sauté chicken until no longer pink. Add sun-dried tomatoes, ravioli, and spinach.

Cover and cook on low until spinach is cooked. Sprinkle with parmesan cheese and serve.

Oven Fried Chicken

Erin and Tommy Gainey

Serves 4-6

4 to 6 chicken breasts

¼ cup shortening

¼ cup butter

½ cup flour (self-rising or plain)

1 teaspoon salt

1 tablespoon paprika

¼ teaspoon pepper

Heat oven to 425°F. In oven, melt shortening and butter in an oven-proof skillet. In a separate bowl, combine flour, salt, pepper, and paprika, and coat each chicken breast. Place chicken, breast side down, in melted shortening and butter.

Cook uncovered for 30 minutes then turn and cook for 30 minutes longer.

THAI CHICKEN

Tracy and Retief Goosen

Serves 4

4 large chicken breasts
(cut 3 diagonal slices on the top
of the breasts to open out the skin)

1 block creamed coconut

2–3 green chilies, chopped

1 tablespoon fresh ginger, chopped

6 garlic cloves, crushed

Box of coriander, chopped
(leave some leaves for garnish)

2 limes, zest off the skin and take out the
juices (save both)

1 teaspoon sugar

1 cup very hot water

Chop the creamed coconut into a bowl, add water, and melt until liquifed. For the sauce, add the chilies, ginger, garlic, coriander, lime juice, lime zest, and sugar, and bring to a slow simmer. Add chicken to this sauce and marinade for 2 hours or 2 days.

When ready to use, grill the chicken until cooked, turning over a couple of times. Baste occasionally with sauce and heat up any remaining sauce for dipping.

TRAVELING BOY'S BURRITOS

Amy Lepard Campbell and Chad Campbell

Serves 4-6

1 pound ground beef

1 package McCormick's™ taco seasoning

½ cup water

12-ounces shredded cheese

Flour tortillas

Jalapeño and onion optional

Cook ground beef until browned, slowly adding taco seasoning and water. Add jalapeños and onions, if desired, and simmer all for 30–45 minutes.

After liquid is gone in meat mixture, add a scoop to a tortilla along with a sprinkle of cheese. Roll up and place in pan. When all tortillas are gone, add remaining meat and cheese to top and bake in a 350°F oven until cheese has melted and tortillas are slightly brown.

CRAB CAKES, MARYLAND STYLE

Nancy and Bob Heintz
Serves 4–6

1 pound lump crabmeat

1 cup vegetable oil (for frying)

¼ cup plain bread crumbs

2 eggs

1 teaspoon dry mustard

2 tablespoons mayonnaise or
Kraft® Miracle Whip

2 tablespoons Dijon mustard

Combine crabmeat, bread crumbs, eggs, dry mustard, mayonnaise, and Dijon mustard in a large bowl, and blend with hands. Shape into patties.

Heat oil. Place patties into the oil and fry until golden brown, about 3–5 minutes per side. If a little sweet and tangy kick is preferred, serve with a prepared seafood mustard sauce.

PINEAPPLE CHICKEN

Amanda Caulder and Dustin Johnson
Serves 4

1 package chicken tenderloins (about 8)
½ cup orange juice
½ cup pineapple juice
1 container Lawry's® Hawaiian Marinade
8 pineapple rings (fresh or canned)

Place pineapple juice and orange juice into a large skillet on medium/high heat. Add chicken tenderloins. Cook until liquid is gone (about 10 minutes). Add Lawry's® marinade and let simmer for another 10 minutes. Place pineapple rings on top and cook until pineapple rings are hot.

CHICKEN AND BLACK BEAN ENCHILADAS

Brittany and Kevin Kisner
Serves 8-10

6–8 boneless chicken breasts
2 cans black beans, rinsed and drained
1 red bell pepper, diced
1 package taco seasoning
¼ teaspoon cumin
1 cup sour cream
1½ cup shredded Mexican cheese
½ cup picante sauce
¾ cup chicken broth
Ground red pepper, to taste
2 cans red enchilada sauce
1 package large flour tortillas

Boil chicken breasts until cooked thoroughly. Reserve broth to use with enchiladas. Chop chicken into bite-sized pieces.

In a mixing bowl, combine chicken, black beans, red pepper, taco seasoning, cumin, sour cream, 1 cup of cheese, chicken broth, and picante sauce. Add ground red pepper for a little spice. Fill tortillas with mixture, fold and lay them side-by-side (folded side down) in a lightly greased casserole dish. Top with enchilada sauce and the remainder of the shredded cheese.

Bake covered at 375°F for 30 minutes. Remove cover and bake at 350°F for about 20 minutes, until cheese is browned and entire casserole is bubbly.

Homemade Spaghetti Sauce with Turkey Meatballs

Sarah and William McGirt

Serves 6-8

MEATBALLS:

1 pound lean ground turkey

½ cup yellow onion, grated

1 garlic clove, minced

2 tablespoons tomato paste

1 egg

½ cup plain bread crumbs

¼ teaspoon salt

¼ teaspoon pepper

SAUCE:

2 28-ounce cans tomato sauce

1 12-ounce can tomato paste

2 tablespoons Worcestershire sauce

2 garlic cloves, minced

½ cup yellow onion, grated

½ tablespoon chili powder

½ tablespoon Italian seasoning

½ tablespoon oregano

½ cup Parmesan cheese

½ teaspoon salt

½ teaspoon pepper

Preheat oven to 350°F. In mixing bowl, combine turkey, onion, garlic, tomato paste, salt, pepper, egg, and bread crumbs. Use a melon ball maker or small spoon to form tiny meatballs. Drizzle olive oil on bottom of a glass baking dish. Add meatballs and bake for approximately 40 minutes. Meatballs will be thoroughly cooked and still moist.

While meatballs are baking, add all sauce ingredients into a large pot and heat on stove on medium. Once meatballs are done, add them to sauce and simmer. Can also choose to cook sauce in a Crock-Pot® for several hours on medium heat. Serve over favorite pasta.

GRILLED TENDERLOIN WITH STRAWBERRY JALAPEÑO WINE REDUCTION

Kristen Koldenhoven and D. J. Trahan

Serves 6-8

4 6-ounce tenderloin filets
(venison, elk or beef)

Salt and pepper

Olive oil

SAUCE:

¼ stick butter

2 fresh jalapeños, sliced thin
(for added spice, do not remove the seeds)

1 ounce balsamic vinegar

¼ cup red wine

3 tablespoons strawberry preserves

Preheat grill to high. Season tenderloins with salt, pepper, and olive oil. Grill filets to desired doneness.

Combine all sauce ingredients in a small sauce pan. Simmer over low to medium heat until bubbly and slightly thickened.

Top each filet with strawberry jalapeño sauce and serve.

CROCK-POT® CHICKEN LASAGNE FLORENTINE

Katie and Cameron Percy
Serves 6-8

1-pound cooked and diced chicken

10-ounce can condensed cream of chicken soup

8-ounces sour cream

1 cup milk

10-ounce package frozen chopped spinach
(thawed, drained and squeezed)

½ cup Parmesan cheese, grated

⅓ cup onion, chopped

1 cup mozzarella cheese

1 package pre-cooked lasagna noodles

Combine chicken, soup, sour cream, milk, spinach, Parmesan cheese, and onion in a bowl. Spread over a layer of lasagna noodles, then cover with mozzarella cheese. Continue this two more times or until all ingredients are used.

Cover with lid and cook on high for 60 minutes, then on low for 3–4 hours.

CHICKEN POT PIE

Michelle and Jeff Maggert
Serves 4-6

4 cooked chicken breasts or
one rotisserie chicken

2 cans cream of chicken soup

1 cup chicken broth

1 cup frozen peas and carrots, mixed

1¾ cups Bisquick®

1¾ cups skim milk

½ stick of butter, melted

Preheat oven to 350°F. Cut cooked chicken into bite-size pieces and spread into the bottom of a non-greased 9x12-inch glass baking dish. Pour the frozen peas and carrots over the chicken. Mix in both cans cream of chicken soup. Mix in the chicken broth and stir everything together. Use more or less of the chicken broth to get the preferred consistency.

In a separate bowl, whisk the Bisquick® and milk together. Pour the mixture over the chicken and vegetables. Top with the melted butter.

Bake in oven at 350°F for 40 minutes or until the top turns golden brown.

Roasted Salmon with Lemon-Basil Teriyaki

Kristy and Parker McLachlin
Serves 6-8

¼ cup sherry
¾ cup soy sauce
1 tablespoon fresh ginger, grated
3 cloves garlic, minced
2 tablespoons brown sugar
1 cup olive oil
¼ cup fresh-squeezed lemon juice
2 cups basil, chopped
2 teaspoons freshly-ground black pepper
1 2-pound salmon fillet
Lemon wedges and parsley for garnish

Combine the sherry, soy sauce, ginger, garlic, and brown sugar in a saucepan, and bring to a boil. Reduce heat to simmer and cook for 10 minutes. Let cool to room temperature. Stir in the olive oil, lemon juice, basil, and pepper.

On a rimmed baking sheet, spread a double layer of aluminum foil, allowing 3 inches of overhang on all sides. Place the fish on the foil and roll up the foil to form a border all around the fish so the marinade will not run onto the pan. Pour marinade over fish and cover with plastic. Refrigerate for 45 minutes. Set aside some marinade to baste the fish.

Preheat oven to 400°F. Place salmon on center rack. Baste the fish from time to time with the marinade until the salmon is opaque. When fish is semi-firm at the center of the thickest part (usually about 40 minutes or less), remove from oven and use a couple of spatulas to transfer it to a platter. Garnish with lemon wedges and parsley.

GRILLED CHICKEN BREASTS WITH FRESH STRAWBERRY SALSA

Jody and John Merrick
Serves 4

4 boneless, skinless chicken breasts
Salt and pepper
1 serrano chile, seeded and minced
1 garlic clove, minced
1 teaspoon chili powder
2 tablespoons raspberry vinegar
¼ cup olive oil

Fresh Stawberry Salsa:
2 cups fresh strawberries
2 tablespoons fresh chopped mint
2 tablespoons sugar
1 serrano chile, seeded and minced
⅓ cup red onion, minced
2 tablespoons raspberry vinegar
Salt and pepper, to taste
¼ cup sour cream

Pound the halved chicken breasts with a meat mallet until they are ½-inch thick. Season with chili powder, salt, and pepper, and place in a large Ziploc® bag or a small baking dish. Whisk together 1 serrano chile, garlic, and raspberry vinegar. Whisk in the olive oil until it is incorporated, then pour over the chicken. Squeeze all the air out of the bag and refrigerate for 2–3 hours.

While the chicken marinates, cut the strawberries and toss them with the sugar and the mint. Cover and let sit in the refrigerator for 1 hour, then add the serrano chile, red onion, and raspberry vinegar to the strawberry mixture. Let the salsa sit at room temperature for 20 minutes before serving.

Preheat outdoor grill on medium/high heat. Remove chicken breasts from bag and shake off excess marinade. Discard the remaining marinade. Cook the chicken until it is no longer pink in the middle – about 5 minutes on each side. Serve with the strawberry salsa on top and a little sour cream.

Braised Beef Brisket

Kelly and Charles Warren
Serves 12

2 14.5-ounce cans low-sodium beef broth
1 cup low-sodium soy sauce
¼ cup lemon juice
5 garlic cloves, chopped
1 tablespoon Hickory Liquid Smoke
1 7–9-pound beef brisket
(can use smaller, just decrease cooking time)

Stir together first 5 ingredients in a large roasting pan. Place brisket in pan, fat side up. Spoon liquid over brisket. Cover tightly with aluminum foil and let chill 24 hours, turning once.

Preheat oven to 300°F. Bake brisket, covered, for 4–4½ hours, or until fork-tender. Uncover and let stand 20 minutes. Pull apart with fork and serve with au jus.

Sweet and Sour Chicken

Beth and Blake Adams
Serves 4-6

1 package onion soup mix
1 16-ounce bottle Catalina dressing
1 18-ounce jar apricot pineapple preserves
4–6 boneless chicken breasts
(cut in cubes and uncooked)

Mix the first 3 ingredients together and pour over the chicken in a casserole dish. Cook at 350°F for approximately 45 minutes.

GRILLED HALIBUT TOPPED WITH BRUSCHETTA

Suzanne and Ricky Barnes
Serves 4

4 Roma tomatoes, diced
3 tablespoons fresh basil, chopped
1½ tablespoons Balsamic vinegar
4 tablespoons olive oil
2 cloves garlic, minced
1 teaspoon salt
1 teaspoon black pepper
4 6-ounce halibut fillets

Prepare grill. In a small bowl, mix together tomatoes, basil, balsamic vinegar, 3 tablespoons olive oil, garlic, 1 teaspoon salt, and 1 teaspoon pepper. Let marinate while preparing the fish. Rub halibut with olive oil. Season fish by sprinkling with salt and pepper on both sides.

Place fish on grill rack. Grill 3 minutes on each side or until fish flakes easily when tested with a fork. Top halibut with bruschetta mixture.

DOLMATHES
(STUFFED GRAPE LEAVES)

Traci and Skip Kendall
Serves 4

DOLMATHES:
2 jars grape leaves
2 pounds ground chuck
1 large onion, chopped
2 eggs
1 tablespoon tomato paste
1 cup rice
1 teaspoon cinnamon, ground
½ cup mint flakes
½ cup parsley (dry)
1 teaspoon salt and pepper

SAUCE:
4 eggs
¾ cup lemon juice

Mix all ingredients except grape leaves in a large bowl. Form small-size meatballs. Place meatballs in center of grape leaf and fold in sides and wrap. Stack evenly into cooking pot. Fill pot with water. Let it come to a slow boil and when it reaches a boil, lower the heat. Cook for 25 minutes.

For the sauce, beat eggs until frothy. Stir in lemon juice. Remove ¾ cup of juice from cooking pot. Add to lemon and egg juice. Pour entire sauce back into cooking pot. Bring back to boil for 1 minute. Remove from heat, then serve.

MEXICAN LASAGNA

Shanna and Jeff Klauk
Serves 6-8

2 tablespoons olive oil
1 15-ounce can black beans, drained
2 pounds ground turkey
1 cup frozen corn
2 packages taco seasoning
8 8-inch flour tortillas
1 small onion, diced
2½ cups Mexican cheese, shredded
1 can stewed tomatoes
2 scallions, finely chopped

Preheat oven to 425°F. Preheat a large skillet over medium-high heat, add 2 tablespoons of extra virgin olive oil. Add turkey and sprinkle with taco seasoning packets and onion. Brown meat until cooked. Add stewed tomatoes, black beans, and corn. Heat mixture through, 2–3 minutes.

Spray a 9 x 13-inch baking dish with non-stick cooking spray. Cut tortillas in half or quarters to make them easier to arrange. Build lasagna in layers of meat and beans, then tortillas, then cheese. Repeat with layers of meat, tortillas, cheese. Bake lasagna 12–15 minutes or until cheese is brown and bubbly. Top with scallions and serve.

CROCK-POT® GREEN CHILE CHICKEN

Richelle and Aaron Baddeley
Serves 6-8

6 uncooked chicken breasts
½ onion, minced
2–3 dashes black pepper
1 cup water
2 small jars Herdez® Salsa Verde
2 heaping scoops sour cream

Put all ingredients, except sour cream, in the Crock-Pot®. Cook on low for 4–6 hours or high for 3–4 hours. After fully cooked, shred chicken with a fork and stir in sour cream.

VARIATION: CAN USE A ROTISSERIE CHICKEN, WHICH REDUCES THE COOKING TIME TO ONLY 1 HOUR.

THAI DUCKLING

Lucy and Aron Price

Serves 4-6

3½ pounds duckling
2 tablespoons peanut oil
1 small pineapple
1 large onion, chopped
3 garlic cloves, finely chopped
2 teaspoons finely chopped ginger
½ teaspoon ground coriander
1½ tablespoons red Thai curry paste
1 teaspoon soft light brown sugar
2 cups coconut milk
Salt and pepper
Garnish with fresh, chopped cilantro

Using a large, sharp knife or poultry shears, cut the duck in half lengthwise, being sure to cut through the line of the breastbone. Wipe the duckling clean inside and out with paper towels. Sprinkle with salt and pepper, then prick the skin all over with a fork and brush lightly with olive oil.

Place the duck, cut side down, on a broiler pan, and broil under a preheated broiler for 25–30 minutes, turning occasionally, until golden brown. Carefully pour off the fat in the pan, as this may burn. Allow the duck to cool a bit, then cut each half into 2 portions. Peel and core the pineapple, then cut the flesh into small cubes.

Heat the remaining oil in a large pan and fry the onion and garlic 3–4 minutes until fragrant and translucent. Stir in the ginger, ground coriander, curry paste, brown sugar, and stir-fry for 1 minute. Stir in the coconut milk and bring to a boil. Add the duck and the pineapple. Reduce the heat and simmer for 5 minutes. Serve over boiled jasmine rice.

Beef and Sweet Potato Burgers

Ashley and Stuart Appleby
Serves 4

1 12-ounce garnet sweet potato, peeled, cut into ¾-inch pieces

1 garlic clove, crushed

15 ounces lean ground beef

2 teaspoons flat leaf parsley, chopped

1 zucchini, grated, with excess water squeezed out

1 egg, lightly beaten

2 tablespoons olive oil

4 mixed grain rolls

1 avocado, sliced

Steam or boil sweet potato until tender, then mash. Combine with garlic, beef, parsley, zucchini, and egg. Form into 4 patties. Heat oil in a large, non-stick frying pan. Cook patties over medium heat for 4–5 minutes on each side or until cooked. Keep warm.

Slice the rolls and toast them. Add the avocado and patty to each roll. Also have the option to add lettuce, onion, and tomato.

WHITE SAUCE CHICKEN

Lisa and Stewart Cink

Serves 6-8

BRINE:

1 cup apple juice

1 cup water

1 tablespoon salt

¼ tablespoon garlic powder

1 tablespoon honey

½ tablespoon dark brown sugar

½ tablespoon soy sauce

½ tablespoon fresh lemon juice

8 boneless, skinless chicken breasts

WHITE SAUCE:

2 cups mayonnaise

1 cup distilled white vinegar

½ cup apple juice

1 teaspoon prepared horseradish

2 teaspoons ground black pepper

2 teaspoons fresh lemon juice

1 teaspoon salt

½ teaspoon cayenne pepper

In a large bowl, combine all brine ingredients and mix well. Add chicken breasts, making sure they are completely covered. Cover the bowl and refrigerate for 1 hour.

Preheat an outdoor grill to 400°F. Place the chicken breasts on the grate directly over the heat and grill for 5–6 minutes on each side, or until golden brown and firm to the touch. The internal temperature should be 160°F.

Mix together ingredients for the white sauce. Pour white sauce generously over grilled chicken breasts before serving .

SOSATIES
(APRICOT SKEWERS)

Candice and Tim Clark
Serves 6-10

2 pounds chicken, lamb or beef, cubed

1 cup apricots, dried

3 yellow onions, sliced into rings

6 tablespoons apricot jam

2 tablespoons brown sugar

3 cloves garlic, crushed

2 bay leaves

2 tablespoons curry powder

2 tablespoons red wine vinegar

1 tablespoon salt

1 teaspoon pepper

6–10 grilling skewers, metal or bamboo
(If using bamboo, soak in water for a few minutes to avoid shavings coming off and burning)

Sauté the onions in vegetable oil, for 1–2 minutes. Remove and dry them off on paper towels. For the marinade, mix together the apricot jam, brown sugar, garlic, bay leaves, curry powder, vinegar, salt, and pepper in a bowl. Add the onion rings to this mixture. Place the cubed meat in the marinade, and place in the fridge for 4–24 hours.

Soak the apricots in water for about 15 minutes, until plump. While waiting for the apricots, prepare the skewers. Remove the meat from the marinade, and alternate a cube of meat, onion, and apricot. Grill at medium heat until cooked through, and baste with the additional marinade.

GARLIC CHICKEN

Ellie and Jason Day
Serves 4

2 tablespoons extra virgin olive oil
1 tablespoon butter
40 garlic cloves, peeled
4–6 chicken thighs with bone and skin
½ cup chicken broth
½ cup dry white wine
Salt and pepper

Rinse the chicken and pat dry with paper towel. Sprinkle with salt and pepper. Add olive oil and butter to a pan on medium/high heat. Place chicken skin-side-down in pan and let it cook for about 5 minutes. Check to see if it is browned then flip it over and cook for another 5 minutes.

After browned, place garlic cloves under the chicken thighs and sauté for about 10 minutes, until garlic is browned. Add the chicken broth and wine. Place the cover on the pan and turn the heat down to low. Let cook for about 30 minutes.

STROMBOLI

Tabitha and Jim Furyk
Serves 4-6

1 pound frozen bread dough
¼ cup Crisco®
1 pound bulk sausage
1 pound mozzarella, grated
½ pound provolone, sliced
½ pound cooked salami
½–¾ pound ham, chopped
¼ pound pepperoni, sliced
½ cup butter, melted
1 tablespoon parsley or oregano
Mustard

Remove dough from the freezer and grease with Crisco. Then cover with a thin, damp cloth and let the dough rise for a few hours. Grease the cookie sheet and use the extra grease on hands to roll out the dough. Lightly spread with mustard.

In the middle of the dough, sprinkle on meats and cheeses. Fold sides over to seal and pinch edges and ends so the meats and cheeses do not leak out while baking. Put folded side down on baking pan. Brush butter on top of loaf and then sprinkle with parsley or oregano.

Bake at 325°F for 15–20 minutes. Watch closely to be sure it does not over-cook.

CHICKEN PICCATA

Jan and Jay Haas

Serves 6-8

8 chicken cutlets, thinly sliced
4 tablespoons oil
2 cups flour
¼ cup white wine
2 teaspoons minced garlic
2 cups chicken broth
2 tablespoons lemon juice
2 tablespoons capers, drained
4 tablespoons butter
Parsley
Lemon slices
Salt and pepper

Salt and pepper both sides of the chicken, then dust with flour. Sauté cutlets in oil until slightly browned. Remove cutlets. Deglaze pan with wine, then add garlic. Cook garlic until brown, and then add broth, lemon juice, and capers.

Return cutlets to the pan and simmer a few minutes. Add butter and cook until melted. Add lemon slices, top with parsley. Serve over noodles.

Robin Love's Beef Stroganoff

Robin and Davis Love III
Serves 4

6 teaspoons olive oil

1 small yellow onion, chopped

1 pound mushrooms, caps only, sliced

2 tablespoons garlic, minced

1¼ pounds beef tenderloin,
cut into bite-size pieces

1 package McCormick®
Beef Stroganoff Sauce Mix

3 cans cream of mushroom soup

1 cup heavy whipping cream

2 tablespoons cooking sherry

2 tablespoons lemon juice

1 16-ounce bag egg noodles

In a large non-stick pot, cook first four ingredients until tender. Add meat and brown on all sides. Add sauce mix and stir until blended. Do not drain.

Stir in the next five ingredients. Add salt and pepper, to desired taste. If sauce seems too thick, add 1 cup of milk (whole or low-fat). Serve over noodles.

Lasagna

Angie and Arron Oberholser
Serves 8

1 box lasagna noodles

1 pound ground beef

1 pound mild Italian sausage

Medium yellow onion

Salt and pepper

1 teaspoon oregano

3 tablespoons parsley flakes

½ teaspoon mustard

2 tablespoons brown sugar

¼ teaspoon garlic salt or powder

2 15-ounce cans tomato sauce

8 ounces mozzarella cheese

8 ounces Swiss cheese

8 ounces Monterey Jack cheese

Parmesan cheese (to taste)

Preheat oven to 350°F. Cook 14 lasagna noodles as directed. In a pan, sauté hamburger, sausage, and onion until browned, then discard grease. Mix the cheeses together in separate bowl and set aside. Mix all other ingredients except cheeses into meat mixture and simmer for 15 minutes.

Spread a little bit of the meat sauce on the bottom of the pan to prevent the noodles from sticking. Line 9x13-inch pan with 4 noodles. Spread one third of the meat sauce over the noodles. Top generously with cheese mixture. Make another layer of noodles, meat sauce, and cheese. Make a third layer of noodles, meat sauce, and the rest of the cheese. Top with Parmesan cheese.

Bake 45 minutes at 350°F. Let sit for 10–15 minutes before cutting.

Lobster Ravioli with Tomato Cream Sauce

Amy and Phil Mickelson

Serves 4-6

1½ cups semolina flour

½ teaspoon salt

2 eggs

2 tablespoons water

2 tablespoons olive oil

2 lobsters (1¾ pounds each), cooked, removed from shell and tails split lengthwise

1–2 cups heavy whipping cream

8 ounces Taleggion cheese, cut into small chunks

4 ounces Emmental or Swiss cheese, cut into small chunks, rind removed

2 teaspoons tarragon, chopped

9.53-ounce jar Rustichella d'Abruzzo Organic Tomato Sauce

Combine semolina flour and salt. Add beaten eggs, water, and oil. Mix to make a stiff dough. Knead 10 minutes or until the dough is elastic. Wrap dough in plastic wrap and let rest for 20 minutes. Roll out using a pasta machine, starting out at the #1 setting and finishing on #5.

Bring a large pot of salted water to a boil. Take a 3-inch cutter and punch out the pasta rounds and place into the boiling water, cooking for approximately 2–3 minutes.

In a small pot, bring the cream to a simmer. Remove from heat. Add two cheeses, whisking to a smooth consistency. Sauce should be thick. Add the tarragon, and season with salt and pepper.

Bring the tomato sauce and cream to a simmer and purée with an immersion blender to make the sauce very smooth.

Plating: Place about 2 ounces of the tomato sauce on the plate then lay the pasta down the center. Spoon the cheese sauce almost out to the edge of the pasta sheet.

Lay the tail meat down with the knuckle tucked in the middle. Place the second sheet of pasta on top of the lobster then place one claw leaned up against the ravioli. Garnish with a tarragon sprig.

Norman Family Roast Chicken

Morgan-Leigh Norman
Serves 4

1 5–6 pound roasting chicken
2 lemons
1 small orange
1 tablespoon lavender buds
1 tablespoon fresh thyme
1 tablespoon fresh rosemary
1 tablespoon fresh oregano
1 tablespoon fresh basil
3 cloves garlic
1 tablespoon honey
1 small yellow onion, quartered
Extra virgin olive oil
2 tablespoons unsalted butter, softened
Sea salt and black pepper

Remove gizzards and clean cavity of chicken completely. Pat Dry. Using a mortar and pestle (can use food processor/blender), add the zest of 1 lemon, lavender buds (fine to leave out if unavailable), thyme, rosemary, oregano, basil, 1 garlic clove, sea salt, and pepper to taste. Grind until it has a paste-like consistency and all the oils have been released.

Add 2–4 teaspoons of olive oil and honey to mortar then grind again to incorporate all ingredients together. (If using food processor/blender, make sure to pulse gently– do not create smooth paste.)

In small bowl, add butter, 1–2 tablespoons olive oil, zest of 1 lemon, and salt and pepper, to taste. Stir to blend together. Using fingers gently work skin away from meat on breast of chicken and gently slather lemon-butter under skin, being careful not to break the skin.

Gently spread lemon-lavender paste all over chicken. If too dry, drizzle a little more olive oil over chicken. Season the chicken with salt and pepper.

Place onion, the other 2 garlic cloves, and 1 lemon, quartered, plus any remaining herbs into the cavity of chicken. Truss the legs of the chicken and place on rack in roasting pan.

Place in oven at 350°F and roast for approximately 1½ hours or until juice runs clear from thigh. Remove from oven and let sit for 10 minutes prior to serving. Pour the roasting juices through a sieve and set aside to serve as jus with chicken.

*Recommended wine pairing: Greg Norman Estates, Eden Valley Chardonnay

Coke Chicken

Nel-Mare and Louis Oosthuizen

Serves 6-8

1 can Coke®
4 tablespoons soy sauce
1 tablespoon vinegar
1 tablespoon brown sugar
Fresh rosemary
6–8 chicken breasts
Salt and pepper

Mix all the ingredients and marinate chicken for 30 minutes in the refrigerator. Place marinated chicken in a skillet over medium heat until it starts to boil.

Reduce heat and let it simmer, until the chicken is cooked and the marinate forms a sticky sweet sauce

Chicken with Roasted Tomatoes and Goat Cheese

Lori and D. A. Points

Serves 4

4 chicken breasts, thin, boneless, skinless
1 can diced fire roasted tomatoes with garlic
1 package creamy or crumbled goat cheese
Tony Chachere's® Original Creole Seasoning
1 cup basil leaves

Sprinkle chicken breasts with Tony Chachere's® Original Creole Seasoning (Use sparingly, as it is spicy). In large, oven-safe skillet, lightly brown chicken breasts over medium-high heat. Pour the can of roasted tomatoes over the chicken. Cover with the goat cheese and basil leaves.

Leave everything in the skillet and place in the oven at 350°F for 8–10 minutes.

CHICKEN NUGGETS

Carrie and Bo Van Pelt
Serves 4-6

¾ cup crushed French's® French Fried Onions
1 tablespoon flour
¼ teaspoon seasoned salt
1 8-ounce tube crescent rolls
1 cooked chicken breast
1 egg, beaten
Poppy seeds

Grease cookie sheet. In a shallow bowl, mix crushed onion rings, flour, and salt. Cut dough into 16 pieces. Cut up chicken into small cubes.

Dip chicken pieces in egg and coat with the dry mixture, Roll up into dough triangles like crescent roll. Brush with extra egg and sprinkle on poppy seeds. Dough does not have to be completely sealed around chicken.

Bake in oven at 350°F for 10–12 minutes or until golden brown.

BAKED SNAPPER

Mandy and Brandt Snedeker
Serves 4

Fresh snapper fillets
3 tomatoes, peeled and sliced thin
½ cup breadcrumbs
1 stick butter
½ cup white wine
2 tablespoons lime juice
½ cup Parmesan cheese
2 tablespoons paprika

Preheat oven to 500°F. Combine butter, white wine, and lime juice in a saucepan. Bring to a boil for 5 minutes.

While the sauce is boiling, place a layer of tomatoes into baking dish and sprinkle with breadcrumbs. Place snapper fillets on top. Pour sauce over fish and sprinkle with Parmesan cheese and paprika.

Bake for 10 minutes then broil for 3–5 minutes until the top is brown.

LEG OF LAMB

Kate and Justin Rose
Serves 6

4 pounds leg of lamb
10 tablespoons butter, softened
1 lemon, zest and juice
2 tablespoons fresh coriander, chopped
3 cloves garlic, crushed
3 cloves garlic, sliced
2 teaspoons cumin, ground
2 teaspoons Harissa® paste or spicy chili paste
2 teaspoons salt
1 teaspoon pepper

For the marinade, combine butter, lemon (zest and juice), coriander, crushed garlic, cumin, paste, salt, and pepper. Massage over the lamb, front and back.

Place the sliced garlic inside the leg of lamb. Place in the refrigerator for 24 hours so the ingredients can soak thoroughly.

Cook lamb at 350°F for an hour, then 300°F for the next hour. Leave to rest for 15–20 minutes before serving.

Bowtie Pasta with Grilled Chicken

Amy Sabbatini
Serves 4-6

4 chicken breasts
6 slices of bacon
1 onion, chopped
1 tablespoon garlic
1 14-ounce can tomato wedges
or diced tomatoes
¼ teaspoon crushed red pepper flakes
½ cup mushrooms, sliced
Salt and pepper
Parmesan cheese
3 teaspoons fresh parsley

Cook chicken breasts and chop into bite-size pieces. Cook pasta according to package.

In a skillet, cook bacon until crisp. Cut into ½-inch pieces and set aside. Sauté onions in bacon grease, then add mushrooms and garlic. Cook until tender. Next, add tomatoes and red pepper and continue cooking for approximately 10 minutes.

When pasta is cooked, drain and pour sauce over top. Toss with grated Parmesan cheese, salt and pepper. Add parsley, chopped chicken, and serve.

Curried Chicken

Rosalind and Charl Schwartzel
Serves 4-6

1½ –2 pounds whole chicken
1 cup ketchup
1 cup chutney
¼ cup Worcestershire sauce
1 tablespoon brown sugar
3½ tablespoons oil
¼ cup curry powder
¼ cup apricot jam

Mix all ingredients together. Pour ⅔ of the marinade over chicken.

Bake in the oven at 350°F for 1½–2 hours, or until chicken reaches internal temperature of 160°F. Use the remaining ⅓ of marinade to baste chicken throughout the cooking process.

DAVID'S PICKLED SHRIMP

Sonya and David Toms
Serves 10-12

5 pounds medium shrimp, peeled and deveined

3 medium red onions, sliced

1 cup bay leaves

1¼ cups vegetable oil

¾ cup apple cider vinegar

1½ teaspoons salt

2½ teaspoons celery seed

2½ teaspoons capers and juice

Dash of Tabasco sauce

¼ cup Lea & Perrins® (Worcestershire sauce)

1 tablespoon yellow mustard

Bring shrimp to a boil and strain. In a container, layer shrimp, onion, and bay leaves.

Mix together remaining ingredients in a saucepan. Bring to a boil then pour over the shrimp. Cover, refrigerate, and stir or toss occasionally. Make this dish at least the day before and serve in a large glass bowl with toothpicks.

VARIATIONS: CAN INCLUDE BUTTON MUSHROOMS, ARTICHOKE HEARTS, OR OTHER VEGETABLES, IF DESIRED.

Sarah's Pot Roast

Sarah and Curtis Strange
Serves 8-10

1 large Vidalia or sweet onion, chopped
1 small bag baby carrots
4–6 large potatoes, peeled and quartered
Salt and pepper
2 tablespoons paprika
1 tablespoon meat tenderizer
4 cups water
4–5 pounds chuck or sirloin roast, excess fat removed

Preheat oven to 350°F. In a large Dutch oven, add the roast and sprinkle with meat tenderizer, salt, and pepper. Cook uncovered for 1 hour.

After 1 hour, remove from oven. Add potatoes, onions, and carrots, paprika, water, and more salt and pepper. Cover with lid, return to oven, and cook at 325°F for 4 hours.

Remove from oven. Uncover and break meat apart to absorb juices. Let sit about 5 minutes while fixing the plates.

Lime Shrimp Lettuce Wraps

Paula Deen
Serves 6

3 tablespoons fresh lime juice
3 tablespoons olive oil, divided
2 tablespoons soy sauce, divided
2 teaspoons grated fresh ginger
1 clove garlic, minced
1 pound medium to large fresh shrimp, peeled, deveined, and chopped
½ red bell pepper, diced
2 green onions, diced
1 (8-ounce) can water chestnuts, drained and chopped
1 head iceberg lettuce, cored and halved
1 tablespoon chopped fresh parsley

In a medium bowl, combine the lime juice, 2 tablespoons oil, 1 tablespoon soy sauce, ginger, and garlic. Add the shrimp and let marinate in the refrigerator for 30 minutes.

In a medium skillet, heat the remaining oil over medium-high heat. Add the bell pepper, green onions, and water chestnuts, and cook, stirring constantly, for 3 minutes. Add the shrimp and marinade, and cook until the shrimp are pink, about 3 minutes. Stir in the remaining soy sauce.

Divide the lettuce into leaves. Spoon about one-quarter cup of the mixture down the center of 1 lettuce leaf. Fold the bottom edge and sides up and over the filling. Repeat with the remaining lettuce leaves and shrimp filling.

CHICKEN SPAGHETTI

Heather and John Rollins
Serves 8

1–1½ pounds boneless, skinless chicken breasts

1 10-ounce can cream of chicken soup

1 10-ounce can cream of mushroom soup

1 10-ounce can Rotel® tomatoes
(I like to use Mexican Rotel® when I want to add a little spice)

1 8-ounce block Velveeta® cheese, diced

1 16-ounce package spaghetti

1 cup shredded cheddar cheese

Salt and pepper, to taste

Preheat oven to 350°F. In a large stock pot, cook chicken in boiling water. Once the breasts are completely cooked, remove them from the water and shred them into small bite-size pieces. DO NOT DRAIN WATER FROM POT.

Cook pasta in large stock pot, drain and put back in the pot. Add chicken, cream of mushroom soup, cream of chicken soup, Rotel® tomatoes and Velveeta® cheese to the pasta.

Stir all ingredients together until the cheese is melted, then pour mixture into a 9x13-inch baking dish. Sprinkle shredded cheddar cheese over the pasta mixture.

Bake for 15–20 minutes, or until cheddar cheese is melted.

Senator Russell's Sweet Potatoes

Sara and Rich Beem
Serves 8-10

3 cups sweet potatoes
¼ –½ cup sugar
(depending on desired sweetness)
2 eggs
½ cup half & half
1 tablespoon vanilla
1 stick butter

TOPPING:
1 cup light brown sugar
½ cup flour
⅓ cup melted butter
1 cup chopped walnuts

Boil sweet potatoes with peels on, then peel away skin when tender. Mash and whip potatoes until smooth. Add sugar, eggs, half & half, vanilla, and butter. Mix well. Put in a buttered 9 x 13-inch dish.

For the topping, mix all ingredients together and sprinkle over top of the sweet potato mixture. Bake at 350°F for 20–30 minutes.

Extra Special Mashed Potatoes

Ryan and George McNeil
Serves 8

4 cups mashed potatoes
1 egg, beaten
8 ounces cream cheese
8 ounces sour cream
½ cup onion, chopped
Salt and pepper
¼ cup extra sharp cheddar cheese, shredded
⅓ cup cooked bacon, crumbled

Combine all ingredients in a bowl and bake at 350°F for 35 minutes. Remove from oven. Add cheese and bacon to the top and finish cooking for an additional 10 minutes.

SLOW-COOKED SWEET POTATOES

Colleen and Joe Ogilvie
Serves 8

8 sweet potatoes (8–10 ounces each)
2 tablespoons canola oil
2 tablespoons trans-fat-free margarine, melted
2 tablespoons honey
6 tablespoons water
2 teaspoons ground cinnamon
½ teaspoon ground nutmeg
Salt and pepper

Scrub the sweet potatoes and pierce with a fork on all sides. Combine oil, margarine, honey, water, cinnamon, and nutmeg in a bowl. Coat each sweet potato with mixture. Place in a large slow cooker. Season with salt and pepper, to taste.

Cover and cook on low for 4–6 hours or until tender when pierced with a fork. Serve hot, like a baked potato. Drizzle with honey before serving.

MACARONI AND CHEESE

Donna Rhodus, on behalf of her son, Josh Teater
Serves 8-10

1 1-pound box macaroni
(cooked per instructions on box)
1 pound Velveeta® cheese
2 cups sharp (or extra sharp) cheddar cheese
½ cup butter or margarine
2 cups milk
Salt and pepper

Preheat oven to 350°F. Place one layer of cooked macaroni in greased or sprayed casserole dish. Put layer of sliced Velveeta® cheese on top of macaroni. Put one cup of cheddar cheese over the Velveeta® cheese. Sprinkle salt, pepper, and ¼ cup of butter on top of mixture.

Repeat steps and add milk to the dish to almost cover the macaroni. Bake for 1 hour. Remove from oven and let sit for 15 minutes before serving.

GRANDMA SA-SA'S GREEN RICE

Tiffany and Chris Stroud
Serves 2-4

½ cup onions, chopped
½ cup celery, chopped
1 cup Minute® rice
1 10-ounce bag broccoli, chopped
½ cup Cheese Whiz®
1 can cream of mushroom soup
1 stick butter

Preheat oven to 350°F. In a small saucepan, sauté onions and celery in butter until onions are translucent. Next, combine remaining ingredients in baking pan and mix in onions and celery.

Bake for 30 minutes and let sit for 20 minutes before serving.

Plantain Cakes

Maria Ochoa and Camillo Villegas
Serves 6-8

6 ripe plantains
(the skin should be almost black)

2–3 eggs, beaten

12 slices of mozzarella cheese

Coconut oil

Peel the bananas and cut into chunks of about ½ inch. Fry in hot oil until lightly browned. Remove and crush until they are flat.

On top of each slice of banana, place 1 slice of mozzarella cheese and cover with another slice of banana.

Soak the cake in egg and fry in a pan with hot oil to melt the cheese and wait until the cake is golden brown. Pat off excess oil, let cool and serve.

Zucchini Casserole

Audrey and Marc Leishman
Serves 8-10

6 zucchinis, sliced thin

1 can Pillsbury® crescent rolls

1 large bag mild cheddar cheese
(We use Sargento®)

1 medium-size yellow onion, chopped finely

2 eggs

1 tablespoon Italian seasoning

1 stick butter, sliced

Extra virgin olive oil

Salt and pepper, to taste

Preheat oven to 350°F. Place zucchinis, onion, and butter in a large skillet. Add a splash of extra virgin olive oil. Cover and simmer, occasionally mixing, for about 15 minutes or until zucchini appear translucent.

In a large mixing bowl, beat two eggs. Add Italian seasoning, salt, pepper, and entire bag of cheese. Once zucchinis are cooked, pour the contents of skillet (including juice) into the mixing bowl. Combine egg and cheese mixture with the zucchinis.

In a casserole dish, roll out the crescent rolls. Pour zucchini mixture on top of crescent rolls. Bake for 20–25 minutes. When the crescent rolls are browned, the casserole is ready. Let it sit for 10–15 minutes before cutting.

GARLIC CHEESE GRITS

Amy and Justin Bolli

Serves 6-8

6 cups water

2 teaspoons salt

1½ cups grits (not instant)

½ cup butter

3 eggs, beaten

1 16-ounce bag shredded sharp cheddar cheese

2–3 cloves minced garlic

Cayenne pepper to taste

Bring water and salt to a boil. Pour in grits, stirring continuously so they do not get lumpy and all of the water is absorbed. Slowly add pats of butter and continue to stir.

Add eggs and stir quickly so they do not cook before blending into the mixture. Then stir in cheese, garlic and cayenne pepper.

Pour mixture into 2½-quart greased dish. Bake at 350°F for 75 minutes.

GAGGEE'S SWEET POTATO SOUFFLÉ

Sybi and Matt Kuchar

Serves 6-8

3 cups sweet potatoes, cooked and mashed

¾ cup white sugar

⅓ cup butter, softened

1 teaspoon vanilla extract

1 4-ounce can pineapple, crushed

2 eggs, beaten

½ cup milk

TOPPING:

1 cup coconut, flaked

⅓ cup all-purpose flour

1 cup packed brown sugar

1 cup pecan pieces

⅓ cup butter, melted

Preheat oven to 350°F. Combine mashed sweet potatoes with white sugar, butter, vanilla, pineapple, and eggs. Mix together and pour into a baking dish sprayed with Pam®.

Mix all topping ingredients together and spread on sweet potato mixture. Bake for 35 minutes.

ARMENIAN RICE

Ami and Robert Garrigus
Serves 8

¼ pound butter
½ small onion, finely chopped
3 slices bacon, cubed
3 cups Uncle Ben's Long Grain Rice®
½ teaspoon garlic salt
3 tablespoons soy sauce
1 package shaved almonds
1 6.5-ounce can mushrooms
3 cans beef bouillon
3 cans beef consommé

Simmer butter, onions, and bacon for 5 minutes in frying pan. Add rice and cook until slightly brown. Add garlic salt, soy sauce, almonds, and mushrooms, then stir until heated through.

Place contents in large casserole dish. Add 2 cans of bouillon and consommé. Cook, covered, for 3 hours at 250°F. Stir every 30 minutes. Add remaining bouillon and consommé, as needed.

PARTY POTATOES

Lauren and Bobby Gates
Serves 8-10

5 pounds russet potatoes
8 ounces cream cheese, softened
½ cup butter, softened
1 cup sour cream
Milk
Garlic salt to taste
Chives (fresh or freeze-dried)

Peel, cube, and boil potatoes until tender. While potatoes are cooking, place cream cheese, butter, and sour cream into mixer, and beat until creamy.

Drain cooked potatoes and while still hot, slowly add them into the cream cheese mixture. Add milk to obtain desired consistency. Add garlic salt and chives to taste. Mix until creamy (do not over-mix).

Pour potatoes into a buttered 13 x 9-inch casserole dish. Place pats of butter over potatoes and bake at 350°F for 45 minutes.

Tim's Irish Potato Dressing

Holly and Tim Finchem
Serves 6-8

5 pounds Idaho russet potatoes, peeled
2 large onions, chopped
1 bunch celery stalks, chopped
Turkey drippings*
Salt and pepper

Cut the potatoes in half and boil until fork-tender. While potatoes are boiling, add the chopped onion and celery to a roasting pan. Stir in a few tablespoons of the turkey drippings and broil until vegetables are tender, stirring occasionally.

Drain the potatoes and coarsely mash with a fork. Add the potatoes and a few more tablespoons of drippings to the vegetable mixture and combine. Add salt and pepper, to taste. Bake at 350°F for 1–1½ hours.

*It's best to make this dish while the turkey is cooking so be sure to have turkey drippings on hand (drippings also can be purchased at some restaurants).

HEAVENLY VEGETABLE CASSEROLE

Amy Palmer-Saunders

Serves 12

1 package frozen
French-style green beans

1 package frozen baby lima beans

1 package frozen small peas

3 green peppers – seeded and
cut into narrow strips

SAUCE:

1½ cups heavy whipping cream

1½ cups mayonnaise

¾ cup grated Parmesan
or cheddar cheese

Fresh ground pepper

Touch of salt

Place the first four ingredients in just enough boiling salted water to keep from burning. Cool until frozen vegetables are thawed and separate with a fork. Drain and cool. Butter a casserole dish of appropriate size. Place the barely cooked vegetables in the dish.

In a separate bowl, mix the sauce ingredients. Cover vegetables with the cream-mayonnaise-cheese sauce.

Bake, uncovered, in preheated 325°F oven for about 50 minutes, or until brownish and puffy on top.

NOTE: HAVE THE OPTION OF BAKING IMMEDIATELY OR HOLDING IN REFRIGERATOR TO BE PARTY-READY AHEAD OF TIME.

Finishes

DESSERTS

CHOCOLATE CHIP CREAM CHEESE CUPCAKES

Ruby and Graham DeLaet
Makes 24 cupcakes

FILLING:
1 8-ounce package cream cheese
1 egg
⅓ cup sugar
Pinch of salt
2 cups chocolate chips

BATTER:
3 cups flour
2 cups sugar
1 teaspoon salt
2 teaspoons baking soda
½ cup cocoa
⅔ cup vegetable oil
2 cups water
2 tablespoons vinegar
2 teaspoons vanilla

Beat together all filling ingredients very well. Stir in the chocolate chips. Set aside.

Sift dry ingredients together. Make a well in the middle. Pour in liquids and beat well. Fill paper-lined cupcake tins ⅔ full of batter. Top with a heaping teaspoon of cream cheese mixture.

Bake for 20 minutes at 350°F or until firm to the touch. Let cool for at least 20 minutes before eating.

CHERRY-BERRY PIE

Carolyn and Jim Herman
Serves 6-8

1 14.5-ounce can sour cherries
½ cup sugar
1 21-ounce can cherry pie filling
1 pint fresh blueberries
1 pint fresh strawberries
2 tablespoons corn starch
1 frozen pie crust
1 refrigerated pie crust, rolled
2 eggs, whites only
1 tablespoon sugar, granulated or brown

Preheat the oven to 425°F. In a large bowl, mash the sour cherries and sugar together and let stand for approximately 1 hour. Add the cherry pie filling, fresh blueberries and strawberries. Add the 2 tablespoons cornstarch and fold together gently.

Remove the frozen pie shell and allow it to come to room temperature, approximately 15 minutes. Pour the cherry-berry mixture into the room temperature pie shell.

Unroll the second piece of dough and place it over the cherry-berry mixture, crimping the edges together well with the tines of a fork. Brush the top with the egg whites, then sprinkle the sugar on the top of the pie. Make a couple of slits in the crust for the steam to escape.

Cover with foil and bake at 425°F for 15 minutes. Decrease temperature to 375°F and bake for an additional 45 to 50 minutes, or until the filling starts bubbling. Pie is best when served cool, which allows the corn starch to hold the filling together. Add a scoop of whipped cream or vanilla ice cream.

Pavlova

Alana and Nick O'Hern
Serves 6-8

6 egg whites, room temperature
1 ½ cups caster sugar (fine sugar)
1 tablespoon corn flour
1 teaspoon white vinegar or lemon juice
Dash of vanilla

Preheat oven to 350°F (180°C) Beat egg whites until stiff and glossy. Gradually add caster sugar, beating until dissolved after each addition. Fold in corn flour, vinegar, and vanilla during the mixing time. (To test, rub mix between fingers to make sure sugar is all dissolved.)

Spread mix into a 7–8-inch circle pan. Do not squash or flatten, but shape the sides up and in toward the center. Put into hot oven for 3–4 minutes, then turn oven down to 250°F for about 1¼ hours. Turn oven off and leave in oven to cool. DO NOT OPEN OVEN UNTIL COOLED OR IT WILL CRACK. After oven has cooled a bit, leave door ajar.

Cover the Pavlova with fresh whipped cream and top with fruit. Aussies love to put strawberries and kiwi fruit on top of the whipped cream, then to pour a little passion fruit pulp over the top.

Red Velvet Brownies

Tahnee and Chris Kirk
Serves 6-8

BROWNIES:

1 4-ounce bittersweet chocolate baking bar, chopped

1 cup butter

2 cups sugar

4 large eggs

1½ cups all-purpose flour

1 1-ounce bottle red liquid food coloring

1½ teaspoons baking powder

1 teaspoon vanilla extract

⅛ teaspoon salt

CREAM CHEESE FROSTING:

1 8-ounce package cream cheese, softened

3 tablespoons butter, softened

2 cups powdered sugar

⅛ teaspoon salt

1 teaspoon vanilla extract

Preheat oven to 350°F. Grease bottom and sides of a 9-inch square pan.

Stirring at 30-second intervals, microwave chocolate and butter in a large bowl until melted and smooth. When melted, whisk in sugar. Add eggs, one at a time, making sure to blend after each addition.

Gently stir in flour, food coloring, baking powder, vanilla, and salt. Pour mixture into greased pan and bake for 44–48 minutes or until a toothpick inserted into the center comes out clean.

While the cupcakes are baking, beat cream cheese and butter with an electric mixer until creamy. Slowly add the powdered sugar and salt. When blended, stir in vanilla. When brownies are completely cool, frost with cream cheese frosting.

Healthy Version Chocolate Chip Cookies

Emily and Daniel Summerhays
Makes 3 dozen

4 cups whole wheat flour

2 teaspoons baking soda

1 teaspoon salt

2 teaspoons cinnamon

2 cups applesauce

1 cup vegetable oil

1 cup honey

6 ounces semi-sweet chocolate chips

¾ cup chopped walnuts

Mix together all ingredients. Spread out on cookie sheet.

Bake for 20 minutes at 350°F. Cut into squares.

Mom's Carrot Cake

Sheri and Steve Pate
Serves 24

1¼ cup vegetable oil
2 cups sugar
3 eggs
2 teaspoons vanilla
2 cups flour
2 teaspoons baking soda
1 teaspoon baking powder
½ teaspoon cinnamon
½ teaspoon salt
13 ounces crushed pineapple
3 cups shredded pineapple
2 cups raw shredded carrots

FROSTING:

8 ounces cream cheese
½ cup butter, softened
1 pound confectioners sugar
2 teaspoons vanilla
¾ cup chopped pecans

Cream together the vegetable oil, sugar, eggs, and vanilla. Add in the flour, baking soda, baking powder, cinnamon, and salt, until just mixed. Add into the mix the crushed pineapple, shredded pineapple, and raw shredded carrots.

Pour into a 13 x 9-inch pan and bake at 350°F for 45 minutes.

While the cake is baking, beat cream cheese and butter with an electric mixer until creamy. Slowly add the powdered sugar. Stir in the vanilla and chopped pecans. Allow the cake to cool, then frost

Apple Pie

Lorie and Hunter Haas
Serves 6-8

FILLING:

5 or 6 large tart apples, preferably Granny
Smith

¾ cup sugar

2 tablespoons flour

1 teaspoon cinnamon

¼ cup butter, cut into 12 pieces

Dough for two piecrusts

PIE CRUST INGREDIENTS:

2 cups all-purpose flour

1 teaspoon salt

¾ cup butter or shortening

6 tablespoons cold water

FOR THE PIE CRUST:

Mix salt and flour. Add the butter and blend with a pastry knife. Begin adding cold water to make dough soft. Roll out on floured surface.

FILING:

Preheat oven to 375°F. Place one pie crust in a pie pan. Place apples in the unbaked pie shell. Mix sugar, flour, and cinnamon, and sprinkle over the apples. Dot apples with the pieces of butter. Cover the pie with the remaining pie crust. Crimp upper and lower pie crusts together to seal. Slit upper piecrust with a knife 8 to 10 times.

Bake for 15 minutes. Lower temperature to 350°F and bake for 45 minutes, or until pie bubbles and crust is browned. Let sit for at least 15 minutes before serving.

VARIATION: SPRINKLE THE PIE WITH CINNAMON AND LARGE SUGAR CRYSTALS (LIKE SUGAR IN THE RAW) BEFORE BAKING.

Gooey Butter Coffee Cake

Sally and Hale Irwin
Serves 16

1 box yellow cake mix
1 stick butter, melted
2 eggs
1 tsp. vanilla
8 oz cream cheese
3 eggs
1 box powdered sugar

Grease a 9"x13" pan with nonstick cooking spray. Beat together the cake mix, melted butter, eggs, and vanilla. Spread the mixture on the bottom of the pan. (Note, the mixture will be thick).

Beat together cream cheese, eggs, and powdered sugar. Pour over the top of the previous mix.

Bake at 325°F for 40–50 minutes on the middle rack of the oven. Edges will be browning slightly and the middle will jiggle, but do not over bake as it should be "gooey" in the middle. Sprinkle with sifted powdered sugar when cool.

The Key to Scott's Heart Banana Pudding

Jen and Scott Stallings
Serves 12

1 can Eagle Brand® condensed milk
1 large Kraft® Cool Whip
2 small boxes vanilla instant pudding
1 box vanilla wafers
4 bananas

Mix pudding as directed on box. Add Eagle Brand® milk and ½ tub of Kraft® Cool Whip. Mix together.

Make a layer of wafers and bananas. Next, pour mixture on top and keep layering. Put in refrigerator and let set before adding the final layer of Kraft® Cool Whip on top.

VARIATION: ADD AN EXTRA BOX OF WAFERS TO THE TOP OR TO HAVE ON HAND TO GARNISH.

Strawberry Pretzel Dessert

Amy and Chris Tidland

Serves 8-10

FIRST LAYER:

2 cups crushed pretzels
½ cup sugar
¾ cup melted butter
⅓ cup chopped pecans

SECOND LAYER:

8 ounces cream cheese
1 cup sugar
9-ounce tub Cool Whip®

THIRD LAYER:

1 6-ounce package strawberry Jello®
2 cups boiling water
10 ounces frozen strawberries

Mix the ingredients for first layer, press into a 13 x 9-inch glass dish (sprayed with cooking spray) and bake at 350°F for 10 minutes. Let cool.

Whip together second layer ingredients until blended and add to the top of pretzel mixture

Dissolve Jello® then add 10 ounces of frozen strawberries. When this mixture is almost set, pour over the second layer. Chill together and serve.

Chewy Cake

Ruth and Larry Moody

Serves 10-12

1½ cups Bisquick®
1 box brown sugar
4 eggs
Chopped nuts
Coconut – optional

Combine all ingredients and pour into an 8x10-inch pan. Bake at 350°F for 30 minutes. Cool and cut.

OREO® BALLS

Courtney and Kevin Streelman
Makes 2 - 3 dozen

1 package OREO® cookies, crushed

8 ounces cream cheese

1 package white or chocolate almond bark

Blend the crushed OREO® with the cream cheese, using a hand mixer or blender (or for the lazy cooks in the group, a spoon will do fine). Roll mixture into pecan-size balls. Refrigerate 30 minutes–1 hour.

Melt almond bark and dip each ball so that half of the ball is coated in (white) chocolate. Allow to harden on wax paper.

Brenda's Brownies

Brenda and Tag Ridings
Serves 8

1 stick butter
1 cup sugar
3 tablespoons cocoa
2 eggs
1 teaspoon vanilla
¾ cup flour
½ cup chopped black walnuts

Melt butter in 8" square pan. Combine sugar and cocoa in bowl and mix well with a spoon to break up cocoa. Add eggs, vanilla, and mix well. Then add flour, melted butter, and walnuts.

When all ingredients are combined, pour back into the square pan and bake at 325°F for 25–35 minutes. Check with a toothpick and do not over-bake.

Pineapple Upside Down Cake

Amanda and Jason Dufner
Serves 8-10

CAKE:
1½ cups plain flour
2 teaspoons baking powder
¼ teaspoon salt
1 stick butter (room temperature)
1 cup sugar
1 teaspoon pure vanilla flavoring
2 large eggs, separated
½ cup milk
¼ teaspoon cream of tartar

TOPPING:
4 tablespoons butter
½ cup light brown sugar
1 can pineapple, sliced

Melt butter and brown sugar in large iron skillet. Remove from heat and cool. Arrange pineapple slices on top of brown sugar and butter. Set skillet aside.

Cream butter and sugar, then add vanilla and egg yolks. Mix well. Combine the mixture with the flour, baking powder, salt, milk, and cream of tartar. Beat egg whites until stiff, not dry then fold into the batter. Spread batter over sugar mixture in skillet.

Bake at 350°F for approximately 45 minutes. Invert onto cake plate.

BANOFFEE PIE

Diane and Luke Donald
Serves 8

1½ cups Graham cracker crumbs
10 tablespoons butter, melted
1½ cups whipping cream
¼ cup powdered sugar
Splash of banana extract
2–3 bananas, sliced
2 cans Dulce de Leche**
1 Cadbury Flake® candy bar, crumbled***

Combine 1½ cups graham cracker crumbs and 10 tablespoons melted butter. Press into a pie plate and bake in 350°F oven for 7 minutes. (For convenience, can use a store-bought graham cracker pie crust.)

Warm the Dulce de Leche just slightly in the microwave until it loosens a bit, or if home made Dulce de Leche has been prepared, let it cool down to room temperature. Spread into the bottom of the cooled pie crust.

When cooled, place the banana slices on top of the Dulce de Leche.

Whip the cream with the powdered sugar and vanilla and spread on top of the bananas.

Crumble the Flake bar over the whipped cream. If the Cadbury Flake bar was not available at the grocery store, shave some chocolate over the top or just omit.

**Can be found in most supermarkets near the sweetened condensed milk. Always an option to make it by pouring 2 cans sweetened condensed milk into a glass baking dish and covering the dish with foil. Place the baking dish in a larger pan and add water (bain marie) and bake at 300°F for 1½ hours until the color changes.

***Can be found in supermarkets in the British food section.

ECLAIR CAKE

Mary and Steve Hulka
Serves 6-8

CAKE:

1 1-pound box graham crackers
1 small box French vanilla instant pudding
3½ cups milk
9 ounces Cool Whip® (thawed)

FROSTING:

2 packages pre-melted unsweetened chocolate
2 teaspoons clear Karo® syrup
2 teaspoons vanilla
3 tablespoons butter, softened
1½ cups powdered sugar
3 tablespoons milk

Butter a 9 x 13-inch pan. Line pan with graham crackers (cutting to fit). Combine pudding and milk, and beat for 2 minutes. Blend in Cool Whip® and pour half of mixture over graham crackers. Place a second layer of graham crackers on pudding (cutting to fit) and pour remaining pudding mixture on top of this layer. Cover top of pudding with third layer of graham crackers, again cutting to fit. Cover and refrigerate for 2 hours.

While cake is in the refrigerator, combine all the frosting ingredients and beat till smooth. Frost the cake and refrigerate for 24 hours before serving.

VARIATION: FROSTING CAN BE STORE-BOUGHT PRE-MADE MILK CHOCOLATE FROSTING OR MADE FROM THE RECIPE.

HOMEMADE VANILLA ICE CREAM

Leot and Vaughn Taylor
Serves 8-10

4 eggs
1 cup sugar
2 tablespoons vanilla
½ pint whipping cream
2 cans Eagle Brand® Sweetened Condensed Milk
1½ quarts whole milk

Combine first five ingredients with a mixer. Pour into ice cream churn, add milk up to line, stir with spoon, and then churn. Makes approximately 4 quarts of ice cream.

If using a larger churn, add more of each ingredient. For example, if using a 5-quart churn add ½ more of each ingredient.

WACKY CAKE

Margaret Gay, on behalf of Kimberly and Brian Gay
Serves 20

3 cups plain flour
6 tablespoons cocoa
2 cups water
2 teaspoons vinegar
2 teaspoons soda
2 cups sugar
1 teaspoon salt
⅔ cup oil
2 teaspoons vanilla

Icing:
1 cup sugar
1 cup milk
1 cup coconut
1 teaspoon vanilla
½ stick Oleo
3 tablespoons flour
1 cup chopped nuts

Sift dry ingredients into ungreased pan. Make 3 holes and pour oil, vinegar, and vanilla into separate holes. Pour water over all. Mix with a fork (do not beat).

Bake at 350°F for 30 minutes in a 13x9x1.5-inch pan or until done. Leave in pan and then frost top of cake while still warm.

Combine the following icing ingredients: sugar, milk, coconut, Oleo, and flour, and cook until very thick. Remove from heat and add vanilla and nuts. Spread on cake while still warm and cut into squares.

Barbara's Cheesecake

Barbara and Jack Nicklaus

Serves 16

CRUST:

1½ cups graham cracker crumbs

2 tablespoons sugar

1 teaspoon flour

¼ cup butter, melted

FILLING:

2 pounds cream cheese, softened

1 cup sugar

2 eggs

2 teaspoons vanilla

TOPPING:

2 cups sour cream

¾ cup sugar

¾ teaspoon vanilla

½ teaspoon lemon juice

Combine all ingredients for crust in a medium mixing bowl. Press into a 10-inch spring-form pan. Bake in a 350°F oven for 5 minutes. Remove from oven and allow pie crust to cool. Turn off oven and open door to cool the oven.

Mix all ingredients for filling in a bowl and pour over the cooled crust. Place in cold oven and turn to 350°F for 30 minutes. Combine all topping ingredients and pour over baked cheesecake. Return to oven for 8 additional minutes. Chill overnight.

BUCKEYES

Brenda and Mark Calcavecchia
Makes 100-120 balls

1 pound unsalted butter, softened
2 pounds creamy peanut butter
3 pounds powdered sugar
24 ounces semi-sweet chocolate chips
½ block paraffin wax

Add peanut butter to butter, then add powdered sugar. (helpful to use a large mixer as it gets hard to mix at the end.) Form into 1-inch balls and chill on waxed paper on a long cookie sheet or jelly pan.

Melt chocolate chips in double boiler and cut wax into small pieces and add to chips. Pick up the balls by sticking a toothpick into top. Dip into hot melted chocolate. Leave a part on the top open with peanut butter showing. Replace on waxed paper and refrigerate till chocolate hardens. Remove toothpicks and cover holes.

VARIATION: HAVE THE CHOICE TO STIR SOME SOLID VEGETABLE SHORTENING INTO THE CHOCOLATE IN PLACE OF THE PARAFFIN WAX. IN THE CASE OF THIS RECIPE, ⅓ CUP SHOULD SUFFICE.

AUNT DALE'S BREAD PUDDING

Jennifer and Glen Day
Serves 8-10

1 loaf of bread, cut into 1-inch cubes
1 quart milk
3 eggs
1 cup sugar
1 cup powdered sugar
2 teaspoons vanilla
2 sticks butter
½ teaspoon cinnamon
12 Hershey® Kisses, melted
6 teaspoons water

Place sliced bread into a 9x13 oven-proof dish. Combine milk, eggs, sugar, and 1 teaspoon vanilla, and pour evenly over bread. Cut one stick of butter into pieces and place evenly on top of bread mixture. Sprinkle with cinnamon.

Bake at 350°F for 45–50 minutes.

For the topping, combine Hershey® kisses, 1 stick butter, powdered sugar, 1 teaspoon vanilla, and water. Mix well and pour over bread pudding after baking. Let rest for 20 minutes, and serve.

Rickie Fowler's Favorite Cookies

Taylor Fowler, Sister of Rickie Fowler
Makes 3 dozen

2 sticks butter, unsalted
¾ cup dark brown sugar
¾ cup sugar
1 tablespoon pure vanilla extract
2 large eggs
1 teaspoon salt
½ teaspoon baking soda
1¾ cups flour
3 cups oatmeal
1 cup semi-sweet chocolate chips

Slightly soften the butter, add both sugars, then mix. Next, add the vanilla extract and eggs. Resume mixing then add the salt and baking soda.

Continue to mix, and slowly add the flour. When flour is mixed thoroughly, add oatmeal and mix well. Lastly, add the chocolate chips.

Roll the dough in golf ball-size balls and place on a baking sheet. Bake at 375°F for 8–10 minutes or until slightly brown.

Harvey's Wallbanger Cake

Heather and Charles Howell III
Serves 12

1 box Duncan Hines® Classic Yellow Cake Mix
1 small box vanilla instant pudding
4 eggs
¾ cup oil
¾ cup orange juice
¼ cup Galliano® Liqueur
¼ cup vodka

Icing:
1 cup confectioners' sugar
1 tablespoon orange juice
1 tablespoon Galliano® Liqueur
1 teaspoon vanilla

In a bowl, combine all the cake ingredients, and mix with an electric mixer. Pour into floured bundt pan and bake for 45 minutes at 350°F or until toothpick comes out clean.

While the cake is baking, mix icing ingredients together and pour over warm cake.

APPLE CRISP

Jackie and Sean O'Hair
Serves 8

¾ cup flour
2 cups oats
1 cup packed brown sugar
1 teaspoon cinnamon
¾ cup butter, melted
6 apples, peeled and sliced

Spray casserole dish with Pam®. Spread enough apples in the pan so that they cover the bottom, 1–2 inches thick. Next, mix all dry ingredients until crumbly. Spread mixture on top of fruit and pat down.

Bake at 350°F for 35–45 minutes or until slightly browned and apples are tender.

VARIATION: CAN ADD FROZEN BLUEBERRIES OR CRANBERRIES TO THE APPLES OR COMPLETELY SUBSTITUTE THE APPLES WITH PEACHES IF PREFERRED.

CHOCOLATE CHIP PUMPKIN COOKIES

Amy Churchill, on behalf of Victoria and Heath Slocum
Makes 24 cookies

1 cup butter
1¼ cups brown sugar, packed
1 cup pumpkin butter
1 egg
2 teaspoons vanilla
2½ cups flour
1 teaspoon baking soda
2 teaspoons cinnamon
1 teaspoon cardamon
½ teaspoon freshly grated nutmeg
¼ teaspoon ginger
1 teaspoon salt
1 tablespoon orange zest
1½ cups dark chocolate chips or chunks

Cream butter and sugar in medium-sized bowl. Add egg, vanilla, and pumpkin butter. Mix well.

In separate bowl, mix together dry ingredients. Add dry ingredients to wet ingredients and stir to combine. Stir in orange zest and chocolate chips and set in refrigerator for 1 hour. These cookies don't spread much so be creative in making shapes. Sprinkle with sea salt before baking, if desired.

Bake for 15–18 minutes in a 350°F oven.

RECOMMENDATION: MAKE IN SMALLER BATCHES AND FREEZE THE DOUGH FOR FUTURE USE AS THESE COOKIES ARE CRISP AND CHEWY FRESH OUT OF THE OVEN.

MAHAN DR. PEPPER® CAKE

Kandi and Hunter Mahan
Serves 12

1 can Dr. Pepper®, room temperature
1 cup powdered sugar
¼ teaspoon cinnamon
¼ teaspoon sugar
1 box yellow cake mix
4 eggs
¾ cup vegetable oil
1 box vanilla instant pudding

Prepare the icing first by mixing 3 tablespoons Dr. Pepper® and 1 cup powdered sugar. Set aside until cake is done.

Spray two 8-inch-round cake pans. Dust inside of cake pans lightly with cinnamon and sugar. Mix all remaining ingredients together and pour evenly into cake pans.

Bake at 350°F for 35–45 minutes. When slightly cooled, place cakes on top of each other on a cake platter and pour on icing.

MILLIE'S FUDGE PIE

Sandy and Kenny Perry
Serves 8

2 frozen pie crusts*
2 cups sugar
½ cup plain flour, sifted
½ cup cocoa, sifted
4 large eggs
2 sticks butter, melted
2 teaspoons vanilla

Combine half the melted butter and eggs. Beat well. Add more butter slowly and beat again. Add the remaining ingredients and mix well. Pour into pie crust and bake at 350°F for 30–35 minutes.

*NOTE: IT IS BEST TO THAW CRUSTS FOR A FEW MINUTES, PUNCTURE WITH A FORK A FEW TIMES AND BAKE THE CRUSTS FOR ABOUT 10 MINUTES PRIOR TO FILLING. THIS PREVENTS A DOUGHY CRUST IN THE MIDDLE OF THE PIE.

PEACH AND HUCKLEBERRY COBBLER

Dowd and Webb Simpson
Serves 8

6 peaches, peeled and sliced
1 cup huckleberries,
blackberries or blueberries
2 teaspoons lemon zest
2 teaspoons freshly squeezed
lemon juice
½ cup sugar
¼ cup flour
1 package sugar cookie dough

Preheat oven to 350°F. Combine peaches, huckleberries, lemon zest, and lemon juice, and let the fruits absorb the juices for about 10 minutes. Next, add the sugar and flour.

Mix gently and allow the mixture to sit for about 5 minutes. Spoon the mixture into a rectangular glass cooking dish or individual ramekins.

Unwrap the sugar cookie dough. If the dough has pre-cut squares, squish each square so it is slightly flat, and place one on top of each ramekin (if there is leftover dough, go back and place a second squished square on each ramekin), or space evenly throughout the glass dish (in this case, the cookie dough should touch and slightly overlap).

Place the dessert in the center of the oven and cook for about 40–45 minutes. The topping should have golden edges and the fruit juices should bubble. Serve warm with a scoop of vanilla ice cream.

THIS BOOK WAS MADE POSSIBLE THROUGH THE SUPPORT AND GENEROSITY OF THE FOLLOWING CORPORATIONS AND INDIVIDUALS WHO BELIEVE IN THE MISSION OF OUR ORGANIZATION.

Special Thanks

Since 1988, the PGA TOUR has been an integral part of who we are and what we have accomplished as a nonprofit entity. The TOUR's charitable platform is the foundation on which the PGA TOUR Wives Association has built our charitable endeavors to support outreach programs and services to aid children and families in need. We are proud and blessed to be a part of the PGA TOUR family and to have the TOUR as a supporter and advocate for the work that we do in the community and in the world.

Our sincere thanks to the PGA TOUR and its partners, tournaments, volunteers, and employees for helping us achieve our goals and mission. Because we truly believe, like the TOUR, that "Together, anything's possible."

Our organization maintains a commitment to helping children and families in need. With support from longstanding partners like MasterCard, we are able to further the charitable initiatives of the PGA TOUR, PGA TOUR Wives Association, and our tournaments. We appreciate their standing with us to further this important cause.

The PGA TOUR Wives Association sincerely thanks LandCastle Title for its ongoing support of our philanthropic endeavors and its belief in our mission.

Corporate Sponsors

Charles Schwab

FedEx

Joseph Frumkin

Innisbrook Resort and Golf Club

Mark and Debi Rolfing Foundation

Michelob ULTRA

Nature Valley Granola Bars

Northwestern Mutual Foundation

Wasserman Foundation

PTWA FAMILY AND FRIENDS

Kelly and Matt Bettencourt

Nancy and Ross Berlin

Amanda and Steven Bowditch

Jennifer and Michael Bradley

Amanda and Jonathan Byrd

Heather and Ben Crane

Candace and Ben Curtis

Dina and Steve Flesch

Stacy and Charley Hoffman

Traci and Skip Kendall

Meagan and Martin Laird

Amanda and Justin Leonard

Shauna and Troy Matteson

Sarah and William McGirt

Jody and John Merrick

Athena Perez

DeAnna and Carl Pettersson

Lori and D. A. Points

Heather and John Rollins

Dowd and Webb Simpson

Courtney and Kevin Streelman

Leot and Vaughn Taylor

Amy and Mark Wilson

Virginia and Leslie Wilson

Acknowledgments

Twenty-five years ago, a few women came together and decided that they could make a difference. Those women, and those who followed, laid the foundation for what is today the PGA TOUR Wives Association. We want to acknowledge those women and individuals who were visionary enough to see that they could use the platforms available to them to enhance the philanthropic efforts that were already underway through the PGA TOUR. Because of their unique situations, they knew they could raise additional awareness for those in need. And they did. So, to those who blazed the trails for all who came after, we want to say thank you.

Pasty Graham	Maria Floyd	Jody Andrade	Winnie Palmer
Gail Murphy	Marcia Colbert	Sarah Strange	Barbara Nicklaus
Bonnie McGowan	Sue North	Sally Hoch	Holly Finchem
Patti Inman	Gail Nelson	Betty Sigel	Susan Bowes
Verity Charles	Pam Tewell	Sharon Funk	
Vivienne Player	Vickie Waldorf	Sally Irwin	
Cathy Stockton	Judy Beman	Sherri Pate	

Writing these stories and compiling the photographs and recipes for this book took thousands of hours and many hands. We would like to thank the following individuals for their time and efforts in making this book a reality.

BOOK COMMITTEE MEMBERS

Kelly Bettencourt, co-chair	Jennifer Gillis	Sarah McGirt
DeAnna Pettersson, co-chair	Patsy Graham	Kristy McLaughlin
Heather Crane	Stacy Hoffman	Sara Moores
Ruby DeLeat	Brittany Kisner	Courtney Streelman
Katelyn DiCristofano	Meagan Laird	Mary Wieland
Lauren Gates	Holly Letzig	Amy Wilson

OUR TALENTED WRITERS

Melanie Hauser	Laury Livsey	Stacy Hoffman
Kelly Bettencourt	DeAnna Pettersson	Amy Wilson
	Sara Moores	

OUR EDITORS

Kelly Bettencourt	Katelyn DiCristofano	Stacy Hoffman
Stacy Hoffman	DeAnna Pettersson	Amy Wilson
Meg Briggs	Jodi Herb	Melissa Good
Meagan Laird	Mary Wieland	

And to the women who have served on the PGA TOUR Wives Association Board of Directors,
past and present, for their leadership and vision.

2012–2013

Amy Wilson, president

DeAnna Pettersson, vice president of membership

Kelly Bettencourt, vice president of fundraising

Meagan Laird, vice president of community outreach

Stacy Hoffman, vice president of communications and secretary

Sara Moores, executive director

And prior years, from the beginning . . .

1989–1990

Susie Mahaffey, president

Beth Fabel

Bonnie Faxon

1990–1991

Susie Mahaffey, president

Beth Fabel

Bonnie Faxon

Bonnie McGowan

Gail Murphy

1991–1992

Beth Fabel, president

Bonnie Faxon

Bonnie McGowan

Linda Wadkins

Sue Sindelar

Patti Arnold Inman

1992–1993

Bonnie Faxon, president

Bonnie McGowan

Linda Wadkins

Bonnie Jones

Cindy Brown

1993–1994

Bonnie McGowan, president

Patti Inman

Kris Dodds

1994–1995

Patti Inman, president

Cissye Gallagher

Vicky Waldorf

Kris Dodds

Cathi Triplett

Laura Flannery

1995–1996

Patti Inman, president

Cissye Gallagher

Cathi Triplett

Rhonda Edwards

Chris Gump

Linda Paulson

1996–1997

Cissye Gallagher, president

Rhonda Edwards

Cathi Triplett

Lou Ann Lancaster

Kathy Wrenn

Ashley Langham

Patti Inman

1997–1998

Cissye Gallagher, president
Judy Brisky
Chris Gump
Jennifer McCarron
Lauren McGovern
Suzy Johnson
Patti Inman

1998–1999

Judy Brisky, president
Chris Gump
Lauren McGovern
Regina Stankowski
Beth Kendall
Cissye Gallagher

1999–2000

Jennifer McCarron, president
Beth Kendall
Ashley Langham
Mary Sutherland
Lisa Cink
Suzie Johnson
Judy Brisky

2000–2001

Jennifer McCarron, president
Margaret Horgan
Jennifer Day
Lisa Cink
Kris Dodds

2001–2002

Jennifer Day, president
Marci Blake
Selena Nobilo
Dory Faxon
Diane Wentworth

2002–2003

Marci Blake, president
Nicole Chalmers
Selena Nobilo
Diane Wentworth
Ann Herron

2003–2004

Marci Blake, president
Nicole Chalmers
Selena Nobilo
Jenny Rollins
Berdene Pappas

2004–2005

Dory Faxon, president
Jennifer Day
Selena Nobilo
Nicole Chalmers
Amy Quigley
Stephanie Sterling

2005–2006

Dory Faxon, president
Jennifer Day
Amy Quigley
Amanda Byrd
Heather Crane
Selena Nobilo
Stephanie Sterling

2006–2007

Dory Faxon, president
Heather Crane
Kate Phillips Rose
Amanda Byrd
Heather Gove
Missy Durkin

2007–2008

Dory Faxon, president
Heather Gove
Kate Rose
Julie Petrovic
Amy Wilson
Heather Crane
Amanda Byrd

2008–2009

Amy Wilson, president
Sandy Perry
Kate Rose
Julie Petrovic
Heather Gove
Dory Faxon

2009–2010

Amy Wilson, president
Sandy Perry
Shauna Matteson
Kate Rose
Angie Oberholser
Julie Petrovic

2010–2011

Amy Wilson, president
Dowd Simpson
Shauna Matteson
Stacy Hoffman
Kelly Bettencourt

2011–2012

Amy Wilson, president
Dowd Simpson
Athena Perez
Stacy Hoffman
Kelly Bettencourt

Index

Player Profiles and Recipes

FAMILY RECIPES

ck, Phoenix • Blue Star Families • Books-A-Go-Go • Boys & Girls Club of Denver • Boys & Girls Club of Las Vegas
Kids Club • Camp Twin Lakes • CARE USA • Carousel Ranch • Casa de Esperanza • Casting for Recovery • Catholic Charities Archdiocese of New
of Southern California • Children's Flight of Hope • Children's Healthcare Charity Inc. • Children's Healthcare of Atlanta • Children's Home Society
Foundation • Compassionate Friends • Crescent Academy • Crisis Nursery • Crusade for Children • Cystic Fibrosis Foundation • Cystic Fibrosis Fo
al • Elizabeth Glaser Pediatric AIDS Foundation • Emory University, Robert Trent Jones, Jr. Scholarship Fund • Evans Scholars Foundation • Everyb
ws Air Force Base • For Every Child • Free Arts for Abused Children of Arizona • Friends of Oakland Parks and Recreation / Ace Kids Golf Program
Two Shoes Foundation • Great Lakes Adaptive Sports Association • Greater Boston Food Bank • Greater Hartford Jaycees • Haiti Project • Happily
Hope Center • House of Hope • How 'Bout a Hug for Foster Kids Foundation • Hurley Medical Center • Indiana University Foundation • Indiana U
Home • Leukemia Society of America • Love146 – End Child Sex, Slavery and Exploitation • Make-A-Wish Foundation • Martha's Village and Kitch
New York • Morning Star Women's Auxiliary • Multiple Myeloma Research Foundation • Nancy Reagan Drug Rehabilitation • National Childhood
dation • Northeast DuPage Special Recreation Association (NEDSRA) • Operation Tom Sawyer • Orlando Regional Hospital • Orlando Regional H
en's Center • Pro Kids Golf Academy • Quad Cities River Bend Food Bank • Quad Cities United Way - Flood Relief Fund • Renaissance Learning C
ald House of Fort Worth • SAFEchild • Salesmanship Club of Dallas • Salvation Army • San Fernando Valley Child Guidance Center • Seamark Ra
s • St. Joseph's Villas • St. Jude Children's Research Hospital • St. Michael's Special School • Starlight Foundation • Sunrise of Pasco County • Sunshi
rbird Junior Golf Foundation • Time for Teens • TPC Village • Unified Theater • United Friends of the Children • United States Blind Golf Associat
cs Authority • Venture Out • Violence Prevention Center • Waccamaw Youth Center • Walter Reed Medical Center • Whaley Children's Center • W
on • Adam's Camp • ALSAC / St. Jude Children's Hospital • American Cancer Society • American Cancer Society, R.O.C.K. Camp • American Juni
n School Bell • Athletes and Entertainers for Kids • Atlanta Children's Shelter • AVON Walk the Course Against Domestic Violence • BETA Club •
A-Go-Go • Boys & Girls Club of Denver • Boys & Girls Club of Las Vegas • Boys & Girls Club of Phoenix • Boys & Girls Clubs • Boys & Girls Clu
USA • Carousel Ranch • Casa de Esperanza • Casting for Recovery • Catholic Charities Archdiocese of New Orleans • Central Florida Children's Hor
Hope • Children's Healthcare Charity Inc. • Children's Healthcare of Atlanta • Children's Home Society of North Carolina • Children's Hospital of S
scent Academy • Crisis Nursery • Crusade for Children • Cystic Fibrosis Foundation • Cystic Fibrosis Foundation of Indiana • Domestic Violence Pr
ion • Emory University, Robert Trent Jones, Jr. Scholarship Fund • Evans Scholars Foundation • Everybody Wins! / Links to Literacy • Fairway Hous
Abused Children of Arizona • Friends of Oakland Parks and Recreation / Ace Kids Golf Program • Friends of Retarded • George Mark Children's Ho
ssociation • Greater Boston Food Bank • Greater Hartford Jaycees • Haiti Project • Happily Ever After League • Healing Hands • Hearts, Hands & H
Kids Foundation • Hurley Medical Center • Indiana University Foundation • Indiana University Foundation, Delta Gamma Lectureship Fund • Ka
ex, Slavery and Exploitation • Make-A-Wish Foundation • Martha's Village and Kitchen • MCI Ronald McDonald House, Milwaukee • Meeting Stre
na Research Foundation • Nancy Reagan Drug Rehabilitation • National Childhood Cancer Foundation • Nationwide Children's Hospital • New Or
RA) • Operation Tom Sawyer • Orlando Regional Hospital • Orlando Regional Hospital Arnold Palmer Children's Hospital • Our Military Kids • Pa
Bank • Quad Cities United Way - Flood Relief Fund • Renaissance Learning Center • Riley Children's Hospital • Ronald McDonald Children's Chan
• Salvation Army • San Fernando Valley Child Guidance Center • Seamark Ranch • Seniors for Kids • Shell Junior Golf • Shriners Hospitals for Chile
ael's Special School • Starlight Foundation • Sunrise of Pasco County • Sunshine Acres • Target House • The Achievement Academy • The First Tee o
ed Theater • United Friends of the Children • United States Blind Golf Association – Junior Golf Program • United Way • University of Iowa Founda
aw Youth Center • Walter Reed Medical Center • Whaley Children's Center • Winnie Palmer Hospital • Wolfson Children's Hospital • Women Playi
an Cancer Society • American Cancer Society, R.O.C.K. Camp • American Junior Golf • Angelwood • Arnold Palmer Hospital • Arrowhead Ranch
en's Shelter • AVON Walk the Course Against Domestic Violence • BETA Club • Bethany Home • Betty Griffin House • Blessings in a Backpack, H
f Las Vegas • Boys & Girls Club of Phoenix • Boys & Girls Clubs • Boys & Girls Clubs of Northeastern Pennsylvania • Brave Kids • Buckhorn Child
ry • Catholic Charities Archdiocese of New Orleans • Central Florida Children's Home • Cerebral Palsy of Northeast Florida • Child Development R
care of Atlanta • Children's Home Society of North Carolina • Children's Hospital of Southwest Florida • Cities in Schools, Inc. • Clarke School for
Fibrosis Foundation • Cystic Fibrosis Foundation of Indiana • Domestic Violence Project • Dreams Come True of Jacksonville • Duke Children's Ho
Evans Scholars Foundation • Everybody Wins! / Links to Literacy • Fairway House • Family First of Monterey County • Family Services of the Piedm
ation / Ace Kids Golf Program • Friends of Retarded • George Mark Children's House • Georgia Council on Child Abuse • Girls Inc. of St. Louis • G
es • Haiti Project • Happily Ever After League • Healing Hands • Hearts, Hands & Hooves of Northeast Florida • Heritage Classic Foundation • Hilt
niversity Foundation • Indiana University Foundation, Delta Gamma Lectureship Fund • Kapalua Art School • Kenter Canyon Elementary Foundatic
tion • Martha's Village and Kitchen • MCI Ronald McDonald House, Milwaukee • Meeting Street • Meyer Center for Special Children • Minority G
habilitation • National Childhood Cancer Foundation • Nationwide Children's Hospital • New Orleans Children's Hospital • Nicklaus Children's Hea
nal Hospital • Orlando Regional Hospital Arnold Palmer Children's Hospital • Our Military Kids • Pace Center for Girls • Palm Beach Habilitation
f Fund • Renaissance Learning Center • Riley Children's Hospital • Ronald McDonald Children's Charities • Ronald McDonald House • Ronald Mc
Guidance Center • Seamark Ranch • Seniors for Kids • Shell Junior Golf • Shriners Hospitals for Children • South Bay Children's Health Center Asso
ise of Pasco County • Sunshine Acres • Target House • The Achievement Academy • The First Tee of Monterey • The First Tee of San Jose • The Kids
States Blind Golf Association – Junior Golf Program • United Way • University of Iowa Foundation, The Carver Family Center for Macular Degene
aley Children's Center • Winnie Palmer Hospital • Wolfson Children's Hospital • Women Playing for Time • Wood Trust Fund • YMCA Youth Shelte
C.K. Camp • American Junior Golf • Angelwood • Arnold Palmer Hospital • Arrowhead Ranch • Assistance League of Las Vegas • Assistance League
estic Violence • BETA Club • Bethany Home • Betty Griffin House • Blessings in a Backpack, Hawaii • Blessings in a Backpack, New Jersey • Blessin
& Girls Clubs • Boys & Girls Clubs of Northeastern Pennsylvania • Brave Kids • Buckhorn Children's Home • California Museum of Science and In
Child Development Resources • Children's Aid and Family Services